EVERYTHING

QUICKBOOKS ONLINE

Everything you Need to Know to Master Bookkeeping and
QuickBooks Online Accounting for All Users + Professional
Hacks, Tips & Tricks for Organized and Effortless Accounting

CARTY BINN

CONTENTS

INTRODUCTION

The accounting software program QuickBooks was created and is sold by Intuit. QuickBooks products were first released in 1983 and are primarily targeted at small and medium-sized enterprises. They provide cloud-based payroll services, on-premises accounting applications, and versions that accept payments from companies.

Intuit was established in Mountain View, California, by Scott Cook and Tom Proulx in 1983. After its Quicken program for personal financial management became popular, the company created comparable services for small business owners.

The Quicken codebase served as the foundation for QuickBooks' first release, which was a DOS version. The codebase for the Windows and Mac versions was different and was based on In-House Accountant, which Intuit had purchased. Small business owners who lacked professional accounting knowledge were big fans of the software. Because of this, the program rapidly accounted for up to 85% of the market for small business accounting software in the US.

As of 2013, it still held the lion's share of this market. However, early iterations of the system did not satisfy professional accountants, who complained about insufficient security measures such as a lack of an audit trail and a lack of compliance with conventional accounting norms.

QuickBooks Online is a cloud service provided by Intuit (QBO). Instead of paying a one-time price, the user opts for a monthly membership and only uses a secure Web browser to log in to the software. Intuit offers fixes and automatically updates the software on a regular basis. However, the application also contains pop-up adverts for additional premium services.

With 624,000 subscribers as of May 2014, QuickBooks Online led the pack for an online accounting platform. Compared to Xero, which as of July 2014 has 284,000 clients.

The cloud version of QuickBooks is a unique product from the desktop version, and it offers numerous features that function differently.

Intuit declared in 2013 that it had "rebuilt from the ground up" QuickBooks Online with a framework that enables clients to personalize the online version of QuickBooks and allows third parties to develop small business applications.

PART 1

GETTING STARTED WITH QUICKBOOKS ONLINE

CHAPTER 1

WELCOME TO QUICKBOOKS ONLINE

What is QuickBooks Online?

QuickBooks Online is a cloud-based accounting solution that helps small businesses manage their accounting, income, spending, payroll, and more. All accounts are accessed through the online login interface, which includes custom feeds and charts, custom invoice creation, 'Pay Now' buttons, and mobile websites, all with auto-synchronization. The native mobile apps for Android and iOS enable on-the-go sales receipt capture, expense monitoring, cash flow management, account balance tracking, time tracking, transaction review, purchase order management, client communications, and more.

Multiple users can examine detailed reports and accounts of the company finances on one dashboard thanks to QuickBooks Online's automatic syncing of an entire business finance profile. The software generates billing and invoice solutions that are all mobile-compatible and print-friendly, as well as trade, profit, and loss sheets. Users can design their own unique reports and feed within the dashboard so that companies only see the information that is most important to them.

Users of QuickBooks Online can add users, change permissions, and track payments, sales history, and invoice details by navigating through the dashboard. Intuit GoPayment, QuickBooks Online Payroll, Shopify, Xero, Salesforce, Square POS, and other third-party applications are all fully integrated with QuickBooks Online.

Checking on QuickBooks Pricing

The QuickBooks Desktop product selection from Intuit has been upgraded. In place of one-time purchase licenses, they now only offer QuickBooks Pro and Premier as Pro Plus and Premier Plus subscriptions. It is no longer possible to buy a QuickBooks Desktop once.

The modified version and price are shown below as of October 2022.

Products for QuickBooks Desktop 2023 are now accessible. No discounts are offered on any desktop goods, and the full MSRP is being sold across all channels.

Desktop Version

QuickBooks Pro	$ 549
QuickBooks Premier Plus	$799

The pricing of QuickBooks can actually be canceled at any point in time but the service is billed in monthly periods with no option or a refund or portion. You can also not create new transactions upon the expiration of your subscription but there is an option for your accounting records and run reports to be viewed for a minimum of one year.

QuickBooks subscription pricing

The online version of QuickBooks is available in six different versions and price points often times most people choose one of all of them. Check the table below for the pricing;

Version	Monthly	Annually	Users
Self-Employed	$15	$180	1 billable user + 2 accountant users
Simple Start	$30	$360	1 billable user + 2 accountant users
Essentials	$55	$660	3 billable users + 2 accountant users
Plus	$85	$1,020	5 billable users + 2 accountant users
Advanced	$200	$2400	Up to 25 billable users + 3 accountant users

Accountant	$0	$0	No limit

QuickBooks provides you the opportunity of choosing between a 50 percent discount for the first three months of your chosen subscription or it gives you a free trial for 30-days. There is also a possibility of you being offered a discount during the 30- day trial. If you have any plans to make use of QuickBooks continually I would advise you to take the plan as you might not have such an offer during the period of your trial. The 50 percent discount will of course save you a lot of money whereas the 30-day trial is an opportunity for you to test the software if it meets all of your needs and more without having to make any form of financial commitment. If you finally decide QuickBooks is not meant for you, you will have to cancel your subscription but the trial will end on the 30th day.

Payroll and time track pricing

There might be a need for you to include additional functionality such as payroll and time tracking. The table gives you an idea of the cost implication;

Version	Monthly	Annually
Core	$65($45/Month + $5/employee x5 employees)	$780
Premium	$115($75/month + $8/employee x5 employees)	$1,380
Elite	$175($125/month + $10/employee x 5 employees)	$2100

Note that all of QuickBooks Payroll plans has the features below;

- Calculating tax payments automatically and also paying them electronically.

- Processing both federal and state quarterly and annual reports, and also preparing W-2 and 1099 forms.
- Paying employees with printed checks or with the use of the direct deposit.
- Processing payroll for employees who work in your company's state or in a different state.
- Keeping payroll tax tables up to date without the need to install updates as it's done with the QuickBooksDesktop Products.
- Making use of the QuickBooks payroll mobile app in paying employees, electronically filing tax forms, viewing previous paychecks, and also paying taxes electronically.

Furthermore, when you establish QuickBooks payroll, there is a need for you to attach your bank account and also provide your tax identification numbers. Ensure you are ready to commence payroll with an immediate effect before you decide to embark on a QuickBooks payroll subscription.

Other add-on pricing

QuickBooks payments allows the use of electronic payments from customers and also entails per-transaction fees rather than monthly subscriptions. The table below shows the current rate as of the time of this writing;

Payment Type	Rate per Transaction
ACH Bank payments	1% up to a maximum of about $10 per transaction (with this, a customer inserts bank information online)
Swiped credit card	2.4% plus 25 cents (mobile reader available)
Invoiced credit card	2.9% plus 25 cents (customers will be able to insert credit card online)
Keyed credit card	3.4% plus 25 cents (you will be able to enter the credit card information online)

QuickBooks Payments deposits money from qualifying credit or debit card transactions directly into your bank account the following business day. The payments and also deposit transactions will then be recorded into your books automatically though this process is dependent on the funding date.

Comparing QuickBooks Features

For the optimal user experience, QuickBooks has a ton of features built right in. I'll talk briefly about these qualities and what they imply in the parts that follow;

QuickBooks Online Self-Employed

Independent contractors including real estate agents, Uber and Lyft drivers, and freelancers should all use QuickBooks Self-Employed. With your protected login, you may access it from any computer with an internet connection, much like QuickBooks Online.

It has special capabilities including the capacity to track business and personal expenses from the same bank account and transfer data to TurboTax that are unavailable in QuickBooks Online and QuickBooks Desktop. Even your expected quarterly tax payments will be calculated, and you will receive a reminder when they are due.

QuickBooks Simple Start

Offering bookkeeping features is QuickBooks Simple Start. Business owners may better manage their bookkeeping, billing, and money thanks to these capabilities.

It provides a single online interface through which users can: access reports, track their income and expenses, and send invoices.

By automating these procedures, admin time can be reduced. Information is digitally stored by QuickBooks Simple Start. You no longer need to manually enter client or business information every time. Additionally, it can lessen the chance of human error.

Numerous bookkeeping capabilities are available with QuickBooks Simple Start. These functions consist of 1099 contractor administration, basic reporting, estimations, receipt management, income, and spending tracking, mileage tracking, sales and sales tax tracking, and invoicing.

QuickBooks Online Essentials

Businesses with up to three users may handle accounts receivable, track income and spending, and keep an eye on payables using QuickBooks Online Essentials (money owed to suppliers). Additionally, it allows you to conduct accounts payable aging reports so you can stay on top of bill due dates. Additionally, you can communicate with your accountant to make tax season simpler.

The number of users is the primary distinction between QuickBooks Online Essentials and QuickBooks Online Plus. While Plus permits up to five users, Essentials only allows up to three. The features that come with each are the second distinction to take into account. In addition to adding the option to maintain inventory (a very useful feature for those who sell things), Plus also offers the ability to track project profitability.

QuickBooks Online Plus

The best accounting software for firms that sell both goods and services is QuickBooks Online Plus. You get everything that Simple Start and Essentials offer, plus the ability to track inventory costs and quantities, make purchase orders, and monitor project profitability, including labor costs, payroll, and expenses with job costing. All of these features are available with QuickBooks Online Plus. Additionally, you can communicate with your accountant to make tax season simpler.

Usage limits for QuickBooks Simple Start

QuickBooks Element	Use Limit
Annual transactions	350, 000
Chart of accounts	250
Classes and locations	40 combined; further, you cannot track your balance sheet by class.

Billed users	1 for Simple Start, 3 for Essentials, 5 for Plus
Unbilled users	2 Accountant users for most plans, 3 for Advanced; unlimited reports-only users in plus and Advanced; Unlimited time tracking-only users in Essentials, plus, and Advanced.

QuickBooks Simple Start, Essentials, and Plus all have hard limits on the chart of both accounts and the number of classes and locations. Once you have them maxed out, there will be a need for you to deactivate accounts, classes, or locations in order to make some space available, or else you will have to upgrade to an advanced subscription.

Essentials, and Plus

The QuickBooks Essentials and QuickBooks Plus intermediate plans are two of the options. Whom they are designed for is the main distinction between QuickBooks Essentials and Plus. Essentials are made for service-based companies without any tangible goods to sell. Its main goals are to help you track your revenue, manage your bills and spending, and collect payments.

On the other hand, Plus is for product- or service-based enterprises that need to manage project profitability, create purchase orders, and keep track of inventory. It also has slightly more sophisticated reporting as a result of these enhanced features.

You can use free mobile apps that can assist you in managing your business on the move because both are a component of QuickBooks Online. Each subscription also includes automated workflows, reports that are suited to your company, and automatic data backup.

QuickBooks Online Advanced

The most potent version of QuickBooks Online, QuickBooks Online Advanced, is made for companies with more complicated financial and accounting requirements. To focus on important decisions and advance to the next level, QuickBooks Online Advanced offers deeper insights, greater serenity, and increased productivity.

Accounting software called QuickBooks Online Advanced is cloud-based and geared for growing and mid-sized companies. All of QuickBooks' essential accounting capabilities are included in QuickBooks Online Advanced, which also offers strong tools including customizable business analytics, revenue and cash flow dashboards, bespoke user roles for 25 people, and online backup and restoration. Batch invoicing and automated procedures help save time and money. Employees may access real-time data from multiple locations via the mobile app, which also tracks mileage.

QuickBooks Online Accountant

Software for managing accounting practices on the cloud is called QuickBooks Online Accountant. It aids bookkeepers and accountants in the editing, inspection, and correction of customer transactions. Accounting professionals are eligible to participate in the QuickBooks Online ProAdvisor program for free after they register. QuickBooks Online Accountant features bookkeeping for your company built around QuickBooks Online Advanced in addition to client tools, giving it plenty of ability to meet all your bookkeeping needs.

Below are some of the best needs of QuickBooks online accountant;

- Searching for free accounting practice management software by businesses and accountants One of my top picks for the greatest accounting practice management software, QuickBooks Online Accountant is accessible to accountants for free, despite the fact that it might seem too good to be true.

- Businesses who wish to manage both their clients' finances and their own operations in one location: Thanks to the software's flexibility, you can view all of your client's financial information from a single dashboard. To handle your own books, you'll also have access to QuickBooks Online Advanced.

- By promoting your services in a unique Find-a-ProAdvisor profile, which comes free with certification as a QuickBooks ProAdvisor, QuickBooks Online Accountant enables you to get the leads you desire. The Intuit Marketing Hub also offers a library of templates and instructions for growing your brand and turning leads into customers.

A very nice welcome indeed! I'm confident that after reading about the features mentioned above, you are fully informed about QuickBooks Online. The following chapters will offer more information by outlining all the things that can be done using both QuickBooks Online and QuickBooks Online(QBO) Accountant (QBOA). Make sure to write down the acronyms because they will be utilized in the upcoming chapters, which also include exercises you should complete. Hold on, read, study, and practice!

CHAPTER 2

CREATING A QUICKBOOKS ONLINE COMPANY

Upon signing on to QuickBooks Online, you are then automatically prompted to create a company of your own. You can begin by inserting necessary data from scratch, importing your data from QuickBooks Desktop if applicable or importing lists like customers and vendors alongside some other importing inventory items.

Signing Up for QuickBooks Online

You've chosen to utilize QuickBooks for your company after all. A general guideline for your account is that activities done in QuickBooks Online should correspond to what is actually taking place. All transactions, including those for tracking sales and making bank deposits, fall under this. While some actions, like submitting invoices, must be taken entirely within QuickBooks, for the most part, the activities you record were carried out elsewhere.

Make sure your accounting accurately captures each stage of each transaction whether you handle a credit card payment, pay your staff using QuickBooks Payroll, or obtain a loan from the bank. That entails comparing the recorded transactions on your actual bank statements to the names, dates, payment options, and totals.

- Begin **by visiting quickbooks.intuit.com/pricing.**

- Search **for four boxes** that describe the **Simple Start, Essentials, Plus, and Advanced subscriptions**. If you would like to make use of QuickBooks Self-Employed, move downwards beyond the boxes towards the freelancer and independent contractor part. You can also choose to pick between a 30-day free trial and three months of reduced prices for **Simple Start, Essentials, and Plus**. Note that the **Advanced subscription** does not offer a free trial but you can choose to gain access to the drive at qbo.intuit.com/redir/testdrive_us_advanced.

- If you would like to sign up for a free trial, choose **the slider button** at the top of the **QuickBooks version** in order to have the free trial for 30 days activated. Note that if you choose to pay to buy the software immediately, you will save more and pay less for your subscription because discounts do not apply to the free trials. Also, be aware that promotional pricing normally comes to an end after three months.

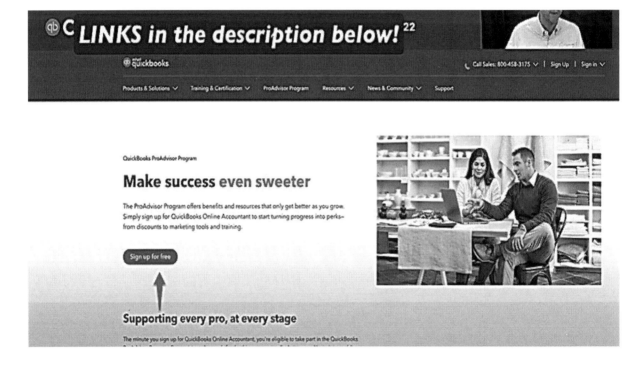

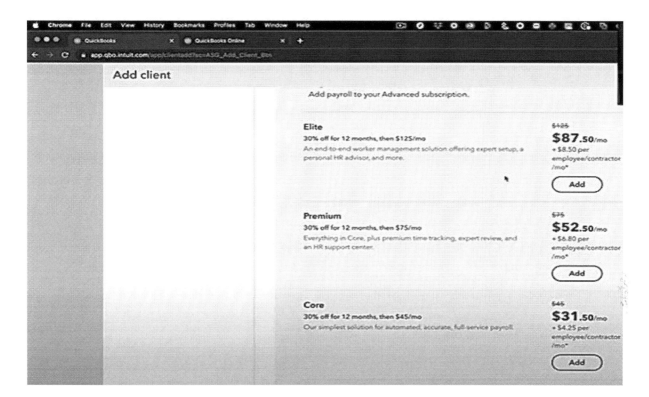

Exploring Your New Company

Companies in QuickBooks online have the same characteristics as any other typical company in the outside world. Here are some of these characteristics:

You may access your company's dashboard by logging into your QuickBooks account.

- Account and Settings can be found by **clicking** the **gear button**.

- Next, choose the **Company tab** from the **Account and Settings section**.

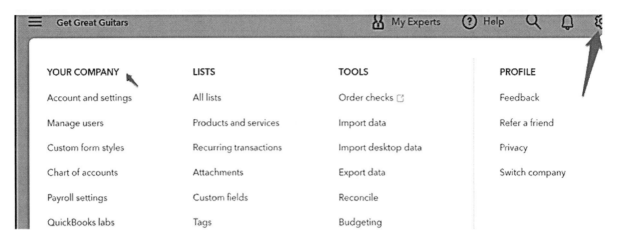

Company name

- To modify the information (as regards the name of the company), click **anywhere** in the firm name area, including the pencil symbol.

- Click **Save** after making the necessary adjustments.

Three items are listed in the firm name section:

Company logo: Import your company's logo to add it to the forms that you create. You must store your logo on your computer as an image file. To import your logo into QuickBooks Online, adhere to these procedures;

- You should click **the gray square** next to the company logo.

- The logos you previously uploaded to QuickBooks Online are shown on the following screen. If your logo is already there, **choose** to include it in the list of your company's details. Click the **blue plus sign** if the logo you want isn't already shown.

- QuickBooks offers a popup that allows you to explore your computer and choose the **logo image file**.

  ○ Click **Open** to go back to the previous screen and see a thumbnail of your new logo after choosing the image file. The logo is then saved in your QuickBooks Online account so that you won't need to refresh it when you customize forms.

- Ensure that the logo you would like to add has been highlighted then click on the **Save** button.

Company and legal name: Put your company name exactly how you want it to appear on forms and invoices. The name listed by the IRS for your business should be the same as your official business name. On tax documents such as Form 1099 and payroll tax returns, the legal name will be used. Uncheck the box and enter your legal name if it differs from the firm name you wish to appear on your invoices.

EIN: The IRS number that was given to you ought to correspond to this. Use your Social Security number if you're self-employed. Because EINs are private information, QuickBooks may ask you to verify your login before accessing or editing the EIN.

Type of company: To input or modify your company type information,

- click the **pencil icon** or **any other location** on the Company Type section.

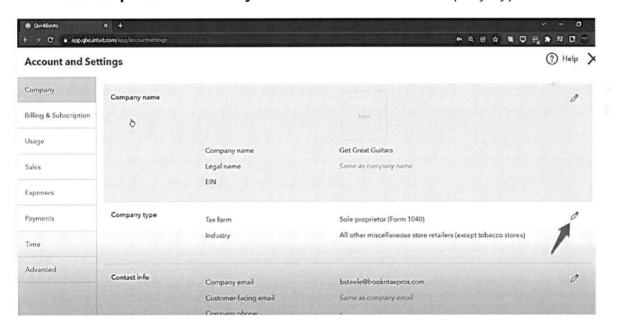

- Choose **your taxable entity type** from the drop-down menu adjacent to the Tax form field by **clicking on it**.

Sole Proprietorship: If you are the only person running your business, you are a lone proprietor. Use Schedule C to report any income or losses (Form 1040).

Partnership: If you run your firm with two or more partners, choose this business category. Form 1065 is used by partnerships to report their business's profits and losses.

S corporation (S-corp): A corporation that chooses to be an S-corp reports on Form the 1120S and transfers corporate income, loss, and taxes through to its shareholders.

A c corporation (C-corp): Rather than going through to the owners, a corporation that meets the requirements to be a C-corp is taxed independently from them. C-corps file reports using Form 1120.

Nonprofit organization: Nonprofits are tax-exempt businesses that prioritize social goals over financial gain. They disclose their yearly activity on Form 990.

Limited liability company (LLC): If you're not sure whether to file taxes as a single proprietor, partnership, or S-corp, choose this company structure.

Company's contact info

- To enter **contact details for QuickBooks and your clients**, click **anywhere** in the Contact info section, including the pencil symbol.

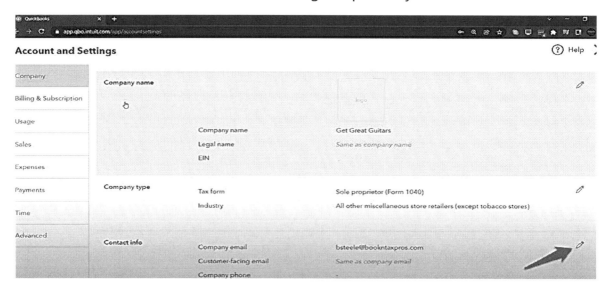

Email: The email address that QuickBooks will use to get in touch with the administrator is your business email. Your clients' sales forms, like invoices, will include the customer-facing email address. Uncheck the option and enter the proper address if this is different from the QuickBooks administrator's email address.

Company Phone: Enter the phone number that will be printed on the sales forms consumers receive.

Website: For it to appear on all of your sales forms, enter a website address.

Company Address

To input or modify your company's address information, click the pencil icon or any other location in the address area. The corporate address, customer-facing address, and legal address are all listed separately in this QuickBooks Online version.

Company address: The firm address, which serves as the business's physical address, is what you use to send payments to QuickBooks.

- Click **Save** after making the necessary adjustments.

Customer-facing address: This address, which can be seen on your invoices and other sales documents, should be where clients should send their payments. Uncheck the box and input the right customer-facing address if it differs from your corporate address. For modifications to be saved,

- click **Save**.

Legal address: Your tax filings must be sent to the legal address, which must coincide with the address you have on record with the IRS. Again, you must uncheck the option and provide the legal address if this is different from the company address.

- Click the green **Save button** once you are pleased with the address you have provided.

Reviewing the QuickBooks interface

If you're a seasoned Desktop user, the differences between QuickBooks Desktop and Online can be rather noticeable. But we can't just base everything on appearances!

Some desktop users switching to QuickBooks Online could encounter a challenging learning curve. Although they have identical functionality, the two different systems that they are intended to run on have different interfaces. Once mastered, however, QuickBooks Online's more streamlined design may make your accounting simpler than QuickBooks Desktop. It only requires a grasp of the layout.

Your emphasis will be split between the header bar and the navigation bar as you navigate QuickBooks Online.

Header bar

The header bar, which runs along the top and has navigation options to the right, appears once you have logged into the QuickBooks Online service.

We have access to anything we need to enter by using the "+ icon." Consider this the location to use when introducing any new types of transactions. Our Customers, Vendors, Employees, and Others are clearly categorized in the frame that appears. It helps to consider these as transactions of the incoming payment variety, goods that need to be paid off, payroll, and adjusting/banking entries. This resembles the flowchart on QuickBooks Desktop's home page!

The "gear icon" gives you access to the budget, audit log, settings, limits, and import/export features for your company file.

Navigation bar

The user interface's left side is occupied by a vertical navigation bar that provides rapid access to QuickBooks' features.

- **Banking**: gives access to locations that can immediately download information and display matches for past bank transactions and bill payments. This function is more useful than the desktop version because it doesn't open a new window but instead displays Name, Account, Customer, and Class in a drop-down menu. There is still a "Batch Actions" option to add new transactions to the bank register if the system has correctly identified transactions. The best feature of QuickBooks Online bank feeds is the ability to check previously inserted or matched transactions and undo them if an error was made.

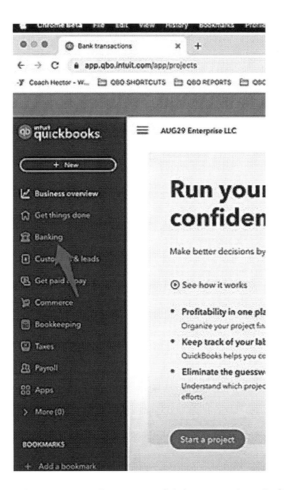

- **Sales**: access to the Customer Center, which contains information on your clients, invoices, products, and services. Live charts that are updated in real-time at the top of these sections display which clients/invoices are past due and which goods are running low on stock. Although it doesn't replace reporting, this toolbar is an excellent method to quickly monitor your business.

- **Expenses**: gives access to information about vendors and expenses. A running tally of open and past-due bills still appears at the top along with vendor information. To make it apparent which account the invoices and expenses are going to, the account is displayed as a category under the expenses tab. This is a fantastic tool to make sure expenses are entered properly for each individual vendor.

- **Workers**: gives contractors and employees access to payroll. The system performs an excellent job of displaying which suppliers are contractors (a check box situated in the vendor description section) and the amount paid out, as was already mentioned. If your business employs a lot of contractors, QuickBooks Online enables regular check-ins to ensure that all pertinent information has been gathered, which makes filing time a snap.

- **Reports**: gives you access to all reporting features and any customized reports you may have saved in your favorites. All your overview, A/P, A/R, employee, and other reports will be gathered together to assist you to identify the report that is most suited for your purposes in the online edition, which strives to organize everything by what you need.

The fact that checks and deposits cannot be input directly into a bank register in QuickBooks Online is a major distinction. The Online edition of QuickBooks demands that transactions be entered individually via the "+ icon" in the header bar, despite the fact that this would appear as a convenient option in QuickBooks Desktop.

It is true that this method requires more time. When using QuickBooks Desktop, it can be simple to scroll through new entries in the register and unintentionally make mistakes that end up costing your company money. The QuickBooks Online approach of inputting transactions one at a time slows down bookkeepers enough to evaluate the work and possibly spot errors before they snowball rather than having them rush through a register. This extra time spent upfront can prevent spending even more time later on locating and correcting errors.

Updating the Chart of Accounts

A list of all the accounts that QuickBooks utilizes to keep track of your financial data may be seen in the chart of accounts. These accounts are used to classify transactions on a variety of forms, including tax forms, reports, and sales forms. Every account has a transaction history that details how much money you have in it and how much you owe.

The chart of accounts is the cornerstone of sound accounting, thus it's crucial to comprehend it and put it up properly.

- Select **Settings > Chart of accounts**, to access and examine your chart of accounts.

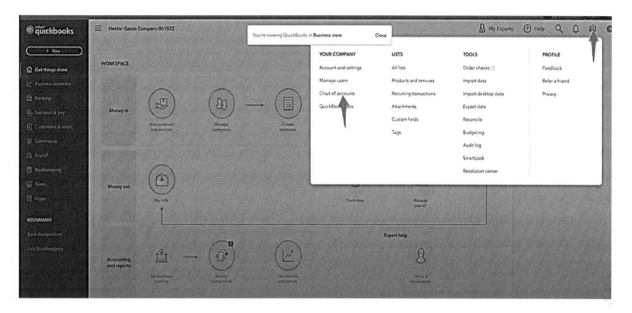

The column name, type, and detail type are used to organize the accounts. The information that appears on important financial reports like the Balance Sheet and Profit & Loss statements depends on the account types and detail kinds.

The transaction history and current balance can be reviewed in many accounts' account histories. You can run a report to view transactions on accounts that don't have a history.

- Select **Account history or Run a report** from the **Action column** to view the history or reports from your chart of accounts list.

Editing or inactivating accounts

Organize and keep your chart of accounts uncomplicated. You can make an account inactive if you don't intend to use it anymore. In order to give you access to historical transaction data for reporting purposes, QuickBooks makes accounts inactive rather than destroying them.

You can quickly make an account inactive if you've never used it or if the balance is $0. Active accounts, however, will require a little more effort. Data removal from one account has an impact on all the others because balanced accounts depend on one another.

Things you should know before making an account inactive

- Except when merging two accounts, it is impossible to permanently delete one.

- Transactions made on an inactive account remain there. Any deactivated (deleted) account transactions are not affected.

- A transaction linked to an inactive account cannot be edited. You must first restore the account before you can properly alter or delete the transaction. After that, go to the register and remove each individual entry. The account should then be examined and corrected to have no balance before being deactivated.

- Correct the balance to zero before designating an account inactive on the balance sheet. If the balance is not zero, QuickBooks Online automatically creates an adjustment entry to bring the inactive account's balance to zero. The automated entry is identical to posting to prior years because it posts to the Opening Balance Equity account. The entry can result in the filing of inaccurate tax information.

Making an account inactive

When you deactivate an account that has a balance, QuickBooks generates a journal item. Thus, the remaining balance is transferred to another account. Existing transactions remain on your financial records and don't vanish. However, QuickBooks won't update the journal item or shift the balance back if you choose to utilize the account again.

Certain accounts need extra steps before they can be rendered inactive:

- Change **the account that the products or services** are tied to if they use the account. Alternatively, you can **deactivate any products or services** that use the account.

- Invoice **your clients** for the billable costs, time, or charges if you want to eliminate an income account that has pending charges. The account can then be deleted.

- You **must delink any recurring transactions** that are connected to an account.

- Move **the subaccounts** to a separate account on your chart of accounts if the account contains subaccounts. Subaccount-containing accounts cannot be deleted.

Now all seems set and almost completed, to complete the process of inactivation simply follow the steps below;

- Scroll to **Settings** then choose **Charts of accounts**.

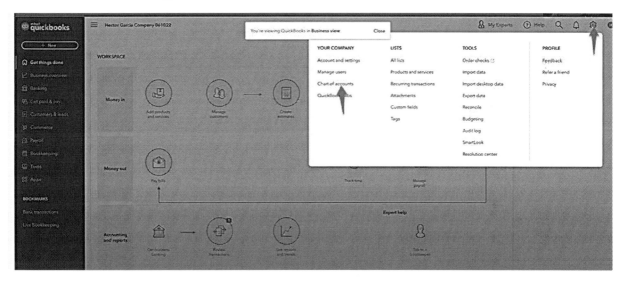

- Locate the account you would like to delete.

- Click on the **Action dropdown** then choose the **Make inactive** option.

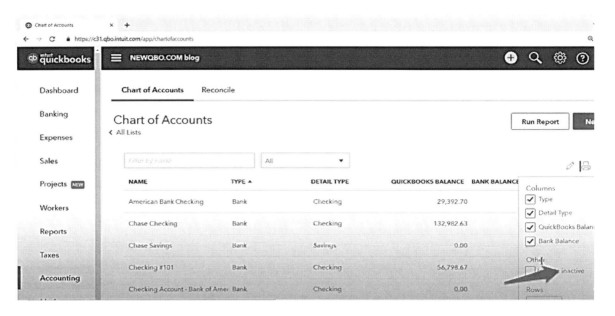

You will still notice dormant accounts and associated transactions when you run reports. They are part of QuickBooks to maintain accuracy. Some reports can be customized to hide inactive accounts, however, doing so may reduce their accuracy.

You can view your inactive accounts in your chart of accounts by following the steps below;

- Click on **Settings** then choose the **Chart of accounts**.

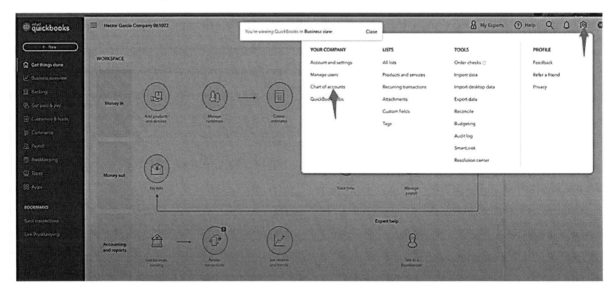

- Close to the printer icon, and choose the **Settings icon**.

- Choose the **Include inactive** checkbox.

Adding account numbers

The list of accounts you employ to classify finances expands along with your firm. Don't worry if your chart of accounts is large. By allocating numbers, you can keep your accounts organized and simple to locate.

By default, the account numbers feature is disabled. Here is how to activate it.

- Locate **Settings** then choose **Account and settings**.

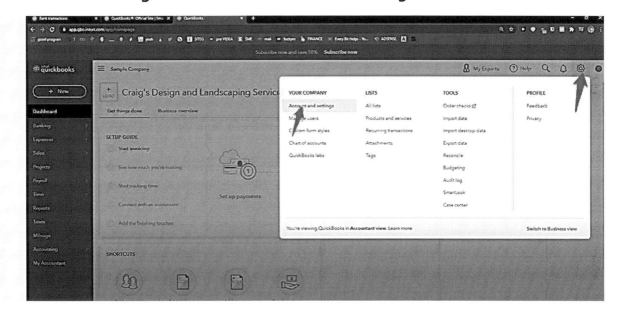

- Choose the **Advanced tab** option.

- Click on **Edit** in the Chart of accounts section.

- Switch on **Enable account numbers**. If you would like to have the account numbers displayed on reports and transactions, choose **Show account numbers**.

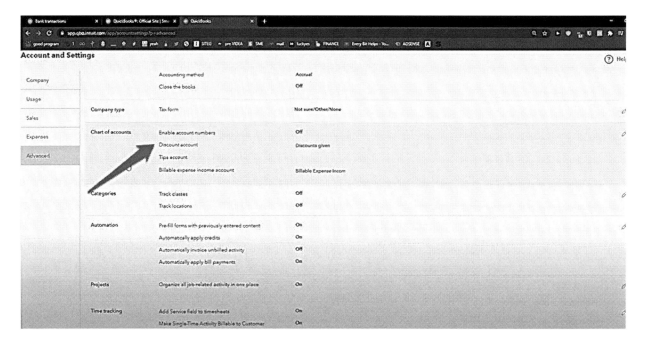

- Click on **Save** then **Done**.

Now that you have switched on account numbers, follow the steps below to make use of it;

- Locate **Bookkeeping** then click on **Chart of accounts**.

- Click on **Batch edit** located at the top of the **Action** column.

- Add account numbers in the **Number column**.

- Upon completion of the above-listed steps, click on the **Save** button.

Now, searching for particular accounts in the Chart of Accounts or adding transactions will take less time. Utilize the numbers you gave the accounts to quickly locate them.

Importing a chart of accounts

Your chart of accounts is used by QuickBooks to organize all of your accounting. QuickBooks personalizes your chart of accounts when you set up your business. You can import your existing accounts from another QuickBooks Online or Desktop company file or a spreadsheet of custom accounts in place of manually entering all of your accounts.

A Google Sheets, Excel, or CSV file can be used to import your chart of accounts but before importing there will be a need for you to format your spreadsheet, upload the spreadsheet, and map your spreadsheet fields to the QuickBooks field then you can begin to import your chart of accounts. I will walk you through all of the above-listed steps.

Formatting spreadsheet

- Open **an existing account spreadsheet or start a new one**. Alternatively, you can import **your chart of accounts** from a different **QuickBooks firm**.

- Ensure there are columns in your spreadsheet such as **Account name, Type, Detail Type, and Number.**

- Add an **Account Number column** if you're organizing your accounts by numbers. If you don't utilize account numbers, you can skip this step.

- When adding a sub-account, use the following format in the **Account Name column: Sub-account is the primary account**. Utility: Gas, as an illustration.

- Save your spreadsheet in **Google Sheets, Excel, or CSV** format if everything appears to be in order.

Upload spreadsheet

- Sign in to **QuickBooks Online**.

- Choose **Settings** then click on **Import Data**.

- Select **Chart of Accounts**.

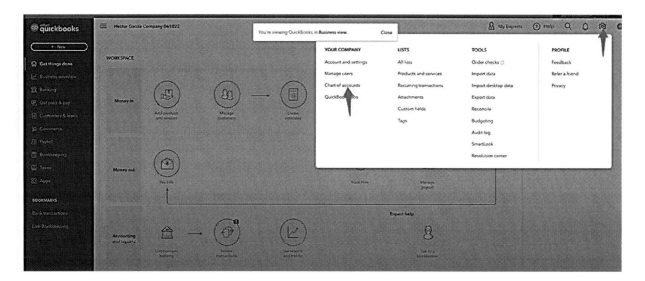

- To upload a file from your computer, click on **Browse** then choose the file you would like to upload then choose **Open**.

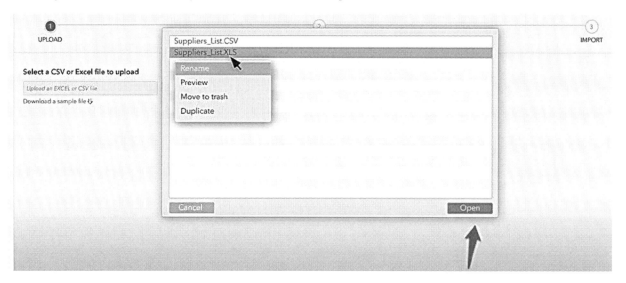

- Or rather if you would be uploading from **Google Sheets**, choose to **Connect** to sign into your **Google account**. Click on the **correct file**.

- Click on **Next**.

Mapping spreadsheet fields to QuickBooks fields

Once your spreadsheet has been uploaded, map your accounts so they will import properly.

- Locate the **Your Field column** then choose the **small arrow icon** and match the names to the QuickBooks Online field for Detail Type, Account name, Account number, and Type.

- If a field doesn't match a column in your spreadsheet, with the exception of Account Name, you can choose **No Match**. If you don't utilize account numbers, as an illustration.

- Click on the **Next button**.

Import your chart of accounts

- Go over the above-listed settings and be sure that all has been done correctly.
- When a field is **highlighted in red**, hover your cursor over it to see what needs to be fixed.
- Any account you don't wish to save can be **unchecked.**
- Select **Import** if everything looks good.

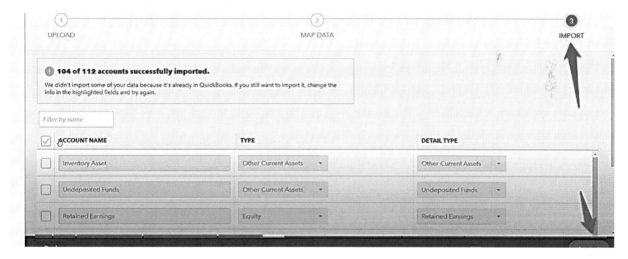

Reviewing Company Settings

You can view and modify your firm name, address, contact information, and Employer Identification Number on the Company tab (EIN). Additionally, you can modify your settings for Intuit marketing.

Company preferences

Usage statistics

In QuickBooks, usage limits refer to the most accounts or users you can have concurrently. You have a specified use cap based on your subscription. The number of billable users, charts of accounts, classes, locations, and tags you can add to QuickBooks are all subject to these restrictions.

By subscription, usage restrictions change in QuickBooks Online. The cap only applies to active (or invited) users, accounts, classes, locations, and tags.

The number of things you have for each usage limit is displayed on your usage limits dashboard. To view the most recent usage restrictions, if you are an accountant, sign in directly to your client's account.

Sign in to **QuickBooks Online** as an admin.

Locate **Settings** then choose **Account and settings**.

Click on the **Usage tab**.

Don't worry if you reach your use caps and are unable to add any more users or accounts. You have two options: increase your subscription level or decrease your usage. You must assess use for each company if you run more than one.

Sales preferences

You may create payment terms, personalize your sales forms, and control what information appears on customer forms under the Sales tab. Additionally, this is where you enable functions like automatic reminders and progress billing.

Customizing sales forms

You may create appealing, expert-looking invoices, estimates, and sales receipts with the help of QuickBooks Online.

Customizing the look and feel of sales forms is a quick and easy approach to improving communications inside your company. To create forms that are appealing, you don't need to be a designer. Additionally, you get to choose which information your customers view and only include that which is essential to your company.

You may make and customize sales receipts, estimates, and invoice templates. How to modify your sales forms is provided here.

Create a new template

- Locate **settings** then choose **Custom form styles**.

- Choose a **New style**.

- Choose a **sales form type** you would like to create a template for.

Customize the appearance

- Click on the **Design tab**.

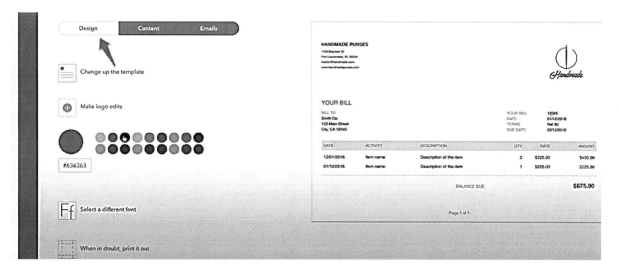

- Name **your template**.

- Click on **Change** up the template in order to choose your preferred layout. Note that these layouts are fixed.

- Choose to **Make logo edits** in order to make adjustments to your logo or completely hide it.

- Select **the (+) addition icon** on the image to alter the logo. Choose from your **previously stored logos or enter a new one**. One logo may be used at a time, although you may store several logos.

- Select **the size and placement icons** to change the logo's size and location.

- Select the **Hide logo** to conceal the logo.

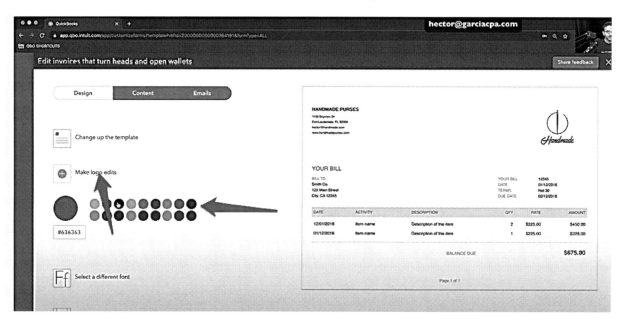

- Select **Try other colors**, try out different hues. For a really unique color, you can input a **HEX code**, which is a six-digit combination of numbers and characters for a color.

- Click on **Select a different font** in order to change the size of the font.

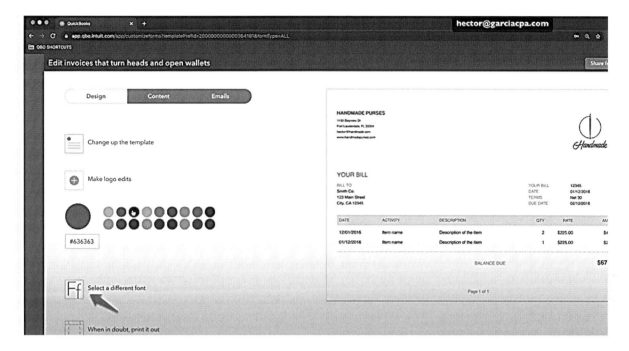

- In order to change the margins, choose **Edit print settings**. If you send printed forms to your clients, this is crucial.

Customizing the info on your forms

- Choose the **Content tab.**
- To begin changing a section, choose **the header, table, or footer** on the example form. Each section will be edited independently.
- You can display specific fields on your form by checking the boxes next to them. Then, to alter the sample form, choose a new part (header, table, or footer).
- When you are almost done fixing your changes click on the **Done button**.

Expenses preferences

You may enable billable expenses and purchase orders on the Expenses page, as well as personalize the email notifications that go along with purchase orders.

Payment preferences

You can connect an existing QuickBooks Payments account to QuickBooks Online under the Payments tab or set up online payments there. Once connected, you may control merchant information, and business owner data, and specify where QuickBooks should record deposits automatically.

Time preferences

The Time tab allows you to determine the start of the workweek, keep account of the services your team provided while working for a client, and choose whether or not to let staff members and vendors know how much you charge for their services.

Advanced preferences

In QuickBooks, you can enable additional features by clicking the Advanced tab. Some are not always turned on. For instance, you can enable categories to track goods and services in a specific manner. The start and end of your company's fiscal year are also set here. You can also enable this option here if your business interacts with several currencies.

QuickBooks Online Apps

You may select and switch apps for your business and clients from one location by using the Apps tab.

Find apps

- From the left side of the menu, choose **Apps**.
- Navigate to the **Find apps tab**.
- To find specific apps, type **their names** into the search field or choose a category from the **Browse drop-down menu**.

Installing an app

- Once you have found your **preferred app**, choose **its tile** in order to see the reviews from other people and also the pricing.
- To begin the signup process, click on **Get App now**.
- Choose your firm or you can also choose a client from the Install for **Your Client drop-down menu**.
- Click on the **Install button**.
- Authorize **QuickBooks** to have your data shared with the chosen app.
- Configure any **sync preferences**.

- Choose **Save & Sync**.

A client cannot sync all applications. If the user chooses any of these apps, they will alert to this restriction. When the app is ready for you to install for your client, you can choose to be notified.

Client apps

To examine and interact with the applications currently connected to the businesses of your clients, go to the Client Apps tab. If the app is one of the cheap ones in the Apps Program, you might get the option to activate it. To make the most of the software, activate it as soon as you purchase it. You can see who connected the app and the support contact details when you choose the app tile. You can choose an action from the drop-down to

- Open **the app**.
- Access **Support** for the app.
- Disconnect **the app from the company.**
- Leave a **Review** for the app.

Note that the drop-down will be made available only for apps that are connected.

Firm apps

You may view or interact with apps related to your firm in the Firm apps tab. You can choose from the drop-down menu for Action:

- Open **the app**.
- Access **Support** for the app.
- Disconnect **the app from the company**.
- Leave a **Review** for the app.

QuickBooks Online Desktop app

For Microsoft Windows (64-bit needed), the QuickBooks Online Advanced Desktop client provides more creative navigation and improvements to speed up workflows. The program was made more stable for power users who spent several hours using QuickBooks Online thanks to its multi-tab and company-switching features. It is especially useful for QuickBooks customers who use more than one QBO Account or access QuickBooks frequently.

If you opt to access QuickBooks Advanced through the QBO Advanced Desktop program for MSW instead of a web browser, you can remain logged in for up to six months unless you deliberately choose to log out. Once you sign in, you can stay signed in, allowing you to access QBO whenever you need to without having to sign in again.

A navigation map view similar to the home page workflows found in QuickBooks Desktop will be available to users. Giving consumers a roadmap of connected actions and processes could speed up and simplify workflows for some users.

Accessing numerous QuickBooks Online firms at once and toggling between them without refreshing each company is another important advantage of the new software. No matter what QBO version your clients are using, you can effortlessly manage them all with this functionality.

Not only will you be able to access all of your clients through your client list, but you will also be able to switch between different client companies as you work throughout the day since Intuit understands that accountants, bookkeepers, and ProAdvisors are multi-taskers.

- Visit **QBO-Accountant or QBO-Advanced** and select the **Gear symbol** to download the app. A button to download the desktop app will be visible.

Easier access to QuickBooks Online.

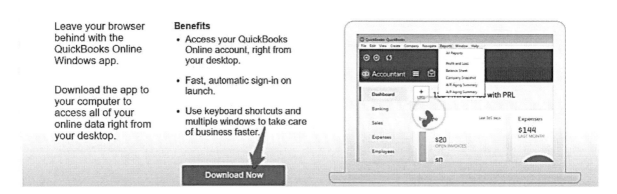

- Your settings may allow the app to install itself automatically. Alternatively, you could be asked to **save the.exe file**; in that case, select **Save** after

37

deciding where to save the file. The installation can then be started by opening the QuickBooks Advanced Setup file.

- A desktop shortcut for the software is **created after installation**. The application ought to launch instantly after installation. Open **the app** from the shortcut if it doesn't.

- Your **user ID and password must be entered** on the sign-in screen. Select **Sign in**

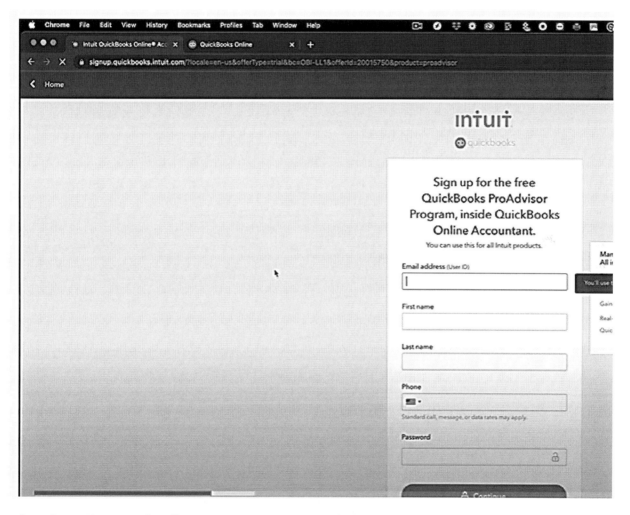

After that. Choose **the firm** you want to open if more than one **QuickBooks Online Advanced** company is displayed. (An error warning will be shown if your user ID does not belong to a QuickBooks Online firm.)

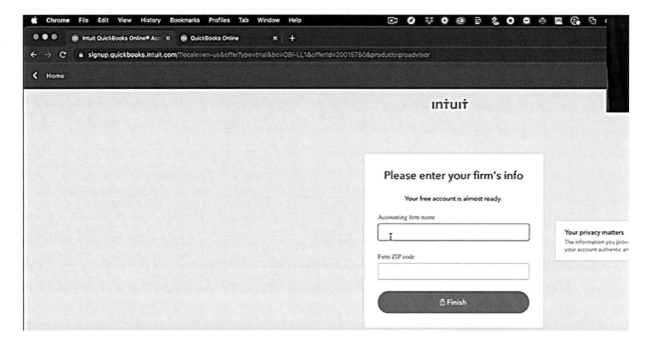

- When using the **Advance Desktop** app for the first time, you can choose how **QuickBooks** will be presented on the home page. (You'll have the ability to alter this setting later.)

Note that **QuickBooks Desktop**-like navigational tools can be utilized to examine accounts. The map view provides rapid navigation to the required work areas by displaying QuickBooks Online operations like sales, costs, payroll, and reporting in workflow diagrams.

- Choose either **Map view or Dashboard view** in the app to move between the navigation map view and the **QuickBooks Online** dashboard view.

QuickBooks Online Mobile apps

Millions of individuals are finding it difficult to escape the "office" in this work-from-home era. However, there can be situations when having access to your accounting information in QuickBooks Online would be quite useful even if you weren't at home or at work.

Free companion apps for the website enable that. The QuickBooks Online mobile app is available for iOS and Android and offers many of the same features as the desktop or laptop version. The actions you take on the app are automatically synced with the browser-based version and vice versa. Both versions offer a user experience that makes doing chores on your mobile device simple and has a similar design and functionality.

You'll see a screen full of shortcuts to the program's primary features once you've downloaded the QuickBooks Online mobile app and entered your login information from the browser-based version. Although this is a condensed description of everything you can accomplish, it directs you to the screens you'll want to visit most frequently. When you select the All tab, a complete list of links for the program, including features like Reports and Products & services that are absent from the shortcuts page, appears.

The app opens two more panels when you

- **click the home icon** in the lower left corner.

One of them is a Dashboard that resembles the one on your browser. It shows a list of your account balances as well as charts for profit and loss, invoices, and costs. To get a list of the most recent activities, select the Activity tab. The list is interactive, just like the majority of the app's features. The transaction underpinning an activity opens when you click on it.

The bottom of the screen has two more links for navigating.

- You may access your selections by **clicking the + (plus) symbol** when you want to add a transaction.
- To access the Shortcuts page, click **the three horizontal lines**. You may access the **Settings screen** by **clicking the gear icon** in the top left corner, where you'll find links to the Company Information, Tax Rates, Overdue Invoice Alerts, and other sections.

QuickBooks App Store

The QuickBooks App Store can be found in QuickBook essentials which you can activate by turning it on. The steps to gain access to it vary, look below for the one that fits best for the web browser you are using;

- Google Chrome: press **Ctrl + Shift +N**
- Mozilla Firefox: press **Ctrl + Shift +P**

- Internet Explorer: press **Ctrl + Shift +P**
- Safari: press **command + Shift +N**

Clear the cache of the default browser if you can see the Apps menu to improve efficiency. However, the site won't appear on the list if you're referring to the App Store. To access it, you'll need to go to their website directly.

QuickBooks Labs

As a component of the QuickBooks Online update, Intuit introduced QuickBooks Labs. This QuickBooks feature is categorized as an experimental plug-in. These have QuickBooks integration. You might want to run the plug-in with a phony company file first in order to safeguard your QuickBooks data.

You would have to rely on Intuit to protect your data since QuickBooks Online does not allow you to easily make a backup copy. You won't be able to restore your data on your own if the plug-in is the cause of the issues. Furthermore, there is no option in QuickBooks Online that enables your administrator to prevent QuickBooks users from enabling such a plug-in. For users with "normal" access, there is also no setting that restricts access to this or comparable services. Another drawback of utilizing a plug-in of this type is that experiments may occasionally disappear from the application, so you can grow accustomed to using something that afterward stops working.

A user may be taken to a brief instructional video before using one of the new experimental plug-ins. Users are sent to the "Intuit Labs" page after selecting the "Learn More" option. These are produced by actual Intuit employees, not by independent software developers.

Don't feel overwhelmed just yet; we're only at the beginning. I have no doubt that this must be fun already. It's good to know that QuickBooks Online allows you to simulate running a business if you don't already have one, and if you have, this program is all you need. You must have studied how to start using QuickBooks Online, including signing up, in the chapter that just ended. You must also have studied the QBO user interface, how to create an account, and how to link account numbers. You must also have learned how to construct a corporation and add all required features.

The other factions, including QuickBooks Desktop, QuickBooks Lab, and QuickBooks Online App, must have also been introduced to you. Make sure to put what you learn into practice because the main objective isn't simply to teach you to read and learn, but also to teach you how to operate and carry out all of the aforementioned tasks. Join the activity and put your knowledge to the test.

Activity

1. Sign up for QuickBooks Online by following the steps listed above.
2. Create a company in your QuickBooks Online, name the company (you could choose to make use of your name), add a logo, and ensure to state the type of company it is.
3. Differentiate between an S corporation and a C corporation.
4. Mention five (5) features present in the navigation bar.
5. Describe the use of the header bar.
6. Go to your charts of accounts and configure them.
7. Mention three (3) things you should know before making an account inactive.
8. Create an account and make it inactive.
9. Create an account and include two (2) account numbers.
10. Import a chart of accounts from Excel into your QuickBooks Online.
11. What is the use of the Usage statistics and the sales preference?
12. Create a template you can make use of in your company account.
13. Differentiate between expense preferences and payment preferences.
14. Install an application in QuickBooks Online.
15. What is a Client app used for?
16. Mention the browsers that can be used in opening QuickBooks Online.
17. Download the QuickBooks Online Mobile App on your smartphone.

CHAPTER 3

IMPORTING FROM QUICKBOOKS DESKTOP AND SAGE 50

If you are not making use of QuickBooks Desktop or Sage 50 then you can choose to skip this chapter and move on to the next else you can glue your face to the book while I take you through converting your data from QuickBooks Desktop or Sage 50 to QuickBooks Online. There is a need for you to carry out these steps for each QuickBooks or Sage company that you wish to migrate. Bear in mind that each set of books that you have kept on your desktop are basically referred to as a company and they will entail a separate QuickBooks subscription fee. Accounting software conversions will always have some edges that are not so smooth hence continue reading and check out what should be expected when you are moving your books from your desktop to the cloud.

Knowing the Ins and Outs of Converting Data

QuickBooks Desktop

Much of the data from your company file can be transferred from QuickBooks Desktop to QuickBooks Online without needing to be manually entered again. Some bits of information, though, won't immediately convert or transfer with your company file.

After conversion, information that will undergo modifications can be handled differently in QuickBooks Online than it was in QuickBooks Desktop, necessitating some adjustments.

Information that won't convert won't be sent automatically with your company file and must be manually included again after migration.

To make sure your information migrates correctly, there are a few things to do before you begin the conversion process; your company files with a backup, A QuickBooks Desktop update Review your overall targets. Keep a copy of your Sales Tax Liability Report. your reports and lists for export.

Your desktop file can now be exported to QuickBooks Online. Depending on the version of QuickBooks Desktop you use, follow the instructions below.

- In **QuickBooks Desktop**, log in **as an admin** to the company file you would like to import.
- Locate the **company menu** then choose the **Export Company File** to **QuickBooks Online** option.
- Click on **Get started**.

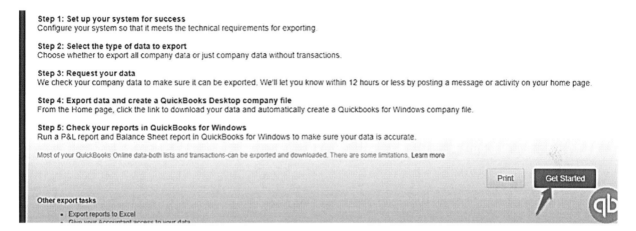

- Choose **Select destination** then sign in to your **QuickBooks Online account**.

Sage 50

The Sage 50 to QuickBooks Online conversion process has certain known restrictions.

Audit trail

Your QuickBooks Online audit trail will not include this information for transactions that were converted from Sage 50. For auditing purposes, you should keep a copy of your Sage 50 backup file. See the Sage 50 pre-conversion checklist.

Cash basis files

For businesses employing the cash foundation of accounting, Dataswitcher does not enable conversions from Sage 50 to QuickBooks Online at this time.

Cash refunds

Refunding a vendor's cash payment is not possible using QuickBooks Online. These transactions, if they exist in your Sage 50 data file, will be transformed into normal journals and won't have a reference to your clients or suppliers.

Check refunds

Refunding a vendor check payment is not supported by QuickBooks Online. These transactions, if they exist in your Sage 50 data file, will be transformed into normal journals and won't have a reference to your clients or suppliers.

Departments

Locations in QuickBooks Online will be the equivalent of Departments in Sage 50. One Department or Location can only be assigned to a transaction in QuickBooks Online. QuickBooks Online will apply one of those Departments across all line items if your Sage 50 transactions use various Departments for each line item. Dataswitcher will in all of these situations always use the Department designated for line item 1.

Foreign currency

Transactions made in a different currency than your home currency in QuickBooks Online will be converted using the historical exchange rate from Sage 50.

Additionally, when Sage 50 files with multi-currency activation are converted, the beginning balances for each currency may be split. Revaluations of currencies used in invoicing won't be recorded as purchases or sales. QuickBooks Online will automatically fix these revaluations for you when you choose matching payments.

Using an online tool to migrate QuickBooks

You don't need to worry if your QuickBooks Desktop is outdated or you don't have access to it. You can move your books with an online tool.

You can make use of the tool if;

- QuickBooks Pro, Premier, Enterprise, or QuickBooks for Mac files are available.
- If you save a backup for Windows, the utility will transport data from QuickBooks company files (.QBW), portable files (.QBM), backup files (.QBB), and QuickBooks for Mac files (.qbb).

- You want to assist your client in switching to QuickBooks Online but you don't have QuickBooks Desktop.
- You wish to transfer a QuickBooks Desktop file to QuickBooks Online even though you don't have QuickBooks Desktop.

Desktop online

There is no need to start afresh. simply transfer your desktop file to a QuickBooks Online business. Follow the steps below to complete the process of having your desktop online;

Get your desktop file ready

- Ensure your **QuickBooks** is up-to-date.

- Press **Ctrl + 1** on your keyboard to check if your total number of targets is fewer than 750,000. The file cannot be converted to QuickBooks Online if the target limit (750,000) has been reached. There is only one choice: either import lists and balances into QuickBooks Online or start from scratch.

- Print **a copy** of your report on your sales tax liability. After your move, you'll need it to submit adjustment entries.

  - Locate the **Reports menu** then choose **Vendors & Payables**. Choose **Sales Tax Liability**.

  - Scroll to the Dates drop-down and choose **All**.

  - At the top from the Print drop-down, choose to **Save as PDF**.

  - Make a choice of the folder you would like to save it in, give the folder a name and choose **Save**.

For Desktop Pro or Premier

- Sign in **as an admin** to the company file you want to import.

- Navigate to **Company** then choose **Export Company File** to **QuickBooks Online.**

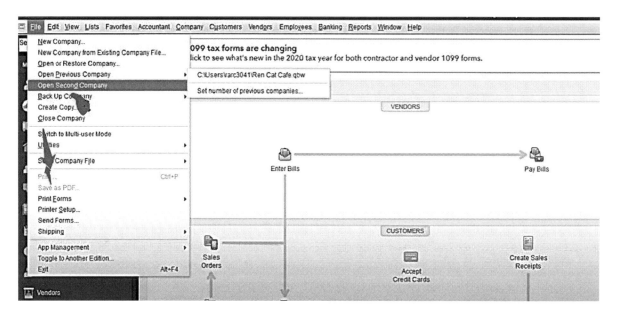

- Click on **Start your export**.

- Sign in **as an admin** to your **QuickBooks Online company**.

- Click on **Choose online company** then choose the **QuickBooks Online company** you would like to replace with your company file.

- Click on **Continue**.

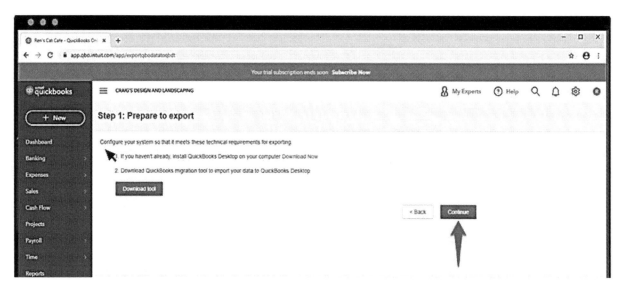

- If you happen to track inventory in QuickBooks Desktop;

  ○ Click on **Yes** to bring them over then insert the as-of-date.

- Click **No** if you would wish to set up new items in QuickBooks Online.

- Insert **Agree** in the text field then choose **Replace**.

- Click on **Yes**, go ahead and replace the data then click on **Replace**.

QuickBooks Desktop Enterprise

Note: Because some of your data won't transfer to QuickBooks Online if you use advanced capabilities (such as advanced reporting and advanced inventory), we advise starting from scratch. Find out more about QuickBooks Desktop Enterprise with cloud support if you wish to continue using these features in Enterprise.

- Sign in **as an admin** to the desktop of the company file you would like to move.
- Press **Ctrl + 1** on your keyboard in order to open the product information window.
- Press **Ctrl + B+Q** and click on **Ok** to show the export window.
- On the export window, click on **Get started.**

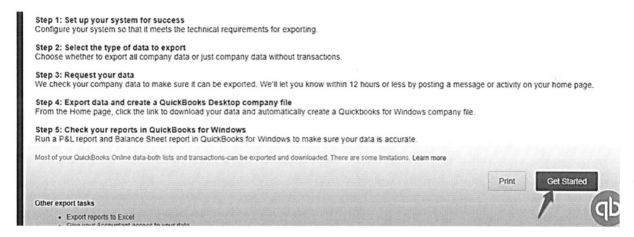

- Sign in **as an admin** to your **QuickBooks Online Company**.
- Click on **Choose online company** then click on the **QuickBooks Online company** you would like to replace with your company file.
- Click on **Continue**.

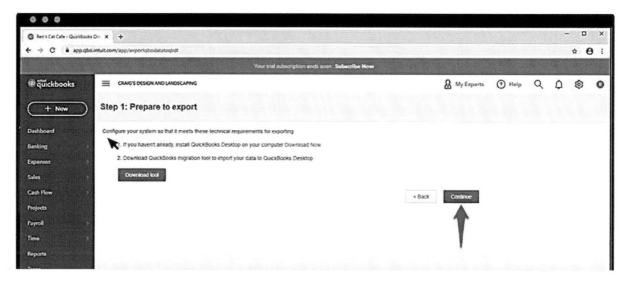

- If you track inventory in **QuickBooks Desktop**;

  - Click on **Yes** in order to have them brought over then indicate the as-of-date.

  - Click on **No** if you would like to set up new items later in **QuickBooks Online**

- Insert **Agree** in the text field then click on the **Replace button**.

- Click on **Yes**, go ahead and replace the data then click on **Replace**.

Using an online service to migrate Sage 50 to QuickBooks online

Do you wish to transfer your Sage 50 accounting data to QuickBooks Online? To move your data automatically, use the Dataswitcher conversion wizard. Any business must take a huge step before switching to accounting software. The transition from Sage 50 to QuickBooks Online can be made simpler with the help of Dataswitcher, a company that specializes in accounting software conversions. Only the accrual-basis accounting system is supported by the converter.

The following data will be free to migrate from Sage 50 to QuickBooks Online for up to two fiscal years: initial balances, both clients and vendors, Accounts Chart, Credits and invoices, Diaries entries, past transactions, and uniform payments.

For an additional charge, Dataswitcher will also convert the data listed below in addition to the aforementioned: 3 years or less of financial data, Inventory things, Employment & Departments (known as Classes & Locations in QuickBooks), Organizational data (address, email, phone number, etc). The Dataswitcher conversion procedure will provide a price quote before you submit your Sage 50 file.

There are some activities in QuickBook Online that you must finish before submitting your Sage 50 file to Dataswitcher and others that are optional. Even if optional tasks may not be applicable to you, we nonetheless advise that you review them.

Delete QuickBooks Online data

Once you start the conversion process, it's critical that there are no previous transactions in your QuickBooks Online file. If your firm does have data, you must remove it from QuickBooks Online before sending your Sage 50 file to Dataswitcher.

Sales Tax

Prior to your conversion, QuickBooks Online shouldn't have had Sales Tax activated. You will need to remove your QuickBooks Online data if it has been activated.

Bank & Credit card accounts

QuickBooks Online may ask you to link your bank and credit card accounts when you first log in. Please wait to perform this until the post-conversion checklist instructs you to do so.

More than one currency

You should enable multi-currency in QuickBooks Online if you use several currencies in Sage 50. Be sure to enable multi-currency after deleting your QuickBooks Online data if you intend to do so, as doing so will reset your settings.

Departments & Projects

The tracking of classes & locations in QuickBooks Online should be enabled if you use departments and projects in Sage 50. Be sure to enable multi-currency after deleting your QuickBooks Online data if you intend to do so, as doing so will reset your settings.

You will have a file named DS CONVERSION.001 (not PRE CONVERSION.001) if you have finished all the pre-conversion checklist items for Sage 50 and QuickBooks Online. You will send this file to Dataswitcher.

You must fill out the online form on the website in order to send your file to Dataswitcher. You'll be taken to the Dataswitcher conversion wizard by doing this.

Double-checking Your Data After Conversion

The actions listed below should be performed after transferring your QuickBooks Desktop file to QuickBooks Online to ensure that your data is prepared for use.

Until you are certain that QuickBooks Online is the correct option for your business, maintain track of your books in both QuickBooks Desktop and QuickBooks Online.

Compare your financial reports

To confirm that your data was correctly copied, compare these reports in QuickBooks Online and QuickBooks Desktop: Profit and Loss standard, Balance Sheet standard.

Review your account detail types

Detail types are given to accounts throughout the process of transferring your data to QuickBooks Online. Undeposited funds, for instance. What the detail type should be, nevertheless, is unclear for the majority of accounts. These accounts receive a general detail type, such as Other Miscellaneous Income, from QuickBooks Online. Later, you can modify this.

Not all of your data in QuickBooks desktop should be lost just because you are switching to QBO. Knowing that you can easily transfer your data from Sage 50 or QuickBook Desktop must be a relief. The just-completed chapter is one that you should make sure you practice and read thoroughly because you will always need to refer to one file or another; as a result, you only need to copy the appropriate file or files.

Activity

1. Briefly describe QuickBooks Desktop.
2. Differentiate between QuickBooks Desktop and Sage 50.
3. Sign into your QuickBooks Online account through the QuickBooks Desktop.
4. Mention two (2) online tools that can be used to migrate QuickBooks.
5. Do all data move during the process of conversion to QBO if yes explain and if no, mention the data that will not be converted?
6. Why is it necessary to double-check your data after conversion?

PART 2

MANAGING YOUR BOOKS

CHAPTER 4

CUSTOMER, VENDOR, AND EMPLOYEE LISTS

Lists are used by QuickBooks Online, just as the QuickBooks Desktop product, to help you save background data that you'll utilize repeatedly. Most of the time, you enter data on the people you do business with customers, vendors, and employees as well as the goods you buy or sell. But you also save lists of other background data, including the accounts your business utilizes and the payment methods it takes. You may discover the information you need to set up buyers, sellers, and the goods you buy or sell in this chapter. Finally, you discover where to find other lists that you might require at the chapter's end.

Adding New Records to a List

The links Sales, Expenses, and Workers in the Navigation bar are used to interact with your clients, suppliers, staff members, and subcontractors. Simply begin by picking the relevant link in the Navigation bar Sales for customers, Expenses for vendors, and Workers for employees and contractors to initiate the process of adding a new customer, vendor, employee, or contractor. Continue reading to discover how to set up a new client.

Creating a new record

In this section that has to do with creating a new record, I will be making use of customers as an example since you definitely cannot do without establishing a customer as they are the soul of a business. Additionally, you can create sub-customers and designate customer types for customers; however, vendors, employees, and other third parties cannot use these functions.

Follow the steps below to set up a new customer in QuickBooks Online;

The Multicurrency option should be turned on before you begin generating people if you have determined that your business needs to use it. This will ensure that you have the fields you need to determine each person's currency available.

- Select **Sales** in the **Navigation bar** then choose **Customers** in order to show the Customers page.

- Select the **New Customer** button located in the upper right corner of the page.

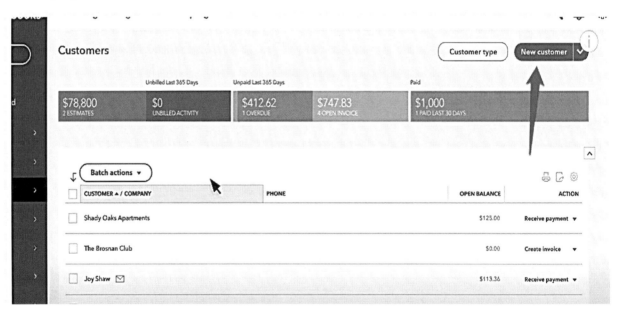

- Insert the **necessary information** as requested.

- Finally click on the **Save button.**

Since you recently added the customer, you won't see any transactions when QBO saves the customer and displays the customer's page with transaction information relevant to that customer. If you select the Customer Details option, you can also view and modify the information you just established for the customer. Click Sales in the Navigation bar, then click Customers to re-display the entire list of customers.

As long as the related person has a balance of $0, you are able to make any client, supplier, or contractor inactive. Click the Action down arrow next to the entry on the right side of the relevant list to render someone inactive. Click Make Inactive in the list that appears.

Using customer types

You can organize otherwise unrelated clients into customer kinds; for instance, maybe you provide some customers exclusive discounts at particular periods of the year. You can use a customer type to make it easier for you to decide which customers will receive the discount.

- Click the **Customer Types button** in the top right corner of the **Customers page** to create new customer types.

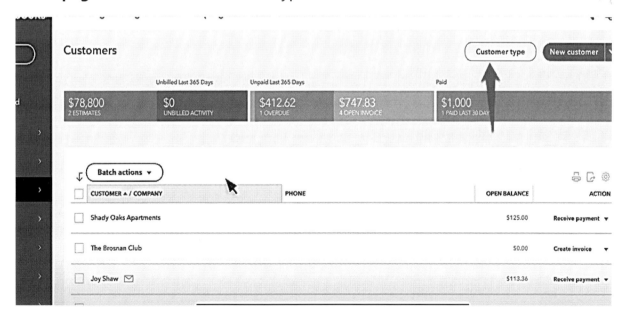

- Next, give your customer type a name and click **Save**. Repeat these steps for each new customer type you want to create.

- Click the **customer's name** on the **Customers page**, then select the b tab to designate a customer category.

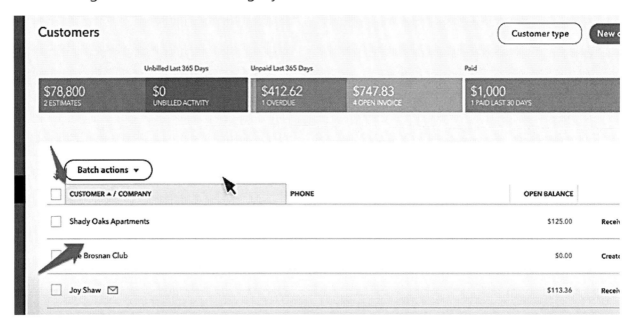

- To re-display the dialog box, click the **Edit button** at the top or on the right side of the **Customer Details page**. In that dialog box, select the **Additional Info tab** to give the customer a customer category.

You can simultaneously assign the same customer type to a group of customers you want, so keep in mind that you don't have to allocate the customer type to each individual client to save time.

Use the Sales by Customer Type Detail report, Sales by Customer Detail report grouped by customer type, and the Customer Contact List configured to add a column for the customer type to see your customers by customer type.

Working with Records

This section will highlight some of the many records that may be used with QuickBooks online as well as how to use them.

Searching lists

The pages for customers, vendors, and employees can all be used in different ways. The Contractors page has fewer features than the others; you can use it to look for contractors and create 1099s. You can sort the list of individuals, export the list to Excel, and take actions on a certain subset of individuals on the list from the Customers, Vendors, or Employees pages that list every individual in those categories.

On any listing page, you can print a simple report by

- selecting the **Print button**, which is located directly above the **Action column**.

Accessing attachments

To maintain track of crucial financial data, you can attach files. You can include things like a customer's contract, a vendor's 1099 form, or an employee's receipt. You have the option to submit images in addition to text documents.

- Simply **drag and drop the item** into the **Attachments box** located at the bottom left of the relevant details page.
- Alternatively, you can **click the box** to bring up the typical **Windows Open dialog box,** allowing you to navigate to and choose the attachment you want to use.

Each attachment is limited to 25MB in size.

- Click the **Show Existing** link below the **Attachments box** to examine papers you've already attached to a person. QBO will then open a pane on the right side of the page with the associated attachments.

Adding attachments to a transaction is another option. You must add the Attachments column to the table on the person's Transaction List page in order to view transactions that have attachments.

- Click the **table gear button** above the **Action column** to display the person's **Transaction List page**.
- Pick **Show More** from the list that appears. When you click the **Attachments check box**, the **Show More** setting changes to **Show Less,** and the **Attachments column** is added to the table grid.

With a paperclip, you can identify it as the column heading. When the Attachments column is displayed for one person, it is also displayed for all individuals of that kind in the Transaction List database. You can view the number of attachments for any given transaction in the column if there are any. The attachments for the transaction are listed when you click the number; clicking one of the attachments in the list opens it.

You add attachments to the various transactions as you create them; only attachments related to transactions and attachments associated with a person appear on the relevant person's page and the various Transaction List pages.

Sorting a list on the Customers and Vendors page

The lists on the Customers and Vendors page can be sorted by name or open balance in addition to the Split View sorting options. By default, QBO arranges the entries on these pages in ascending alphabetical order by name.

Employees can be sorted by status, pay type, alphabetical order, and reverse alphabetical order (active or inactive). Contractors cannot be sorted; by default, QBO arranges them alphabetically.

- Click **Sales or Expenses** in the **Navigation bar**, followed by **Customers or Vendors** to reveal the relevant page; in this example, I'll choose the Customers page. This will let you change the sort order for the **Customers or Vendors lists**.

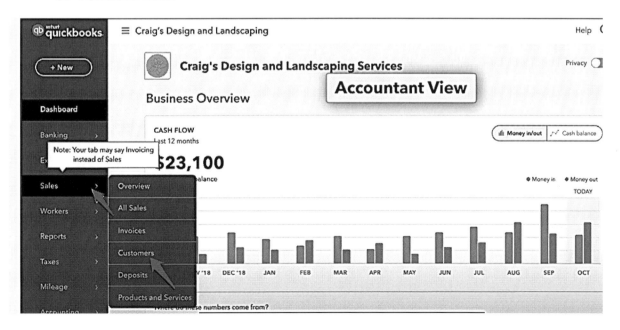

- After that, click **the heading of the column** you want to order by. **QBO** lists the customers in descending alphabetical order if you click the **Customer/Company** column heading.

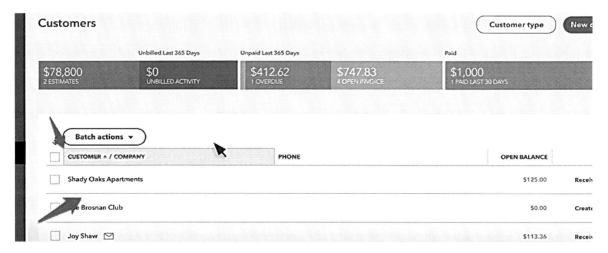

- **QBO** arranges the list in **Open Balance order,** from lowest to highest, if you click the column heading for that column.

Working with a batch of records

When working with clients or suppliers, you can execute certain actions simultaneously for a collection of records.

Changing Setting for Lists

The lists on the Customers page, Vendors page, and Employees page can all be modified to some extent. You may decide whether to display or hide the information like street addresses, attachments, emails, and phone numbers, as well as whether to include or exclude inactive entries from the list. Additionally, you can decide how many entries are shown on each page and how wide the columns are for those entries.

Depending on the list you're using, you can either show or hide some parts. For instance, you can choose to display or conceal address information for customers and vendors but not for employees or contractors.

To view the linked page,

- select the **relevant link** from the **Navigation bar (Sales, Expenses, or Employees).**

- Click the **table Gear button** above the **Action column** at the right edge of the page to modify the data presented in the list. To show or hide information, check boxes can then be **selected or deselected**.

- When done, click **outside the list**.

I advise you to **click in the open space** at the bottom of the Navigation bar when you click outside the list to avoid unintentionally leaving the current page.

Accessing Other Lists

By selecting the gear symbol for Settings in the Heading, you may access lists. Lists is one of the categories that appear.

- Click **All Lists** under the **Lists category.**

After that, a page of lists will appear. There are lists for Recurring Transactions, Product Categories, Custom Form Styles, Payment Methods, Terms, and Attachments in addition to the Chart of Accounts Products, and Services.

You can quickly return to the list view by

- selecting **All Lists** from the breadcrumb navigation under the title after choosing any list to open it in full table format. This course will begin with a look at the list of recurring transactions.

Importing Customers and Vendors

To ensure smooth data imports, you should first grasp the formatting specifications and file size restrictions before importing client files into QuickBooks.

- File sizes have restrictions. The maximum import file size for Excel and Outlook is 1,000 rows or 2MB. You'll need to separate the data and carry out numerous imports if you want to import large files.

- Imports of files could be done incorrectly. The file won't replace your customer list if you have to re-import it after an improper import. Before you re-import the file, remove the incorrectly imported customers to avoid getting duplicates.

- Sub-account import is not possible. Prior to importing them, convert subaccounts to parent accounts; after the import is finished, reverse the conversion.

- There can be only one email address. Only one email address can be supported throughout the QuickBooks import procedure. Additional email addresses can be added afterward.

- All data must have a distinct name. Each entry in the Name box must be distinct. The names of customers cannot be the same.

For Excel customer list

To ensure that the correct data is imported into the appropriate fields, check that your Excel customer spreadsheet is properly formatted and mapped. Open an Excel spreadsheet, or make a new one, and then perform the following actions:

- **View the headers**. Make sure the headers for the columns in the spreadsheet's first row correspond to the information about the customer, such as Name, Email, and Mobile Number.

- **Fill in the sheet.** Put contact information in a new spreadsheet if you're making one. If there is no data in a column, leave it blank.

- **Save the Excel workbook**. Keep track of the file's location and save it as an XLS or XLSX. The information you import corresponds to QuickBooks's invoicing information.

After that, log in to QuickBooks Online and take the following actions:

- Click on **Settings (the gear icon)**
- Click on **Import Data**
- Choose **Customers**
- Navigate to **Select a CSV or Excel file** to upload box then select **Browse**.
- Navigate to your **Excel spreadsheet** then click on **Open**.
- Select **Next.**

- You'll notice a warning if any data is missing. A checkmark will be present if the data is comprehensive. Choose **Next**.
- Make necessary adjustments to the information if need be then click on Import.

Gmail Customers

There are two simple methods for importing customer lists from Gmail to QuickBooks Online. Either export client contacts manually into QuickBooks Online or link Google contacts via Gmail.

Linking Gmail contacts

- From the **QuickBooks Online** dashboard, click **New**.
- Beneath **Customers,** click on **Invoice**.
- You will be in a fresh, empty invoice. Click the **drop-down** arrow next to the **Customer field**, then choose **Add New**.
- Click on **Connect your Gmail Account.**
- To sync your contacts from **Gmail to QuickBooks Online**, click **Accept**.

A Gmail contact can now be selected as a customer in any transaction, but they aren't added to your QuickBooks Online contacts permanently. You'll have to individually add Gmail contacts or import the complete list for that.

At any time, you can

- choose the **Customer field drop-down arrow** and click the **paper clip icon** to unlink your Gmail contacts from **QuickBooks Online**.

Importing customers from Gmail

- Sign in to your **Gmail Account**.
- Select the **Contacts icon** from the right side of the screen.
- To open a new tab, click **(the icon looks like a square with a diagonal arrow)**. Click to **pick the contacts** you wish to export only. If not, move on to the next action.
- Select **Export** from the menu on the left.

- Click **Selected Contacts** to export the contacts you selected, or select **Contacts** to export all contacts.
- Go to **Export as** and choose **Google CSV**.
- Choose **Export.** You'll find the file in your **Downloads folder.**

After that, log in to QuickBooks Online and take the following actions:

- Click on **Settings**.
- Choose **Import Data**.
- Click on **Customers**.
- In the **Select a CSV or Excel file** to upload box, select **Browse**.

- Click **Open** after navigating to the **Google CSV** file you just downloaded.

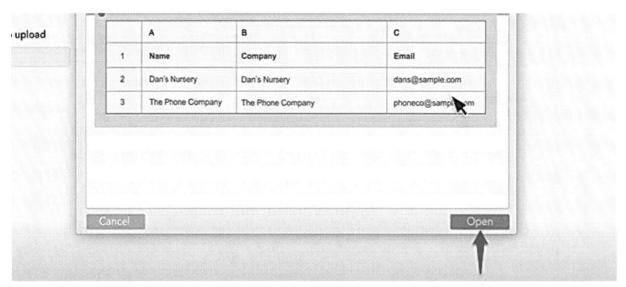

- Select **Next**.

- You'll notice a warning if any data is missing. A checkmark will be present if the data is comprehensive. Choose **Next**.

- Make necessary adjustments to the information if need be then click on **Import**.

Importing lists

You most likely have lists of clients and suppliers if you've been in business for a long. You might be able to save some setup time in QBO by importing them if they are kept electronically.

You can transfer your list information from the QuickBooks Desktop product into your free trial of QBO, which can help you become used to QBO by using list information you're currently familiar with.

List data imports are not the same as QuickBooks Desktop company imports. Be advised that because payroll setup cannot be imported, you cannot import your list of Employees, who are "people." If you import a QuickBooks Desktop firm with employees, you can import employees.

You can import list data from an Excel file or a CSV file, even if you haven't been using QuickBooks Desktop. Most programs, including QuickBooks Desktop, let you export data to a CSV format, which stands for comma-separated values. By chance, Excel can access and save CSV files. So you can open a CSV file, make any necessary changes in Excel, and then save the updated CSV file. Alternatively, you might update the file and then save it as an Excel 97-2003 workbook.

The data must follow a specified format in order to be imported into QBO from a CSV file or Excel workbook. The good news is that QBO gives you the option to download a sample Excel file in order to see the format needed for importing list data. You can use this sample as a model for how to set up the data in your own file.

The actions that come next assume that Excel is already set up on your machine. Use Excel Mobile, a free app from Microsoft, if you don't have a copy of the spreadsheet program. You must sign in to Excel Mobile with your Microsoft account email and password in order to modify your files in Excel Mobile.

The procedures below can be used to download and see the example file for suppliers.

- The Vendors page will appear after you click **Expenses** in the **Navigation bar**.
- In the top right corner of the screen, click **the down arrow** next to the **New Vendor icon**.
- Select **Import Vendors**.
- Select the link for **Download a Sample File**. When you click the link, QBO, assuming you're using **Chrome**, downloads the sample file and shows a button in the Windows taskbar for it.

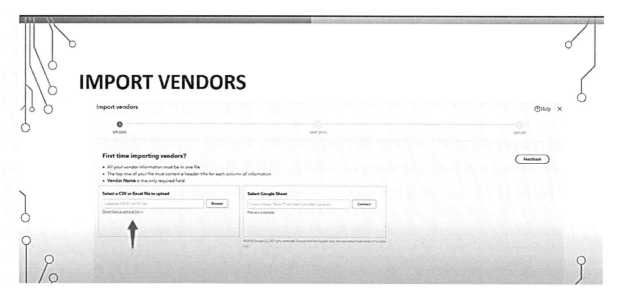

- Click on **the sample file's button** located in the **Windows taskbar**.

- Scroll to the right to view the content of the file and the data kept in each column.

- Model your own file after the example file. You can export lists to CSV or Excel files if you've been using QuickBooks Desktop; see QuickBooks Desktop Help for more information.

If you can match the headings in your data file to those in the sample data file, you'll find that importing your data will go more smoothly. Additionally, your data file cannot be larger than 2MB in size or contain more rows than 1,000. Don't forget to save your data file as a CSV (comma-delimited) file or an Excel 97-2003 workbook.

You can import your list data once you have prepared an Excel or CSV file containing it. Take these actions:

- Ensure your data file isn't opened.

- Display **the import vendors** or **import customers page**.

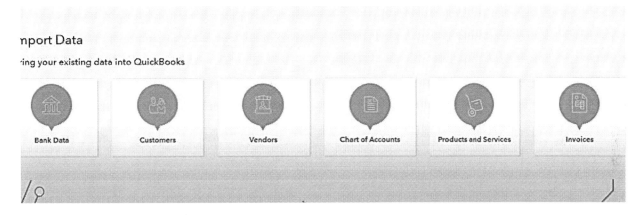

- Click on the **Browse button**.

- Move to the folder where you have saved the file that contains the list information.

- Choose **Open** after **selecting the file**. The name of the file you selected is updated by QBO on the **Import Vendors page**.

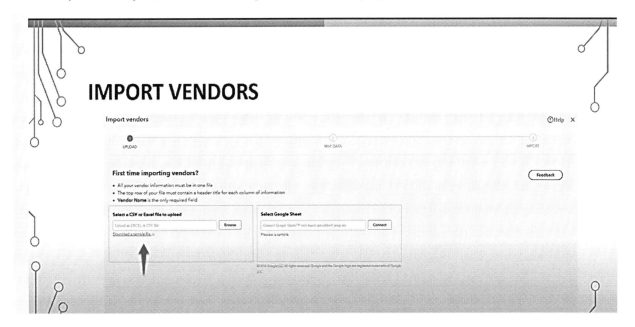

- Choose **Next.** Your file is uploaded by **QBO**, which then shows the Map Data panel.

- Check to see if the fields in your data file and QBO match up correctly. Open the list box next to each QBO field name as necessary and compare it to the labels in your data file as necessary.

- In the bottom right corner of the screen, click **Next**. The records that QBO has located are displayed.

- Verify the accuracy of the data in the records QBO offers to import. Any field's contents can be changed by clicking it and entering new data. Additionally, you can uncheck any row to prevent QBO from importing the data in that row.

- Click the **Import icon** in the lower right corner of the screen once you are certain the data is accurate.

A portion of the data cannot be imported if the Import button is grayed out and unavailable. To find data that cannot be imported, look for a field highlighted in red. If the issue isn't clear, seek assistance from Intuit Support.

After importing the data, QBO notifies users of the number of records imported with a message. The relevant page displays the list you imported.

Exporting lists to Excel or Google Sheets

A list of your clients or suppliers can be exported to Excel. Since uploading your list to an Excel file wouldn't make much sense otherwise, I'm going to assume in this part that you have Excel installed on your computer. You can use the free mobile version of Excel if it's not already installed on your computer.

To display either the Customers page or the Vendors page,

- select the **relevant link** from the **Navigation bar** (Sales or Expenses); in this example, I'll pick the Vendors page. Three buttons are visible on the right side of the page, directly above the Action column. QBO exports the list to an Excel file when the middle button is clicked; in Chrome, a button for the file displays at the bottom of the screen.

- Excel opens the file when you click t**he button at the bottom of the screen**. If you select the **Enable Editing** option in the yellow bar at the top of the window, you can modify the file. Additionally, in order to modify the file if you're using **Excel mobile**, you must sign in using your Microsoft account.

Introducing Spreadsheet Sync

You may sync Excel with your QuickBooks Online Advanced account using Spreadsheet Sync, enabling you to

- Take data out of QuickBooks Online Advanced, edit in an Excel file, and then post back.

- Use the list templates in Spreadsheet Sync, and create fresh data to publish to QuickBooks Online Advanced.

- Create unique reports and update them with the most recent information from QuickBooks Online Advanced.

Note: Spreadsheet Sync can only be opened and managed by QuickBooks Online Advanced admin users.

Spreadsheet Sync can be accessed in a few different ways while using QuickBooks Online Advanced.

- Click on the **Settings icon**.
  - In the dropdown menu, click on **Spreadsheet sync**.

- From the side navigation panel, choose **Reports**
  - Click on the **Caret** close to **Create new report** in the upper right side then click on the spreadsheet.
  - Open **Spreadsheet Sync**.

Installing the Spreadsheet Sync add-in

Opening Spreadsheet Sync from within Excel

- Click **Launch Add-In Spreadsheet Sync** in the Excel navigation bar.

- Choose **Sign in**.

- Insert your **QuickBooks Online user ID** in the task panel then click **Sign in**.

- Insert your **password and click on Continue**.

Managing list records with Spreadsheet Sync

To pull out company data into a spreadsheet;

- If your **QuickBooks Online Advanced account administrator** has only assigned you one company, that company will show up in the Please **pick your company dropdown**.

  - If you have been given access to more than one company, go to Company settings in the Spreadsheet Sync toolbar and click Add new to start using that company's data.

- It should be noted that adding companies to Spreadsheet Sync and setting user permissions both require access to QuickBooks Online Advanced.

To create a spreadsheet report;

- Click on **Build Reports** from the toolbar.

- To choose the report or data table template you want to use, first choose the **Company or Group data** you wish to download. Then choose the data source.

To edit or add data to your QuickBooks Online Advanced account;

- Click **Manage Records** in the toolbar.

- Under the **Records** to create or edit menu, choose **a list template**, then choose the **Company or Group data** you want to change or add to.

Uninstalling Spreadsheet Sync

To stop making use of the Spreadsheet sync all you have to do is sign out.

- Click **Launch Add-In Spreadsheet Sync** in the **Excel navigation bar**.
- Choose to **Sign out**.

The customer, the heart of the business, is discussed in this chapter together with the staff and vendors. You must have learned about record lists in the recently completed chapter, including how to create a new record, how to sort a list on the customers and vendors page, the different types of lists available in QBO, how to import customers and vendors from the previous version of QuickBooks you are using, as well as from Excel and Gmail, and how to use spreadsheet sync. I would suggest that you study and practice diligently because this chapter has a lot of material.

Activity

1. Differentiate between a customer, a vendor, and an employee.
2. Create a record in your QBO and add a new record to a list.
3. The phrase "using customer types" what does it mean?

4. How can you access an attachment in QBO?
5. Modify the settings in your QBO for your lists.
6. Import customers and vendors from the previous version of QuickBooks you are using and if you are new to QuickBooks, highlight the steps to be taken to import customers and vendors.
7. Link your Gmail contacts with your QuickBooks Online.
8. Export the list you have in QBO to an Excel sheet.
9. Create a spreadsheet report.

CHAPTER 5

MANAGING SALES TAX, SERVICES, AND INVENTORY

You have all the tools you need to manage your inventory with QuickBooks Online. Track your inventory, receive reminders when it's time to refill and view insights into your purchases and sales. Non-inventory goods and services can also be entered so you can simply include them in your sales forms.

All purchases and sales should be entered into QuickBooks as inventory. Then, so that you don't have to, let QuickBooks adjust the amount on hand as you work. Once everything is set up, tracking inventory in QuickBooks and adding items to sales forms is simple.

Setting Up Sales Tax

This is much simpler than you would think. With the help of a wizard in QBO, you can be guided through the procedure while being asked simple things like your address and whether you must charge sales tax outside of your state.

Your life will be easier if you put up sales taxes before setting up items. Why? Because QBO makes use of the sales tax data you enter when setting up products. If you don't set up sales taxes first, you'll need to go back and change each item to make it tax-deductible.

For businesses using the accrual basis of accounting, QBO tracks and submits sales tax automatically. Furthermore, if your QBO company accounting foundation is set to accrual, QBO will automatically calculate sales tax on transactions.

If your company operates on the cash basis of account, all you have to do is set your company accounting method to Accrual just before setting up sales tax;

- Click on **settings(gear) > Account and Settings > Advanced.**

After completing the aforementioned settings, add sales tax and switch back to the Cash accounting method. Be advised that the Sales Tax Center will track your sales tax responsibility on an accrual basis; however, you can use the Sales Tax Liability reports to determine the precise amount of sales tax that needs to be paid.

QBO prompts you to set up sales taxes the first time you

- select **Taxes**.
- Select **"Setup Sales Tax"** from the menu.

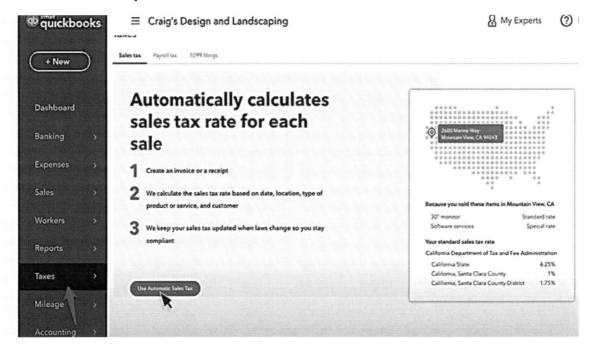

The wizard asks you for your address if you haven't already entered your company's address in QBO. If your address has already been entered, QBO shows it to you onscreen so you may double-check.

- When your address is accurate click **Next**.

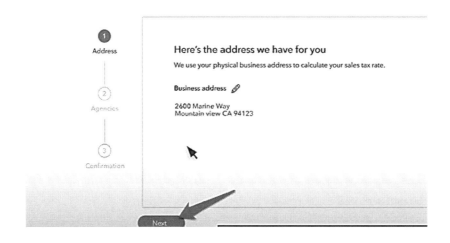

- When the wizard asks if you need to charge sales tax in states other than your home state, you can respond with either No or Yes. If you pick Yes, you must specify the additional states in which you do so. Choose **Next**.

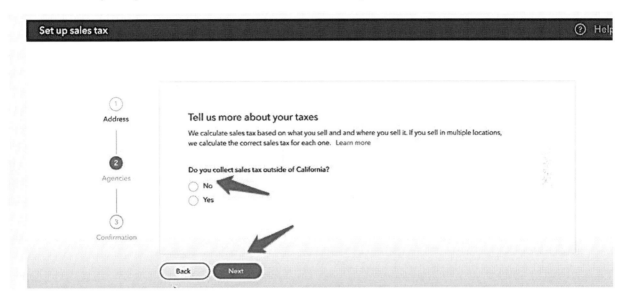

The following questions from QBO concern your current tax year's beginning, how frequently you file sales tax returns, and the day you first began collecting sales tax for your taxing authority.

You can also add and modify tax agencies, rates, and settings in the sales tax center.

Adding tax rates and agencies

- Navigate to **Taxes** the click on **Sales tax.**

- Beneath the **Related Tasks** list located on the right side, click on **Add/edit tax rates** and **agencies.**

- Click on **New** and select **either a single or a combined tax rate.**

- Enter the **tax's name**, the agency you pay, and the rate's percentage. If you only pay one rate to one agency, use that rate.

- Click on **Save**.

Adding a combined rate

Consider putting up a combined tax rate if you have to track sales tax for more than one taxing authority. For instance, you might be required to report and pay sales tax to your state, county, and city.

Below are basic things you should know;

- Your consumer will only see one tax rate on their sales form if you use a mixed tax rate. The sales tax center, however, keeps track of and distributes the proper sums to each agency.

- A combined tax rate might have up to 5 components.

Take the steps below to add a combined tax rate;

- Navigate to **Taxes**, then click on **Sales tax.**

- Beneath the **Related Tasks** list on the right-hand side, click on **Add/edit tax rates and agencies**.

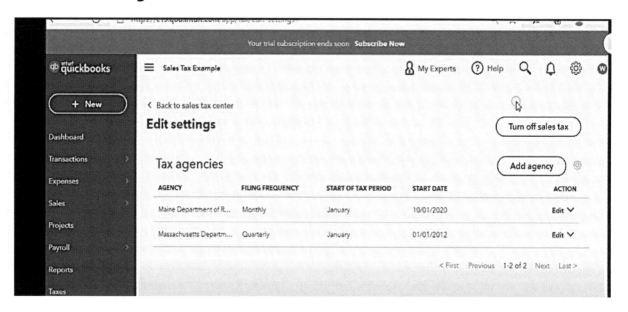

- Click on **New**.

- Choose a **Combined tax rate**.

- Insert a name for the combined rate and the different sales tax requirements.

- If need be, choose to **Add Another Component** to include more than two rates.

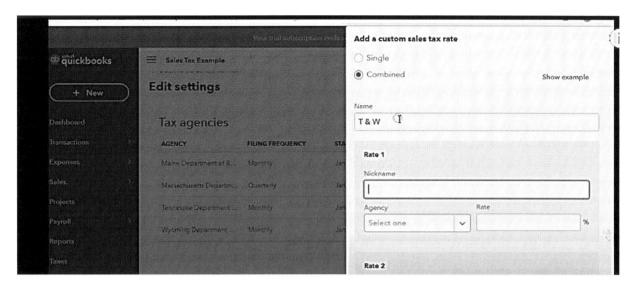

- Click on **Save**.

Upon the completion of this, certain things such as the following will happen;

- The list of Sales Tax Rates and Agencies now includes the new rate.

- The new combined rate is now selectable in forms like invoices.

- The Sales Tax Owing list in the Sales Tax Center allows you to view the sums owed to each agency.

- The Sales Tax Liability report is accessible.

Edit a tax rate

There are basic things you need to know with editing a tax rate such as;

- Sales tax rate can be edited if there is a need to make some changes to it.

- Component rates alone can be edited.

- If you would like to edit a combined rate you have to also make changes to its component rates.

Follow the steps below to edit a tax rate;

- Navigate to **taxes**, then click on **Sales tax**.

- Beneath the **Related Tasks** list on the right-hand side, click **Add/edit tax rates and agencies**.

- Click on the rate you would like to change then choose **Edit**.

- Insert **the new rate** and you can also change the name of the agency if need be.

- Click on the **Save button** when you are done.

Upon the completion of the above-listed steps, below are likely events that might occur;

- Only new transactions are eligible for the new rate.

- The new rate is applied to new transactions created with dates in the past.

- The earlier rate is no longer usable after editing a rate.

- Transactions already made at the older rate are still valid. Unless you specifically choose a different sales tax rate when editing the transaction.

- New transactions made using recurring templates that make use of the modified component are subject to the new rate. The earlier rate and transactions already completed using the template are unaffected.

- Reports provide information on both rates (before and after).

Editing the name of a tax agency

Below are things you should know;

- The Tax Rate field cannot be modified.

- Deactivate the current tax name and rate if the rate needs to change.

- Create a new tax with the desired rate after that.

Follow the steps below to have the name of an agency edited;

- Go to **Taxes**, then click on **Sales Tax.**

- Beneath the name of the agency you would like to edit, click on **rename**.

- Insert the **new name** then click on **Save**.

Changing the sales tax center filter

- Navigate to **Taxes**, then click on **Sales tax**.

- Select your favorite filter from the **Start of Year and Accounting Basis drop-down menu**.

Editing sales tax settings

You can turn sales tax either on or off by simply editing the sales tax settings.

- Navigate to **Taxes**, then click on **Sales tax.**

- Beneath the **Related Tasks** list located on the right-hand side, click on **Edit sales tax settings**.

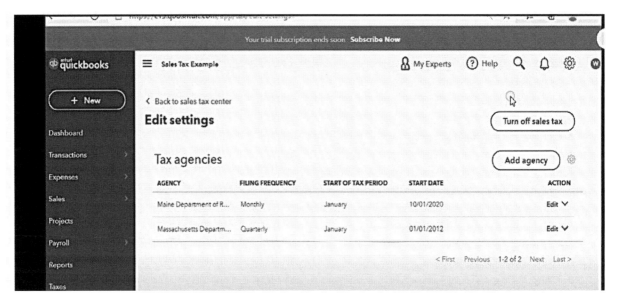

- Click **Yes** if you charge sales tax.

- Configure the options below;

  ○ Decide on a default tax rate. In fresh sales forms, the default rate is automatically chosen. If necessary, you can select a different rate.

  ○ QuickBooks Online remembers the rate you choose for a specific customer and overrides the default rate if you select a different rate for that customer.

  ○ To mark new clients as taxable, choose **Mark**. As a result, the new clients you bring on board are not tax deductible. In the **Tax Info area** of each customer record, you can modify this value for specific clients.

  ○ Mark is the only option; new goods and services are taxed. This indicates that any items you add to a form already have the **Tax column chosen**. If you don't have to charge sales tax, you can clear individual products on a form.

- If you don't charge sales tax, choose **No**. If you have already applied sales tax to previous transactions, you must first take that money back. Otherwise, you won't be able to disable sales tax.

- Click on **Save**.

Deactivating a tax rate

- Navigate to **Taxes** then click on **Sales tax.**

- Beneath the **Related Tasks** list on the right-hand side, click **Add/edit tax rates and agencies**.

- Pick a tax rate name and then click on **Deactivate**.

- Click on **Continue**.

Understanding sales tax liability

Sales tax liabilities are sums of money that businesses must collect from customers and give to federal, state and municipal taxing bodies. On a sales tax liability report, business owners and organizations keep track of their sales tax obligations. The amount of tax paid to state and local tax authorities as well as the amount of tax collected are both listed in this report. Since state and municipal governments are in charge of collecting sales tax, different locations may have different sorts or classifications of sales tax.

Food

The majority of states in the US don't tax food when it's bought for domestic use. However, some governments charge a lesser sales tax on food meant for domestic consumption than they do on other goods. Many states tax food at the same rate as other items, but they also give low-income households rebates. The majority of the time, local governments don't tax food when it is exempt at the federal or state level.

Vehicles

The majority of states charge a sales tax on vehicles bought there. In fact, New York mandates that the car be registered after the sales tax has been paid. In New York, the Department of Motor Vehicles will collect the sales tax from the buyer of the vehicle if they are unable to show documentation that it was paid. For instance, the sales tax on autos in Missouri combines the state and local sales taxes. Not where you bought your car, but where you live determines the local sales tax.

Medical Appliances

In many states, prescription medications are exempt from sales tax. Non-prescription medicines, medical equipment, supplies, and supplies without a prescription are subject to sales tax. Drugs are defined as pills, tablets, capsules, or liquids that cure human ailments in the state of Georgia. Drug products including antiperspirants, mouthwash, toothpaste, and sunscreen, for instance, will be charged in New Jersey even if they include an "active component." Deodorants, toothpaste, and skin care products are taxed in Maryland. Medical devices like lift chairs and wheelchair ramps, for instance, are subject to sales tax in Maryland.

General Merchandise

The majority of states charge sales tax on everyday items. On goods like soda, sweets, and food served at a restaurant, customers must pay sales tax. Both the purchase of computer software and the use of prepaid calling cards are subject to state sales tax. State sales tax is applied to items in the hygiene or grooming category. For instance, the general goods sales tax in the state of New York applies to apparel, housewares, and car parts. Supplies for pets are subject to general sales tax. State taxes apply to jewelry, greeting cards, gift wrap, and school supplies.

Enabling the Automated Sales Tax Feature

For quick and accurate filings, QuickBooks can calculate sales tax for you automatically on your receipts and invoices. Then, it notifies you when your tax payment is due, enabling you to file promptly and preventing late costs.

Follow the steps below;

Learn how QuickBooks calculates sales tax

Based on the following, QuickBooks automatically determines the total sales tax rate for each sale:

- the sales tax exemption status of your client.

- where you sell and ship from.

- The sales tax classification of your service or item.

Tell QuickBooks where you collect sales tax

To effectively compute sales tax and returns, QuickBooks Online keeps track of your state's tax regulations. You can also include additional taxing authorities you pay if you charge sales tax outside of your state.

There are two ways to organize how sales tax is collected:

- Set up the first location for which you will charge sales tax if you recently registered for QuickBooks.

- Check to see if you can transition to the new sales tax system if you still collect sales tax manually.

Include tax categories for your products and services

Depending on where you sell, different laws may apply about how to tax good. Visit our blog to learn how the sales tax on a lemon can vary based on the finished product and the location of the sale.

Any item you sell can be given a sales tax category when you're ready. By doing this, you may tell QuickBooks how much sales tax to charge you based on the specifics of your transactions.

Check customers' info over again

If you send goods or provide services to a customer's address, tax rates may also alter. For example, churches, schools, and other nonprofit organizations are exempt from paying sales tax.

Verify that you have the correct tax status, billing address, and shipping address for your customers.

Keep an eye on sales tax from your customers

After completing the necessary setup, you may begin using the automated sales tax feature. We'll demonstrate its operation and location when you create an invoice or receipt for a client.

Check how much you owe and why

Find out in great detail what taxes you owe and why. Before you prepare and submit your sales tax return, this enables you to check that everything is accurate.

File your sales tax return

In order to prevent late returns and additional costs, QuickBooks Online keeps track of all of your payment due dates in one spot. When the time comes to file, check your debt to make sure everything is correct. Then, you can mail your return or e-file it on the website of your tax office. Following filing, you can maintain track of your new sales tax payment in QuickBooks to update your records.

Converting sales tax from QuickBooks Desktop

One element that does not transfer fully from QuickBooks Desktop to QuickBooks Online is sales tax. You'll see that certain taxes import merely the list and balances, while others convert as journal entries.

On the Chart of Accounting page, there will now be accounts for sales tax payable. Each Sales Tax Agency Payable account in QuickBooks Desktop and each Sales Tax Payable account in QuickBooks Online will have one.

After importing your QuickBooks Desktop company file into QuickBooks Online, you could find some variations in the Sales Tax.

Difference: Your account balances for Accounts Payable (A/P) and/or Accounts Receivable (A/R) are different.

Reason:

- A general journal was established with amounts against A/P (in the case of a tax amount owing) and A/R when you filed sales tax in QuickBooks Desktop (in the case of a refund). The diary was shut off after the bill was paid or the money was received.

- Instead of using A/P or A/R, QuickBooks Online establishes a new suspense account to hold money owed to tax authorities.

- The funds will be transferred from the A/P or A/R accounts in QuickBooks Desktop to this new suspense account in QuickBooks Online if you finished a filing but have not yet made or received payment for that file before switching to QuickBooks Online.

Difference: Your previous sales tax payments or refunds are nowhere to be found (that would have appeared in the bill payments window in QuickBooks Desktop).

Reason:

- These payments and refunds are managed by QuickBooks Online under the Sales Tax Centre.

- For a QuickBooks Online view of your payments and refunds, go to Taxes and choose Sales tax.

Difference: In QuickBooks Online, the liability accounts that you used to track sales tax in QuickBooks Desktop have different amounts.

Reasons:

- You'll notice a difference in QuickBooks Online if you track your sales tax to a separate liability account than your purchase account in QuickBooks Desktop.

- Transactions with tax will track to GST/HST Payable in QuickBooks Online if they had a tax that tracked to GST Payable Purchases in QuickBooks Desktop.

- Your chart of accounts will also differ, but the two accounts will balance when combined, and your tax records will be accurate.

Difference: New expense accounts will only be seen for some of your tax agencies.

Reason:

- If you previously utilized tax agencies that didn't track tax on purchases separately to an account, QuickBooks Online will create a new expenditure account and use it.

- All purchase-related charges were combined into one expense account on the corresponding purchase line item in QuickBooks Desktop.

- Your sales tax amounts will be accurate even though these transactions seem different after being imported into QuickBooks Online.

- The newly formed expense account will now be used to track new transactions made in QuickBooks Online that include this cost tax.

Switching from manual to automated sales tax

Tracking your sales tax returns has never been easier thanks to QuickBooks. QuickBooks automatically calculates sales tax depending on the products you sell, the locations where you sell them, and the shipping locations. QuickBooks will automatically update your tax rates for you whenever your state makes adjustments, such as the sales tax rate.

Here's how to make the switch to QuickBooks Online's new sales tax system and how to view your previous sales tax information after you've made the change.

It should be noted that not everyone has access to this switch option now, but if you don't, you should shortly. And also after converting to automated sales tax, you cannot go back to the previous method.

You will be prompted to match your current tax rates to the official tax agency indicated in QuickBooks when you switch to automated sales tax. You must match all of your tax rates if you have fewer than 20.

It is strongly advised, but not needed, to match all of your rates if you have more than 20. Future sales forms won't be able to use any rates you don't map. You won't see any transactions using the mismatched rates on your Sales tax tab, but you can still get historical data for your rates in the Sales Tax Liability Report and Chart of Account Registers.

Follow the steps below to make the switch;

- Navigate to **Taxes**, then click on **Sales tax**.

- Choose either to **Use automatic sales tax** or **Get Started** if your **QuickBooks** is prepared to make the switch to automated sales tax. A switch should be accessible to you soon if you don't have it now.

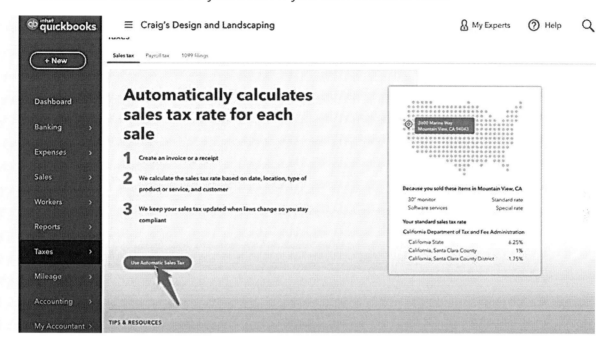

- Verify the accuracy of your company address. If so, choose **Next**. If it isn't, use the **Next button** after clicking the pencil icon to alter the address.

- Match the official state agency's tax rates with your current rates in one of two ways:

    - **Match one rate at a time**: If you only have a few rates, locate and choose the appropriate tax agency for each rate using the OFFICIAL AGENCY NAME option. Verify that it corresponds to the tax agency listed in the YOUR AGENCY NAME box.

    - **Match more than one rate at once**: Select the checkbox next to each tax rate you wish to bulk match, then use the Official agency dropdown in the Bulk Matching window to find and choose the right tax agency. This will match numerous rates to a single agency. then choose **Apply.**

- Click on **Next**
- Check all the rates when you are through and click on **Save**.

- To leave the window, click **the X**; to see a demonstration of automated sales tax, click **Continue**.

You keep all of your previous sales tax information when you transition to the new sales tax. All of your paid sales tax returns may be managed in one location.

- Navigate to **Taxes** then click on **Sales tax**.

- Click on **History**.

- If you wish to check out for more details, click on **View return**.

You can view your information from the sales tax liability report or the chart of account registers if you didn't match all of your rates when you moved to automated sales tax.

If you didn't map all of your rates when you went to automated sales tax and you wish to match up previous sales tax data, you have two choices:

- Speak with your accountant about moving old/new liability accounts using a journal entry. The name of the agency will match the name in the sales tax settings.

- With a journal entry, you can eliminate all liabilities and start over in the sales tax center. Discuss this with your accountant.

Exploring the Economic Nexus Feature

If you need to pay sales tax in another state, you can find out if you do so using the Economic Nexus tool. For sales tax purposes, some businesses never need to add more than one tax authority. This is due to the fact that their business only works in one state and from a single location.

Your online or physical presence in a US state is referred to as your economic nexus. If you do enough business in a state and reach a certain sales threshold, you can be required to pay sales tax to that state. Each state has a different tax rate and threshold.

Activities that create a tax obligation

If you engage in one or more of the following business activities in a state, you may be subject to tax duties there:

- Physical location in the state
- Online sales to customers that are in the state.
- Out-of-state sales.
- Provision of service in the state.
- Business property that is also located within the state.
- Salespeople within the state.
- Independent contractors that are in the state.
- Soliciting orders at trade shows in the state for more than three days in a single year.

You must add the new tax agency to your tax settings and register to collect sales tax if you are conducting business in a state.

State by state differs in their tax duty needs. It's best to research each state's unique nexus regulations. These common company scenarios will make it necessary to file for sales and use tax in a specific state.

Example 1: You run a cupcake shop in New York.

Obligation: State by state differs in their tax duty needs. It's best to research each state's unique nexus regulations. These common company scenarios will make it necessary to file for sales and use tax in a specific state.

Example 2: You run the same cupcake store in New York, but you ship to a second one-man distribution facility in Massachusetts, which is just across the border.

Obligation: There is now a requirement for you to collect sales tax for sales inside of Massachusetts.

You can use a report in QuickBooks Online to determine whether you need to charge sales tax to a particular state. This is how:

- Sign in to your **QuickBooks Online account**.
- Navigate to **taxes** then click on **Sales tax**.
- Click on the **Economic Nexus button**.
- Make use of the dropdown menus to choose a **State and Date range**.

- Select **Run report;** The report displays your transaction count in relation to the state's nexus regulations that you chose. This report contains the following details:

    - ○ **Transaction count**: The number of transactions in the state that falls within the selected date range.
    - ○ **Threshold met**: This is an indication as to if you should collect sales tax for the state. If you have to ensure you register with states where you meet the threshold.
    - ○ **Agency set up**: Whether the state agency has been added to your list of tax agencies in the sales tax settings is indicated.
    - ○ **Date last run**: this displays the date and time when you last executed a report for the state.

Custom sales tax rates

You can choose whether to mark each customer in QuickBooks Online as taxable or not, or you can mark them all as taxable at a default rate. If they are listed as taxable, you may always choose the tax rate to apply to each customer; otherwise, if you haven't yet set up a rate for each of them on the sales form, they will be taxed at the default rate.

Marking a customer as taxable

- Navigate to **get paid & pay or Sales** then click on **Customers**.
- Click the **name of a particular customer** in order to have their details expanded.

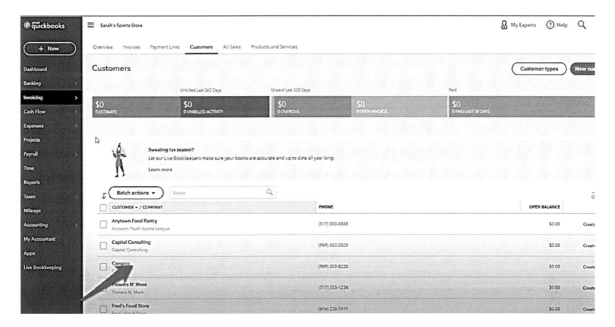

- Click on the **Edit button** at the top.

- Locate the **Additional info** section then check **the box for This customer is taxable**.

- Finally click on the **Save button**.

To set the default tax rates for all of the customers;

- Navigate to **Taxes** then click on **Sales tax**.

- When in the **Related Tasks section**, click on **Edit sales tax settings.**

- To choose the tax you want to act as the default sales tax, select the **Default sales tax selection**.

- Additionally, you have the option of marking either all new clients as taxable or all new goods and services as taxable.

- When all is done and set, click on the **Save button**.

All sales forms are now updated with your new default rate. To modify the tax rate, use the Tax selection on the sales form if you want to charge a customer a different sales tax rate. You will be able to update any previous invoices you unintentionally created without sales tax to include the correct sales tax.

Run a report to see which customers are now identified as taxable if you are unsure of which consumers pay sales tax and at what percentage.

A taxable customer report can be run by:

- Selecting **Sales** tax after going to **Taxes**.

- Then, click **View taxable** customer report under **Related Tasks.**

- Information about the consumer, including whether they are taxable and at what rate, is shown in a report. If necessary, you can further modify this report.

Users that have restricted access for either vendors and purchases (A/P—Accounts Payable) or customers and sales (A/R—Accounts Receivable) are likewise restricted in what they can accomplish in the sales tax center based on their responsibilities.

Auditing your customer list

It's critical to maintain organization and keep track of your clients as your company expands. You can add client profiles to QuickBooks Online so you can include them in transactions or invoices. Here's how to add clients and update your client list.

You may track your clients' future transactions in QuickBooks Online by adding them to the customer list. This is how:

- Navigate to **Get paid & pay or Sales** then click on **Customers**.

- Click on **New Customers**.

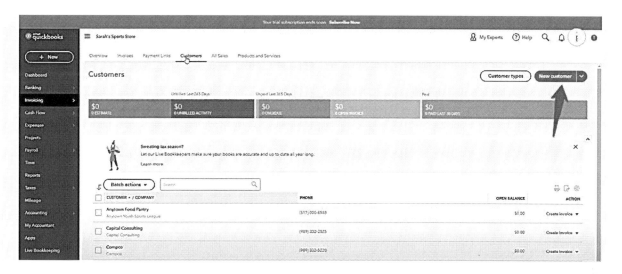

- Enter the information you wish to appear for the customer in the Customer display name area. (This field must be filled in)

- Review each area after that, and insert any more crucial client information.

- If the customer is tax exempt, click the **This customer is tax exempt** checkbox in the Additional details area. Select the reason for their tax exemption in the **Reason for exemption** option after that.

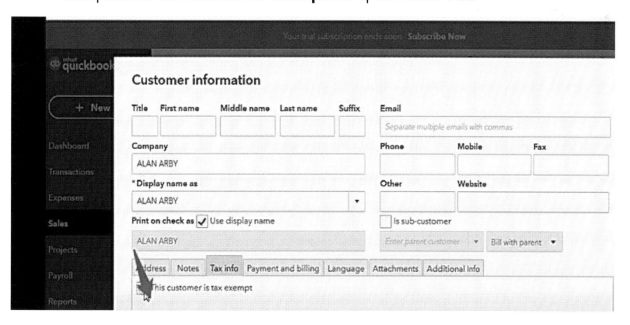

- Click on the **Save button**.

When you modify customer information, other parts of your business file, such as previously delivered invoices, will update to reflect your changes. Additionally, any recurring templates in QuickBooks Online that make use of previously stored data, such as billing, shipping, email addresses, tax status, chosen payment method, and terms, are updated.

This is how to change a customer's information:

- Navigate to **Get paid & pay or Sales** then click on **Customers.**
- Click on the **customer** you would like to update.
- Click on **Edit**.
- Make any changes if needed.
- Click on the **Save button**.

You can mark a customer as inactive to get rid of them, which will make them disappear from lists and menus. All of a customer's transactions will still be accessible on reports even if they are inactive.

Subordinate customers are likewise deleted when a parent customer is deleted. However, a project that is associated with the customer cannot be turned inactive. Delete any projects that are linked to the customer in order to declare them dormant.

- Navigate to **Sales**, then **Customers** under **Get Paid & Pay.**
- To view the customer's profile, click on **their name**.
- Pick **Edit** from the dropdown menu.
- Choose to **Make inactive**. Select **Yes**, and make inactive to confirm.

You can merge the profiles of duplicate customers. The data from the deleted profile is transferred to the profile you want to maintain.

Make sure that neither client has any sub-clients. If they do, you must first convert their sub-customers to regular clients.

- Go to **Sales**, then **Customers**, or **Get paid & pay.**
- The customer profile you want to delete is selected and opened.
- Choose **Edit**.
- Enter **the name** of the duplicate customer profile you want to preserve in the Customer display name field. The names must completely match.

- Choose **Save**.
- Select **Yes** when prompted if you wish to combine the two profiles.

Reporting and paying sales tax

Either you or an accountant can take care of your sales tax management. In the left-side Navigation Pane,

- Select **Taxes**, followed by **Sales Tax**. You are currently within the Sales Tax Center.

Then, you can view all of the unfiled sales tax returns. Additionally, you'll find those that are past due.

- Click the **View Return button** next to the return you want to file on the right side of the page to file and pay a return.

You can now include a sales tax adjustment. A panel will show up on the right side of the screen if you click the Add an Adjustment option.

You must first include a justification for the modification. Credit, prior payments, and prepayments are all included as possible reasons for an adjustment in the selection menu. Another option is Other, which can be used for fines, interest, or rounding errors.

Choose an income account if the justification is because of credit or earlier payment. Choose an expense account if the cause is a fine, penalty, or interest that is owed. If a rounding error caused it, choose an expense account for positive errors or an income account for negative ones.

Then, input the adjustment amount. To complete the adjustment,

- click the **Add button**.

- Click **Record Payment** to return to the **Review Your Sales Taxes page**.

After that, QuickBooks Online computes and displays the amount owed to the tax authority. Here, you'll be able to confirm or modify it.

- By selecting the **Report link** and then selecting **Download Your Full Report,** you may also view details. Your taxes are broken down there under the Sales Tax Liability.

Last but not least, specify a payment date and the bank account that will be used. To complete the procedure, press the Record Payment button.

Working with Products and Services

Everything you might sell to a consumer is listed in Quickbooks Online's Products and Services category. It is comparable to Quickbooks Desktop's Item List. There are two straightforward ways to access Products and Services.

The left-side Navigation Pane is the initial route.

- Select **Sales, followed by Products and Services.**

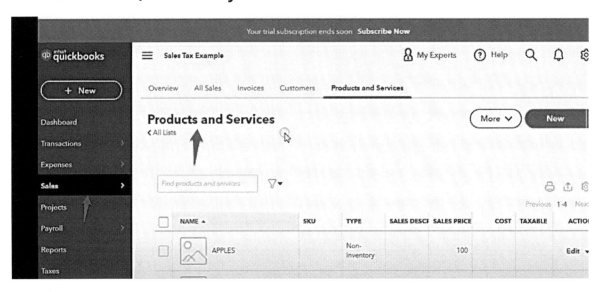

- The second method is to select **Settings by clicking the gear symbol** in the heading. **Products and Services** can be found in the **Lists category**. When you arrive, you will see a list of all the goods and services you have established.

You can access

- **All Lists using the breadcrumb navigation** that is located beneath the **header for Products and Services**. In addition to seeing the chart of

97

accounts that was covered in the prior unit, clicking it will take you to a page of lists.

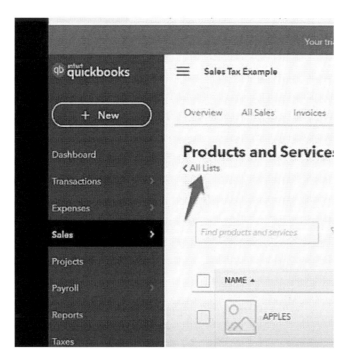

Alerts that let you know whether an item is out of stock or running low will be visible above the table. When either alert is clicked, the product and services table is filtered to only show those items.

Using the search bar, you can look for particular goods and services as well. You can set search parameters like the status, kind, and stock level using the blue triangle next to the search field.

You can print, export to Excel, and modify the table's settings using the icons in the top right corner. There are a number of other columns that can be added but are not by default displayed. These pertain to the purchase order's quantity and the accounts for income, expenses, inventory, and purchases.

There are ten columns in the table that can be shown by default. The majority of the column headings allow you to sort the items in that column in either ascending or descending order by clicking on them.

The name and photo go in the first column.

- By selecting the **Edit link in the Action column**, you may change the name and photo.

The SKUs are listed in the second column. These special codes are used to keep track of inventory. Utilizing SKUs is optional.

The Type is listed in the third column. Inventory, non-inventory, and service are examples of item types. Inventory is used for anything that you wish to keep track of and either buy or sell. Items that you buy, sell, and/or trade but don't need to be tracked are considered non-inventory. Service is for goods and services that you offer and don't have a measurable component.

Sales Description appears by default in the fourth column. This is for the product or service's description. The language submitted here will be printed on a variety of documents, including invoices and receipts.

The sales price column appears next. This displays any sales prices that you have entered and used consistently. Leave this area empty if the price varies on a regular basis.

Cost, Taxable, Quantity on Hand, and Reorder Point are the next four columns.

Adding inventory, non-inventory, and service items

All purchases and sales should be entered into QuickBooks as inventory. Then, so that you don't have to, let QuickBooks adjust the amount on hand as you work. Once everything is set up, tracking inventory in QuickBooks and adding items to sales forms is simple.

Step 1

Ensure you turn on inventory tracking in order for you to be able to add inventory items.

Step 2

Once you have done the above, the settings below will help you add inventory products.

- Select **Products and services under Get paid & pay**.

- Choose **New or Add an item or service**. then decide between non-inventory options, or inventory.

- For the thing you're tracking, enter a **Name, SKU, or Category**. Using categories will help you organize your goods and services so that they are simpler to find.

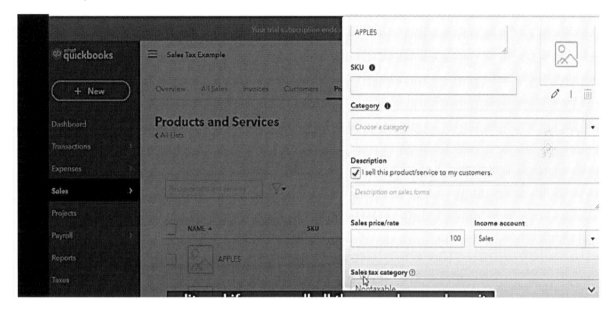

- From the **Unit menu**, choose **the unit**.

- From the **Category menu**, choose the **appropriate category**.

Step 3: Include your product's quantity, point of reordering and inventory asset account

- Include the initial stock amount for your product. Then, in the As of date column, enter the date that you first began recording that amount.

- To receive notifications when it's time to reorder, add a Reorder point. That third rectangle that you see is.

- Inventory Assets should be selected from the dropdown menu for the Inventory Asset account. This account is used by QuickBooks to track the cost of all the stock you have (or inventory value).

Step 4: Add your product's sales, tax, and purchasing info

- On sales forms, include a description of your goods. This is visible on any documents you send to consumers, including invoices and sales receipts.

- Include **the unit cost.**

- Add **the sales rate or price**.

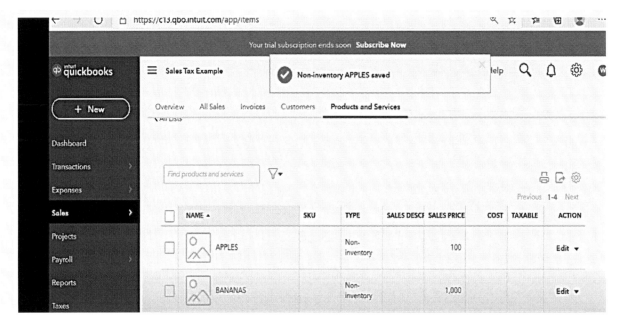

- Find the account you use to track your sales by selecting the Income account drop-down. You can use a QuickBooks income account that has been set up for you. However, if you require a new account, click **+ Add new** at the top of the drop-down list.
- If applicable, tick the Include **Tax checkbox**.
- Choose the **Sales tax category drop-down** and indicate the appropriate tax rate for the purchased item. Set up **sales tax in QuickBooks** if you can't see this drop-down.
- On order forms, include a description of your goods. Bills, purchase orders, and other documents you send to vendors will reflect this.
- Add the **cost of the item**. Don't be concerned if this alters. When you purchase supplies, you can still enter the most recent pricing.

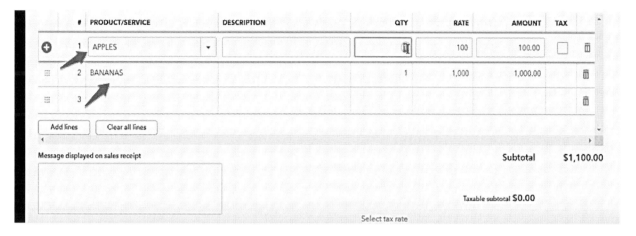

- Choose **Cost of Goods Sold** from the drop-down menu for the expense account. This account is used by QuickBooks to track the cost of the goods you sell.
- If appropriate, click the **Include purchase tax option**.
- Choose the **appropriate purchase tax from the drop-down menu** for purchase tax.
- Reverse charge is added.
- Choose a favorite supplier. You may quickly reorder this product since QuickBooks remembers your favorite provider.
- Optionally select **Advanced**.
- SKU or category addition for the thing you're tracking **Using categories** will help you organize your goods and services so that they are simpler to find.
- Select **Publish and close**.

Reordering inventory items

Using QuickBooks Online, reordering supplies and other items. Once they arrive, keep note of the things to update your inventory. How? Read on.

Step 1: **Check if you have low stocks or items that are out of stock**

Search for low-stock or out-of-stock alerts so you may order what you most urgently need.

- Choose **Products and services** after going to **Get paid & pay or Sales.**

- You can easily identify if you have low-stock or out-of-stock items at the top. To view those items, select **Low stock or Out of stock**.

When an item reaches or falls below its "reorder point," or the point at which you should reorder more stock, QuickBooks knows it is running low.

When you add new products, you can enter reorder points. You can update your existing products to add reorder points if they currently lack them.

Step 2: Create and send a purchase order

You can inform suppliers of the goods you require by sending them a purchase order. In a jiffy, make a purchase order by following the steps below:

- Choose **Products and services** after going to Get paid & pay or Sales.
- Choose **Out of Stock or Low Stock**. Use none of the top filters if you need to reorder both low-stock and out-of-stock items from the same source.
- Choose the **items as necessary.** A drop-down menu is located above the product list.
- Choose to **Reorder** after choosing **Batch activities**. This generates a single vendor's purchase order.
- Fill out the purchase order completely, or add any additional products you need to have the vendor replenish.
- Select **Send and save**.

Step 3: Track when you get your order from your vendor

You can track what you get from a seller in one of two ways:

- If you intend to pay your vendor in the future, create a bill from the purchase order.

- If you made an immediate payment to the seller, make a check or an expenditure from the purchase order.

With this, you can inform QuickBooks that you restocked. The amount on hand is then increased by the number of things you got via QuickBooks.

Creating inventory adjustments transactions

You could occasionally find that you have more or fewer of a certain item than QuickBooks indicates. QuickBooks Online Plus and Advanced users who maintain inventory can manually change an item's quantity to reflect what they actually have on hand without documenting a purchase or sale.

Insert an inventory quantity adjustment

- Click on **New**.

- Choose **Inventory quantity adjustment.**

- Insert the **Adjustment date**.

- Choose the **appropriate account** from the Inventory adjustment account drop-down.

- In the Product area, choose the **desired products**. Note that the description and available quantity are automatically filled in.

- Enter a new quantity or a change in quantity for each item.

- Enter the adjustment's specifics in the **Memo area**.

- When finished, choose **Save and close**.

Establishing categories

All subscriptions that utilize sub-items can use categories in place of those items, with the exception of those that switched from QuickBooks Desktop. Using different Products and Services reports, you can use categories to classify the products you sell and, ideally, gain a better understanding of what your customers are purchasing. Transactions cannot be given a category, and classifications have no bearing on your accounting or financial reports.

You can add new categories as you add products, or if you'd prefer, you can establish categories beforehand and make them available when you add items by;

- selecting **Manage Categories** from the **More menu** on the **Products and Services** list page.

- Clicking the **New Category button** on the **Product Categories** page allows you to add a new category; all you need to do is enter the category name in the Category Information panel that displays on the right side of your screen. Check the Is a Sub-Category box and choose the name of the current category if the new category is a subcategory of an existing one. To create a category,
- click **Save** at the bottom of the screen.

You can change an existing category if necessary by clicking the

- **Edit link** next to it in the table on the **Product Categories page**. The Category Information panel reappears and shows the most recent data for the category. If you want to remove a category, click **Remove** after making your adjustments.

Changing item types

You can alter the kind of service or non-inventory item separately, or you can pick many products and alter their item types all at once.

Be advised that there are various restrictions on changing item types. Particularly, you are unable to convert any Inventory goods into another item kind. You can modify the following things:

- Non-inventory and Service items to Inventory items.

- Service items to Non-inventory items.

- Non-inventory items to service items.

Only when switching from non-inventory items to service items or vice versa are many things changed at once when changing item kinds. You can only change one thing at a time if you need to convert a service item or a non-inventory item to an inventory item.

Given that a bundle is a collection of previously defined things, you cannot transform a bundle into any other item type. QBO automatically updates a bundle with the updated information whenever the item type of an item that is a part of it is changed.

By selecting Edit in the Action column of the Products and Services list, you may alter the type of any individual item. QBO then displays the item in the Product/Service detail panel. At the top of the panel, above the item's name, click the Change Type link. The only modifications you'll see after this are that Bundle isn't an option and the current item type has a checkbox. When you select a new item type, QBO updates the Product/Service Information panel to use that item type. After making any other adjustments, click Save and Close.

Simplifying your invoicing process

To let customers know they owe you money for items or services you provided for them, you enter invoices in QBO. When creating invoices in QBO, you have the option of sending them via email or USPS.

The Invoice with Google Calendar software, accessible in the Intuit App Center, automates the process of transferring event specifics and descriptions from your Google Calendar onto a QBO invoice if you record work you complete on your Google Calendar (to later use in invoicing).

- Simply open a **QBO invoice form** and click the **Google Calendar icon** that shows on the form once you've enabled the interface between your **Google Calendar and QBO**.

You can provide search criteria using a panel that displays to the right of the invoice form. You do this by choosing a Google Calendar, a time frame, and a search term. When you choose to add events to the invoice, QBO imports event details from your Google Calendar, including the title, description, hours worked, and date. This saves you from having to enter the same information twice.

Using the add-on program QuickBooks Invoicing for Gmail, you can also send invoices directly from Gmail and provide your clients the option of making payments online. If you're interested, you may get this software through QuickBooks Labs. It doesn't require a monthly subscription cost, but it does charge per transaction.

Using price rules

You may manage the cost of your goods and services by using pricing rules. Discounts are possible, as well as varying prices for each item. You can also make them available to only specific clients for a predetermined period of time.

Step 1: Turn on price rules

- Select **Account** and **Settings or Company Settings** by going to **Settings**.

- Choosing the **Sales tab**.

- Select **Edit in the Products** and services section.

- Turn on **price rules beta** by checking the box.

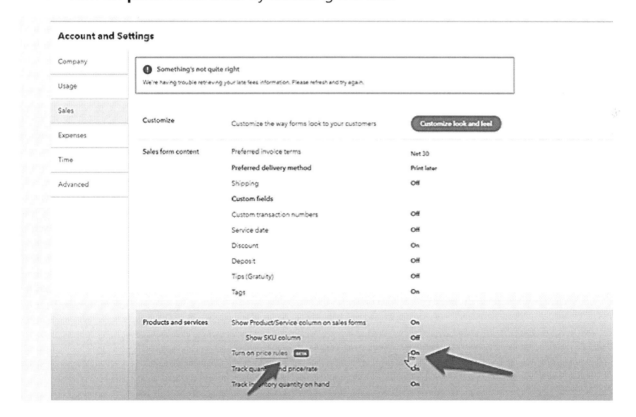

- Choose **Save**, followed by Done.

Step 2: Create a price rule

- Select **All Lists** from the **Settings menu**.
- Choose **Price Rules**.
- Select **Establish a rule**.
- Select the **New** pricing rule after your first rule.
- Finally, you should name your rule.
- Fill the Start date and End date fields with the dates when the rule is in effect.
- By default, price restrictions are applied to all of your clients. Choose a **specific customer** from the drop-down menu under **Select customers** before making your selection. Next, choose to **Add customer**. If you have client types, you can also add them.
- By default, price regulations apply to all goods and services. Choose **a certain type** from the drop-down menu under the **Select products or services heading**. Next, choose the type.
- To choose how much to raise or lower pricing, use the dropdowns for **Set sales price or rate by, Percentage, and Rounding**.
- Select **Apply** when you're ready to put your adjustments into effect. The Adjusted pricing column displays each item's updated price as a result of your customizations. To save your rule, select Save and close.

Keep in mind that as you add items to an invoice, the price rule will automatically be applied. By choosing the rate and viewing all current pricing rules, you can also override the price rule. Also, there is no limit in creating price rules, however, less than 10 thousand works best.

Working with bundles

You can combine products and variants that customers buy at the same time using QuickBooks Commerce. By doing this, you can record your sales without constantly choosing a product. This is how;

A bundle cannot be created until products and variants have been added to your inventory. Utilize the Bundle Converter tool if you wish to produce several bundles.

Creating a bundle

Here's how to put your products together into a bundle to assist you to save time when you record sales.

- Access Inventory.
- Choose **the item** you want to add to the bundle.
- Choosing **Add a Bundle**.
- Select **Save** changes after entering the bundle's name and any other necessary information.
- Add a product or variant from the bundle to the **Variant Name column.** Note: SKU searches are also an option.

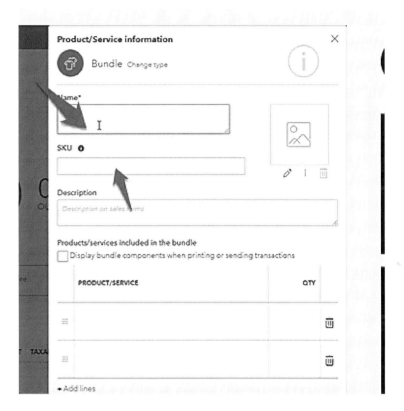

- To add more goods and variants, select **+ Add a variant**. Note: You can change the product and variant quantities as necessary.

- Select **Save adjustments**.

Your B2B store will automatically publish the bundles you build. Here's how to publish via other sales channels.

The only platforms that support publishing products straight from QuickBooks Commerce are Shopify, WooCommerce, and Squarespace. You must first construct the package from the marketplace for Amazon and eBay, then link it to QuickBooks Commerce.

- Access **Inventory**.
- Choose **the bundle** that is contained in the product you want to publish.
- The package you intend to publish should be chosen.
- The **Sales Channels tab** should be chosen.
- Choose t**he sales channels you want to publish** your bundle to from the ACTION column.

Importing and Exporting Products and Services

You can save time by importing a spreadsheet of your goods and services into QuickBooks. I'll walk you through formatting your spreadsheet in Google Sheets or Excel so you can import it right into QuickBooks.

Downloading the sample file

Excel or Google Sheets can be used to construct a spreadsheet listing your goods and services. You may format your spreadsheet to import appropriately by following the instructions in our sample file. The sample file can be downloaded here, along with formatting advice:

- Open **QuickBooks Online** and **log in**.
- Choose **Settings**. Select **Import Data next**.
- Select **Download** a sample file, then open the file.

Importing list

You are now prepared to import your items and services into QuickBooks after creating a spreadsheet with them in Excel or Google Sheets. Remember that once you import a list, there is no going back. Additionally, you can only import 1,000 rows at once. Divide your list into many, more manageable files if it is longer than that.

How to import your file is as follows:

- Sign in to **QuickBooks Online**.
- Click on **Settings** then choose **Import Data**.
- Click on **Product and Services**.

- To upload the file from your computer, select **Browse**. Select **Open** after selecting the file.
- Alternatively, pick **Connect** to sign into your **Google account** and upload files from **Google Sheets**. Select after **choosing the file**.
- Click on **Next.**
- Map out your data. The headers on your spreadsheet are represented by Your Field. Choose the drop-down menu from each that corresponds to a field in **QuickBooks Online.**
- Click on **Next.**
- Cells that are marked in red indicate that they are invalid. Check the spreadsheet cell, then try importing the file once more.
- Select for each good or service with the same name, replace all values. This cannot be undone, so make sure everything looks as it should.
- Click on **Import**.

Exporting list to Excel or Google sheets

Your QuickBooks Online products and services can be exported easily. This implies that downloading the information you typed into your file to your local hard disk is simple.

- Select **Products and services** under **Get paid & pay**.
- Run report can then be chosen by clicking the **More dropdown arrow.**
- Export to **Excel** can be selected after selecting the **Export icon**.

Managing products and services with a spreadsheet system

Your goods and services can be simply added by importing a spreadsheet or by doing it manually in one of two ways. The use of the spreadsheet system is the fastest way to have all your products or services added to QuickBooks.

- Navigate to **Sales** in the left menu. Choose the **sub-tab** for **Products and Services** To import, click.
- Examine the sample **Excel worksheet** that you can download.
- Organize your spreadsheet so that each column's names and order correspond to those in the sample file. Return to the Import screen after finishing, click Browse, and upload your file.

- Connect each **QuickBooks field** to a specific column in your **Excel workbook**. The data from the chosen column will be imported into the chosen QuickBooks field.
- Check your data to make sure everything is accurately mapped, and make any necessary corrections. When finished, click Import.

Given all of the capabilities that QuickBooks Online offers, you must be feeling regret that you didn't learn about it sooner. This chapter just ended is another big one. Every firm deal with tax refunds and provides services, and if they deal in commodities, they must always maintain an inventory.

You should have learned what sales tax is, how to configure it on QuickBooks Online, what sales tax responsibility is, and how to automate the sales tax feature before finishing the just-ended chapter. You should also have learned how to convert your valuable sales to QuickBooks Online. You must also be familiar with the new Nexus function, the auditing of client lists, the management of goods and services, and the application of price rules. You'd agree with me that I'm quite loaded. Make sure you read everything in the activity below, rehearse, and try it.

Activity

1. What do you understand about sales tax?
2. Configure a sales tax in your QBO.
3. Describe what a sales tax liability is.
4. Enable the automated sales tax feature in your QuickBooks Online.
5. Convert your sales tax from QuickBooks desktop(if you have been making use of QuickBooks before).
6. Check your settings in QBO and change from manual to automated sales tax.
7. What is the Economic Nexus feature?
8. Configure how to pay sales tax.
9. Add inventory and service items to your QuickBooks online.
10. Change the order in which you have arranged the inventory items in your QBO.
11. Create an inventory adjustment transaction.
12. List the various item types in QBO.
13. What does the term "price rule" mean?
14. Create a price rule in your QBO.

15. Create a bundle in your QuickBooks Online.
16. Adjust your products and services with a spreadsheet system.

CHAPTER 6

INVOICING CUSTOMERS AND RECEIVING PAYMENTS

The excitement begins right here because the topics covered in this chapter have to do with raising capital, which is the most enjoyable aspect of running a business from the standpoint of any businessperson.

Getting Oriented with Sales Transactions

You can see the status of sales transactions, open invoices, and paid invoices very clearly on the Sales page. From within the page, you can also examine, make, and edit sales transactions.

- Go to **Bookkeeping, Transactions, and then All Sales**, or go to **Sales** and then **All Sales,** to go to this page.

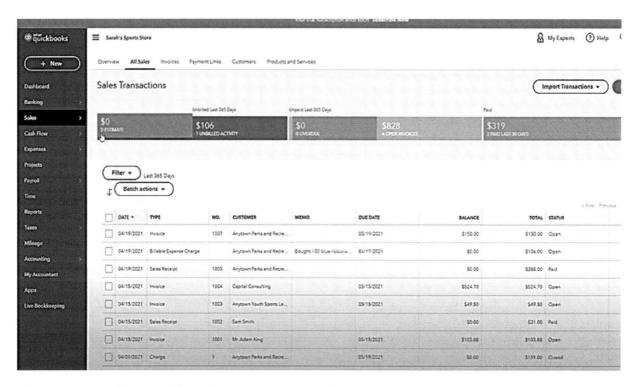

View transaction and invoice status at a glance

The Money Bar, a crucial element of the Sales page, will be visible after you go there. It provides you with a fast view of open and recently paid invoices and quickly displays the status and dollar amounts of your sales transactions. Additionally, it displays any unbilled fees, charges, time activities, or estimates.

The list allows you to view information about certain transactions and can show:

- Estimates
- Invoices
- Sales receipts
- Payments
- Credit memos
- Delayed charges (QuickBooks Online Plus, Advanced, and Essentials only)
- Billable time activities (QuickBooks Online Plus and Advanced only)

The list makes it simple to see any transaction's status and determine if it is Open, Closed, Paid, Partially Paid, or Overdue.

The list is easily customizable so that you can view the data you require:

- To see only the items you are interested in, filter the list.
- View only the info you require by altering the columns.
- In order to work with the data included in lists in different ways, export lists to Microsoft Excel.

Keep in mind that '365 days' is the default view for all transactions. If an invoice was not created during the previous 365 days, the Invoices page won't show up.

Managing sales transactions from the sales page is very easy as you will be able to;

- From the **New transaction dropdown menu, create new invoices, payments, sales receipts, estimates, credit memos, delayed charges, and billable time activity**.
- Do anything about a transaction. For instance, by choosing Receive Payment in the Action column, you can pay an invoice right away from the list.
- Print transactions or packing slips, either for a specific group or an individual (for invoicing and sales receipts).
- Delete, invalidate, or copy transactions.
- Send transactions, and when sending just one, personalize the message that goes with it.
- Update the estimations' status.
- Make more entries for the consumer, such as charges, time activities, and credits (QuickBooks Online Plus, Advanced, and Essentials only).

Creating Invoices

Send your customers an invoice if you expect to get paid for the goods and services you provide in the future. You can include the good or service you're selling in an invoice that you send to your client via email.

I'll demonstrate how to make new invoices as well as how to look through outstanding debts. We'll also provide information on how to manage things if you utilize an external payment processing platform like QuickBooks Payments, where clients can pay their invoices online.

Step 1: Create and send an invoice

Using the old experience

- Click on **New**.

- Choose **Invoice**.

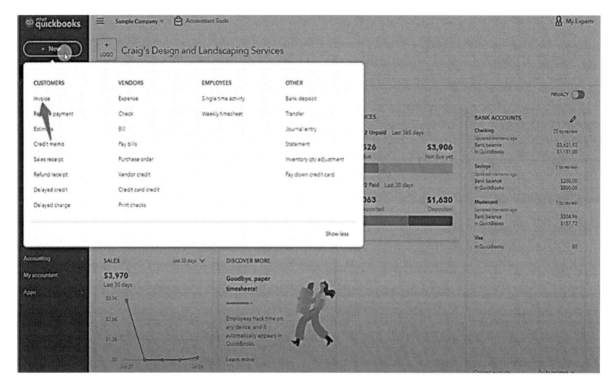

- Choose **a customer** from the **Customer dropdown menu**. Verify that every piece of information, including the email address, is accurate.
- Check the **invoice's date**. Change the due date in the Terms dropdown if necessary. The term "net" denotes how many days there are until payment is expected. The due date can be altered if necessary; the default is 30 days.
- Choose **a product or service** from the **Product/Service column**.

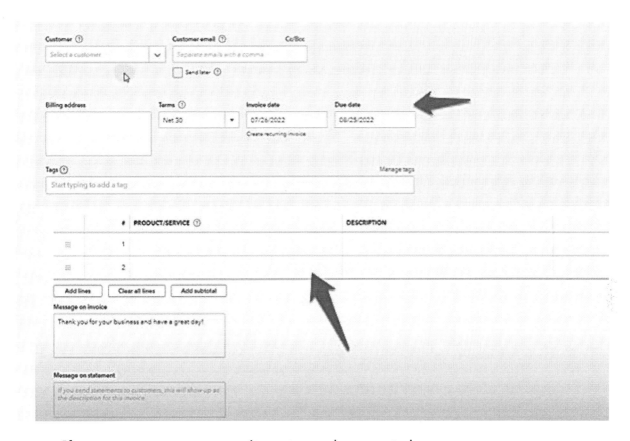

- If necessary, enter a quantity, rate, and amount change.
- If you must charge sales tax, tick the Tax box.
- When finished, you have a number of options for saving or distributing the invoice:
  - When you're prepared to email your customer with the invoice, choose Save and send. If necessary, edit the email, then click **Send and close**.
  - Select **Save and close** to send the invoice at a later time.
  - Choose **Save** to print a printed invoice. Choose Print or Preview next.
  - Choose **Save and share a link** if you want to SMS your customer a link to their invoice.

Step 2: Review unpaid invoices

Unpaid invoices are added to your accounts receivable account by QuickBooks. This account will appear on your balance sheet as well as other financial reports.

- Go to **Get paid & pay or Sales & costs**, then **pick Invoices** whenever you wish to check your invoices. To find out where invoices stand in the sales process, look at the Status column.

Here are a few typical states you might encounter:

- **Due in (days)**: the email has not been invoiced yet.
- **Due in (days) Sent**: the invoice has been sent to the customer.
- **Due in (days) Viewed**: the customer has opened the invoice.
- **Deposited**: invoice has been paid by the customer.
- **Overdue (days)**: the invoice is past the due date and has not been paid.
- **Overdue (days) Viewed**: the customer opened the invoice but hasn't paid the past-due invoice.
- **Delivery issue**: The invoice was not delivered. You might have to check the email address and attempt sending it again.
- **Voided**: The invoice was voided in QuickBooks.

Step 3: Receive payments for invoices

Customers can pay their invoices directly by credit card or ACH transfer if they use QuickBooks Payments. Everything is processed and taken care of for you. QuickBooks records transactions in the appropriate accounts when you receive payments.

You can monitor payments made through an external platform in QuickBooks if you do so.

Creating Billable Time Entries

You must enable the billable time setting if you wish to charge your client straight from the monitored time. This is how:

- Choose **Settings.** Select **Account and settings** after that.
- Choosing the **Time tab**.
- Select **Edit** from the **Timesheet section**.

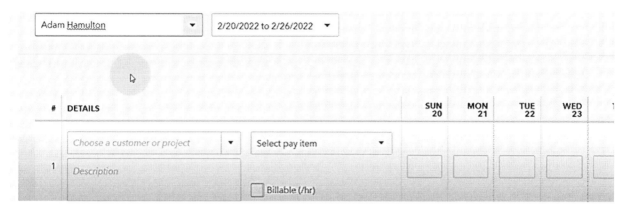

- Activate the setting that says "Allow time to be billed."
- Select the **Show billing** rate to users entering the time checkbox if you want your users to see their billable rate when they enter their time. If you bill clients at a different hourly rate than you pay your employees and subcontractors, you might wish to leave this unchecked.
- Choose **Save**, then choose **Done**.

You can then create a billable time through the Time tab:

- Select **Time**, then **Time entries**, under **Payroll**.
- Choose the user for whom you are adding time, then click **Add Time**.
- If necessary, change the date range in the menu by selecting **This week, Last week, or Custom**. Next, choose the day for which you are entering time.
- To enter a start time and end time, turn on the Start/end times switch and add the number of hours worked.
- Choosing **Add work details**. Next, choose your customer or project from the **Customer/Project dropdown**.
- Switch on **Billable (/hr)** to make the timesheet billable.

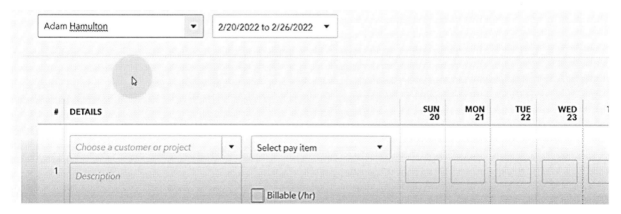

- Add any necessary choices or notes.
- Choose **Done**.
- Select **Add** and repeat steps 4 through 8 if you need to add more timesheets for that employee.
- Click on the **Save and Close option**.

Entering time activities

You can record the total number of hours worked by your employee or vendor for the week on weekly timesheets.

Note:

- Timesheets for each week are not posted transactions. This means that until the contents of the timesheets have been included in a sale for an expense-type transaction, they will not appear on reports like Profit and Loss.

- There can be only one hourly rate per timesheet. You can subscribe to QBO Payroll if you need to enter several hourly rates.

Follow the steps below to complete this process;

- **Choose + New.**

- Select **Weekly Timesheet** under **Employees**.

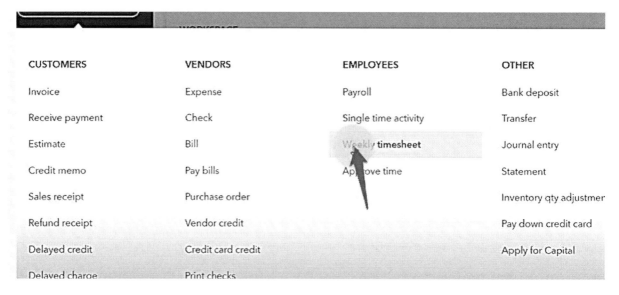

CUSTOMERS	VENDORS	EMPLOYEES	OTHER
Invoice	Expense	Payroll	Bank deposit
Receive payment	Check	Single time activity	Transfer
Estimate	Bill	Weekly timesheet	Journal entry
Credit memo	Pay bills	Approve time	Statement
Sales receipt	Purchase order		Inventory qty adjustmer
Refund receipt	Vendor credit		Pay down credit card
Delayed credit	Credit card credit		Apply for Capital
Delayed charge	Print checks		

- Choose **the employee or vendor's name** and the week you want to record from the little arrow icons.

- Fill in the remaining fields. Note: Click **Settings** under the **Total Hours** to adjust the days available.

  - **Customer or project**: choose the customers or project you would like to bill the activity to or you can also choose to track expenses.

  - **Service**: Choose the service that represents the activity.

  - **Billable**: Choose the checkbox and insert the rate if there is a need for you to bill the activity to the customer.

  - **Location and class**: ensure this feature is turned on.

  - **Description**: Insert a description activity.

  - **Time field**: Insert the number of hours and minutes your employee or vendor spent working on this activity.

- Finally, click on **Save**.

Adding billable time and expenses to an invoice

You can send consumers invoices for particular project-related costs after creating projects (including timesheets). These procedures apply whether you bill consumers a fixed price or a time and materials fee.

Step 1: Decide how you will like to be charged for projects

If you bill for time and materials, you typically invoice clients for the precise costs and labor hours associated with a certain project. To include them in invoices, you must make your project expenses and timesheets billable.

Usually, you don't invoice for specific project expenses if you charge a fixed rate. Instead, you provide consumers with a project-wide estimate. When the work starts, you can turn the estimate into an invoice.

You might occasionally need to charge for particular project expenses, though. One typical instance is when clients request additional work that wasn't originally part of the project plan.

Step 2: Switch on billable expenses

If you have not already, turn on billable expenses.

- Click **Account and settings under Settings**.
- Choosing the **Expenses tab**.
- To expand it, go to the **Bills & Expenses area and pick it**.
- The Make expenses and items chargeable switch should be turned on.
- To save and then exit your settings, select **Save and then Done**.

Step 3: Make project expenses billable

- Navigate to Business overview then click on **Projects** and then open the specific project.

Project expenses

- Select **Choose Add to Project, then Expense**.
- Fill out the form with expenditures.
- Each item's Billable box should be checked.
- Select **Publish and close**.
- From the **Customer/Project dropdown menu**, choose **the project.**
- Choose **Save**.

Project timesheets

- Choose + **New**.
- Click on the **Time entry**.
- Select a **worker**.
- Choose **a day and, if necessary, adjust the date range**.
- To input a start time and end time for that day, turn Start/end times on. Alternatively, enter the number of hours worked.
- Select **To add the project** and make the timesheet billable, provide work information.

- If there is a need for you to make use of a custom rate for this timesheet, click on **Use custom** rate then insert your preferred amount.

- Click on **Done**.

- Click on **Save and Close**.

Keep in mind that your staff members can directly link their time to the project you created if you utilize QuickBooks Time. In order for those timesheets to display in your project, make sure you approve and export them.

Step 4: Invoice your customer for billable expenses

Return to the project's Overview tab after making all of your project expenses and timesheets chargeable.

- Select **Invoice** after choosing **Add to Project**.
- From the **Customer dropdown menu**, choose the **client you want to invoice**.
- Your timesheets and chargeable expenses will show up in the **Add to the Invoice section**. All time and chargeable expenses should be added to the invoice.

- Finish up with the invoice, then **submit it to your client**.

If you wish to submit timesheets or specific expenses as an invoice:

- Enter your **project now.**
- Head over to the **Transactions tab**.
- Locate the timesheet or chargeable expense on the list.
- Select **From the Action column**, choose to **Create Invoice**.
- Finish the invoice, then submit it to your client.

Printing a Batch of Invoices or Packing Slips

When shipping items to customers, a packing slip is a document that lists the item, quantity, and other crucial shipping details.

Print a packing slip in QuickBooks Online

- Select **Customers under Customers & leads**.
- To get a list of the customer's transactions, click on **their name**.
- Choose the **checkbox** next to each invoice or sales receipt for which you wish to print a packing slip from the **Transaction List tab**.
- Print packing slip after selecting the **Batch operations selection**.
- You can choose printing choices, examine a preview, and print from the print preview screen.

Recording Customer Payments

You enter a customer's payment into QBO after receiving it. The following options are available for displaying the Receive Payment window:

- Find the invoice for which you wish to record a payment in the **Sales Transactions list**, and then click **Receive Payment in the Action column**.

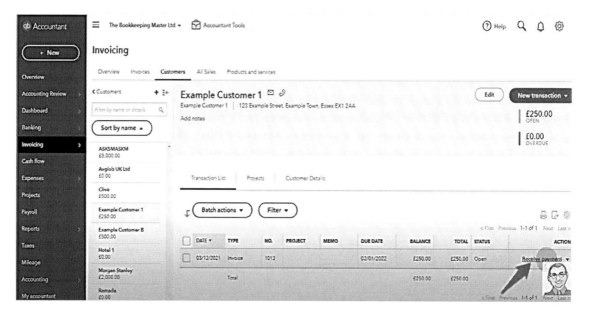

- On the **Sales Transactions page,** you can click the **New Transaction button** and choose **Payment**.

- You can choose **Receive Payment** by clicking the **Create menu**.

- Choose **Projects**, choose the project you're working on, and then click **Add to Project**.

When you select the first option from the preceding list, QBO opens the Receive Payment window with the details of the selected invoice and a suggested payment amount already filled in.

When using the second or third approach, QBO shows a blank Receive Payment window. The Outstanding Transactions section at the bottom of the window appears after you pick a customer, showing all of the customer's open bills.

- Choose a **payment method** at the top of the screen, then choose the account you want QBO to deposit the customer's payment into. The sum of the client's payment should be entered in the **Amount Received column**. Check the box next to each invoice that has been paid with the customer's payment in the section titled **Outstanding Transactions**.

Understanding the Payments to Deposit account

Credit card and ACH payments processed using QuickBooks Payments are deposited into the chosen external bank account. You can think of this as your payments account.

The external bank account that QuickBooks uses to deposit payments can easily be changed. Keep in mind that you can only use one account to collect payments at once.

Change your payments account

To use QuickBooks Payments, follow the instructions for the QuickBooks product you are using. Two primary account settings are as follows:

Standard deposit: By entering your bank routing and account number, you can connect a bank account for customary funding occasions (non-instant deposits).

Updating the Standard Deposit account

- Utilize a web browser to log in to **QuickBooks Online**. Don't utilize **GoPayments** or the **mobile app.**

- Select **Account and settings** from the **Settings menu.**

- Choosing the **Payments tab**. Select **Change bank** under **Standard Deposits** in the **Deposits section**.

- Select **Create** a new bank account.

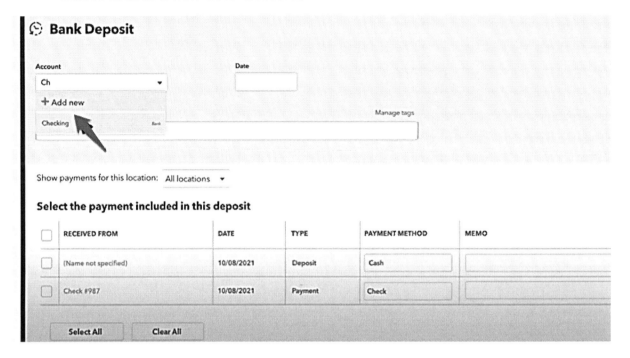

- To modify your bank account, provide the routing number and account number.
- As soon as you're ready, click **Save**.
- Before submitting your request, double-check the bank account information and make sure it is chosen.

Instant Deposit: connect a debit card to finance Instant Deposit transactions. The debit card associated with your QuickBooks Cash account is already set up.

Updating the Instant Deposit account

- Choose **Settings**, followed by **Account and settings**.
- Go to the **Deposit accounts** section under the **Payments tab**.
- To change your instant deposit information, select **Change**. Select the **0% fee option** if you decide to move from your personal debit card to your **QuickBooks Cash debit card**.
- When finished, choose **Save and then Done**.

Customer payments from online invoicing and other sources will begin to be deposited into the new account by QuickBooks.

Remember that this does not alter how payments are categorized by QuickBooks on your chart of accounts. This modifies the bank account that QuickBooks uses to deposit funds.

Recording invoice payments

You can make and send an invoice to your client if they intend to pay you in the future. In order to balance your accounts, you must record customer payments and link them to the appropriate invoices.

Please take note: If you process payments with QuickBooks Payments, we take care of the accounting for you. QuickBooks processes the money and assigns it to the appropriate account when your customer pays the invoice.

To mark an invoice as paid, you must record the customer payment after processing it in QuickBooks. If not, the invoice is left open and shows up on your records as underpaid. An invoice can be paid in full or in part, and QuickBooks keeps track of any unpaid amount.

Single invoice

- Choose **+ New**.
- Choose **to Receive payment**.

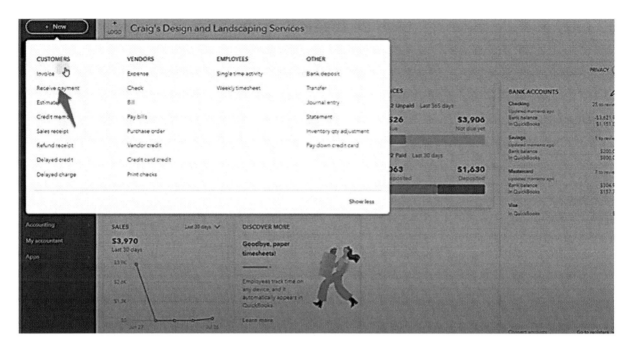

- Choose **the customer's name** from the **Customer dropdown menu**.

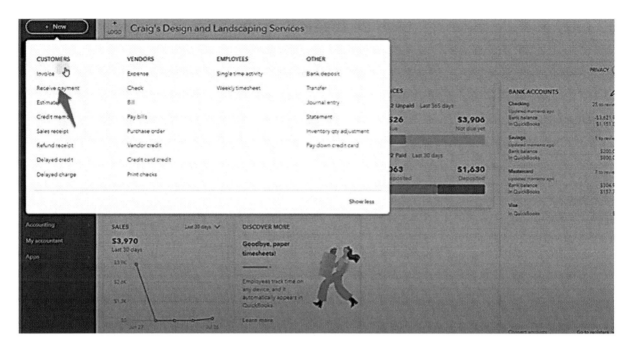

- Choose the **payment method** from the **Payment method dropdown.**
- Choose the account you want to deposit the money into from the **Deposit to drop-down menu**.

- Choose the checkbox next to the invoice for which you are recording the payment in the **Outstanding Transactions section.**
- If necessary, enter the **Memo and Reference number**.
- Select **Publish and close**.

Recording partial payment for an invoice

- Choose + **New.**
- Choosing to **Receive payment**.
- Choose **the customer's name** from the **Customer dropdown menu**.
- Choose the payment method from the **Payment method dropdown**.
- Choose the account you want to deposit the money into from the **Deposit to drop-down menu.**
- Put your customer's payment amount in the **Amount received column**.
- Choose the checkbox next to the invoice for which you are recording the payment in the **Outstanding Transactions section**.
- If necessary, enter the **Memo and Reference number**.
- Select **Publish and close**.

QuickBooks applies the payment to the invoice line items in order when you record partial payments. Up until the payment is finished, additional payments are applied to the subsequent line items.

Having more than one payment in a single deposit

Use the Undeposited Funds account to record the payments in QuickBooks if you deposit multiple checks into the bank at once. This enables you to combine numerous payments into a single QuickBooks deposit transaction. Do this only if your bank combines several payments into one deposit.

Entering a sales receipt

If you utilize a different Point of Sale system, you can enter a single sales receipt to record the overall daily sales in QuickBooks. Or if you merely fail to send invoices to clients. You can do this to save time while maintaining the accuracy of your income reports.

Following is a step-by-step instruction to get you going.

Step 1: Create a customer for daily sales

This customer account will only be used on your "end of day" sales receipt.

- Choose **Customers from Get paid & pay or Sales by going there**.
- Choose **New customer**.
- Specify **Daily Sales**.
- Choose **Save**.

Step 2: Set up accounts for daily sales

Ensure that the accounting for your daily sales are upright. You can declare your income accurately by doing this to a great extent.

Setting up daily sales accounts entails:

- On the Toolbar, choose the **Gear icon**.
- Select **Chart of Accounts** from the **Your Company menu**.
- Click **New** in the top right corner.
- Get these accounts set up:

Name	Category Type/ Account Type	Detail Type	Description
Daily Sales Income	Income	Other Primary Income/Sales of Product Income	For tracking daily sales
Clearing account	Cash and cash equivalents	Bank / Cash on hand	Zero balance account for daily sales
Overage and Underage expense	Expense	Other Business Expenses	For drawer shortages

Step 3: Set up items for daily sales

To keep your things organized, create a category called "Daily Sales":

- On the **Toolbar**, choose the **Gear icon**.

- Select **All Lists** from the **Lists menu.**
- Choose the preferred **Product categories** you want.
- In the top right corner, choose **New Category.**
- The new category is called **Daily Sales**.
- Choose **Save**.

The following items come after setting up the Category:

- On the Toolbar, choose the **Gear icon**.
- Select **Products and Services** from the **Lists section**.
- Click **New** in the top right corner.

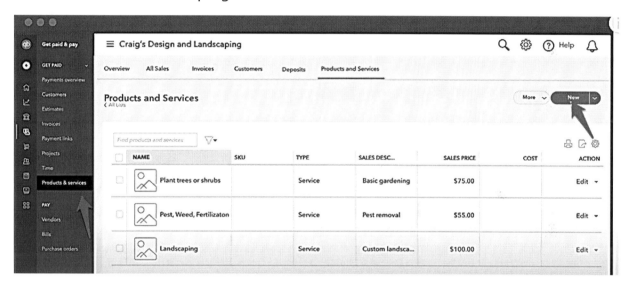

- Set these things up. Note: For each item, be sure to choose **Daily Sales as the Category**.

Step 4: Create a daily sales template

This template will be used each time you need to keep track of daily total sales.

- On the **Toolbar**, choose the **Gear icon**.
- Select **Recurring Transactions** from the list.
- Click **New** in the top right corner.
- Select **Sales Receipt** from the dropdown menu for the **Transaction Type**.
- Make sure the Type is Unscheduled and give your template the name "Daily Sales."
- Decide on **Daily Sales** as the client.

- The following items should be chosen in the Product/Service section;
  - Daily Sales: Daily Sales Income
  - Daily Sales: Cash
  - Daily Sales: Check
  - Daily Sales: Visa/Mastercard
  - Daily Sales: American Express
  - Daily Sales: Overage/Underage
  - Daily Sales: Discover

- Click on **Save template**.

Step 5: Record your total daily sales

Your sales receipt template is now ready. Your "end of day" sales can now be recorded.

- On the Toolbar, choose the **Gear icon**.
- Select **Recurring Transactions** from the **Lists menu**.
- Once you've located your template, choose **Use from the Action selection**.
- Check out the sample breakdown of total daily sales below for a better idea of how your sales receipt should seem.

Recording Bank Deposits

You frequently deposit several payments from different sources at once while making a deposit at the bank. Typically, the bank keeps track of everything as a single record with a single total. The same payments won't match how your bank reported the deposit if you enter them as separate records in QuickBooks.

In these circumstances, QuickBooks offers a unique method for you to combine transactions so that your records correspond to your actual bank deposit. To record bank deposits in QuickBooks Online, follow these steps.

- To combine transactions, add them to your **Undeposited Funds account**.
- After that, merge them using the bank deposit tool.

Step 1: Put transactions into the Undeposited Funds account

Put any invoice payments and sales receipts you want to combine, if you haven't already, into the Undeposited Funds account. Everything that is in this account prior to recording a deposit is here. If you do, QuickBooks handles everything on your behalf. Transactions are processed and moved into your accounts automatically. The Undeposited Funds account is not required.

Step 2: Combine transactions in QuickBooks with a bank deposit

In QuickBooks, every bank deposit generates a unique record. For each of your deposit slips, make one deposit at a time.

- Choose **+ New**.
- Decide on **Bank Deposit**.
- Select the account you want to deposit the money into from the **Account menu.**
- For each transaction you want to combine, tick the appropriate box.
- Verify that the sum of the chosen transactions matches the amount on your deposit slip. As a guide, use your deposit slip.
- Choose **Save and new or Save and close**

Keeping Tabs on Invoice Status and Receiving Payment

By letting them select the due date when seeing the invoice, Schedule Pay encourages timely payment from your clients. Up until the invoice's due date, your customer may select any day to make a payment.

Set up schedule pay for your invoice

The good news is that starting Schedule Pay requires no action on your part. You're ready to go as long as your invoices are configured to accept online payments.

Your clients see the Schedule Pay option when you issue a new invoice after they click the Review and Pay button on their emailed invoice.

Schedule pay won't work if;

- The invoice is Due on receipt.
- Your customer edits the amount to be paid.
- The main amount of the invoice is $50,000 or more.

You can also keep tabs on the scheduled pay status of your customers invoices by taking the steps below;

- Select **Sales**, then **Invoices**.
- Locate the invoice whose payment status you want to verify.
- The activity tracker panel will appear when the status field on that invoice line is selected.

When the Payment Scheduled status appears beneath the section for invoice activity, you know your customer has Schedule Pay set up.

Giving Money Back to a Customer

It occurs. It's unfortunate, but it does happen. There are times when you must refund money that a consumer gave you.

In the event that a customer returns goods to you, send a credit memo. As an alternative, you might give a refund receipt if you need to reimburse a customer for their money, possibly because the customer's goods arrived damaged and they don't want to place another order.

Issuing a refund to a customer

You can reverse a deposit made by a customer who paid you a down payment on an invoice but later backed out of the deal by offering them a refund and applying for credit.

Create a credit memo, and a check to return the deposit, and then record the payment in QuickBooks Online to refund the deposit.

Step 1: Create a credit memo

- Choose **+ New**.
- Click on **Credit Memo**.

- Choose the **Customer's name** that appears on your invoice.

- In the Amount field, enter the invoice's total, including the deposit.

- Choose **Save**.

Step 2: Create a check to refund the deposit

- Choose + **New**.

- Choose **Check**.

- In the **Payee field**, pick the client.
- Select **Accounts Receivable** from the **Category menu** under **Category Details**.
- In the Amount area, enter the deposit's total amount.
- Select **Publish and close**.

Step 3: Record a payment

- Choose **+ New**.
- Click on **Receive Payment**.
- Choose the **Customer's name** that appears on your invoice.
- Verify that the sum of the credits matches the credit memo and invoice that are mentioned under **Outstanding Transactions**.
- Check the boxes next to the invoice and credit memo in the Outstanding Transactions section.
- Select **Publish and close**.

Recording a credit memo

Some customers would rather receive a credit they can use to lower the balance on their subsequent invoice than a refund.

In QuickBooks, credits can be handled in a few different ways. To instantly reduce a customer's outstanding balance, you can create a credit memo. Alternatively, you could enter a deferred credit so they may spend it later.

Read on for more information on the distinctions and how to use them in client transactions.

You can instruct QuickBooks to automatically apply credit memos to client balances or open invoices if you haven't already. To activate the automatic application of credit memos:

- Select **Account and settings under Settings.**
- Choose the **Advanced tab**.
- In the Automation section, click **Edit.**
- Select **Apply for** credits automatically.
- Pick **Save**, then click **Done**.

Recording a credit memo;

- Choose + **New**.
- Click on **Credit memo**.

- Choose the **customer's name** from the **Customer dropdown menu**.

- Enter the credit memo's specifics, including the amount and the date. A custom credit service item can be made, allowing you to rapidly include it as a single line item in credit memos.

- When finished, choose **Save and close**.

Writing off Bad Debt

Bad debt is a risky idea that could result in you losing out on money that is legally yours. Bad debt is essentially when someone owes you money but the sum is rendered invalid. As a result, you incur a deficit in your own assets and are unable to recoup your initial invoiced/loaned sum.

Anyone, whether an individual or a business, is capable of accumulating bad debt. This debt should be recorded in your financial books and gross revenue records even though it cannot be paid back.

It can be difficult to remain in a bad debt scenario. It's crucial that you "pay off" your poor loans, though. Simply put, writing off a bad debt entails admitting that you have suffered a loss. This contrasts with bad debt expense, which is a technique of accounting for potential losses in the future.

You must record uncollectible invoices you send through QuickBooks as bad debts and write them off. This guarantees that your net income and accounts receivable are always current.

Step 1: Check your aging accounts receivable

Using the Accounts Receivable Aging Detail report, examine additional invoices or receivables that ought to be written off as bad debt.

- Select **Reports** from the **Business overview menu**, or go directly to **Reports**.
- Locate and open a report called **Accounts Receivable Aging Detail**.
- Determine which unpaid accounts receivables need to be written off.

Step 2: Create a bad debts expense account

- Go to **Settings**, you can then click on the **chart of accounts**.

- To create a new account, click **New** in the upper right corner.
- Choose **Expenses** from the **Account Type option**.
- Choose **Bad debts** from the **Detail Type menu**.
- Enter **Bad debts** in the Name field.
- Click on the **Save and Close option**.

Step 3: Create a bad debt item

- Choose **Products and Services** from the **Settings menu**.
- Choose **New**, then **Non-inventory**, from the menu on the upper right.
- **Bad debts** should be typed in the Name field.
- Choose **Bad debts** from the **Income account dropdown.**
- Select **Save and Close**.

Step 4: Create a credit memo for the bad debt

- Pick + **New.**
- Decide on **Credit memo**.

- Choose the client from the **Customer option**.
- Select **Bad debts** under **Product/Service**.
- Enter the sum you wish to deduct in the **Amount column.**

- Put **Bad Debt** in the **Message box** that appears on the statement.
- Choose **Save and Close**.

Step 5: Apply the credit memo to the invoice

- Choose **+ New**.
- Select **Receive** payment from the Customers menu.
- Choose the relevant customer from the **Customer selection**.
- Select the invoice from the **Outstanding Transactions list**.
- Select the **credit memo** from the **Credits section**.
- Click on the **Save and Close option**.

Reviewing and Creating Transactions with Spreadsheet Sync

The kinds of templates offered by Spreadsheet Sync for pulling data to run a report or publishing data to QuickBooks Online Advanced. Spreadsheet Sync templates come in two different categories.

- **List templates:** In your QuickBooks Online Advanced account, they are used to add or amend lists of corporate data. Accounts, Classes & Departments, or Vendors & Customers are examples of list-type templates.

  - List data will become dropdown options in the **transaction templates of Spreadsheet Sync after being uploaded.**

- Transaction template: The purpose of business documents like invoices and bills, purchase orders, and estimates are to add to or modify business activity.

  - After entering new list data, choose **Update Sheet** from the toolbar to update the options in a posting template dropdown.

Every business relies heavily on money, and this chapter must have made you aware of that as well. You should have learned how to handle sales transactions, create an invoice, enter billable time, insert time activities, add billable time and expenses to an invoice, print invoices, record customer payments, comprehend how payments to deposit accounts work, record invoice payments, enter sales receipts, record bank deposits, monitor invoice status, and payment, reimburse customers, and more in this chapter.

This chapter should be carefully read, understood, and analyzed.

Activity

1. Describe all that sales transactions entails.
2. Create an invoice.
3. Create a billable time entry.
4. Insert time activities.
5. Include billable time and expenses in the invoice you have created.
6. What is a packing slip?
7. Receive and record payments from customers.
8. Record invoice payments.
9. Insert a sales receipt.
10. Record bank deposits.
11. Issue a refund to a customer in the form of credit.
12. How can a bad debt be written off?

CHAPTER 7

PAYING BILLS AND WRITING CHECKS

Spending money is never as much fun as earning it, but having to pay bills is a necessary part of life. The transactions you utilize in QBO to fulfill your financial commitments are examined in this chapter.

If you start using QBO after you've been in business for a while and have some unpaid debts, you can enter those bills as instructed in this chapter to use them as a learning tool. Be sure to enter any checks you've written that haven't yet cleared your bank into QBO if you recorded an opening bank account balance. Make sure to enter into QBO all the checks you've written this year, even if they have cleared the bank, if you didn't record an opening bank account balance or you entered a bank account balance as of December 31 of the previous year.

You can display the Expense Transactions page by selecting Expenses from the Navigation bar to record the majority of expense-related transactions. To choose a transaction type, click the New Transaction button.

The Create icon changes to an X when you enter the menu, and expense-related transactions appear in the Vendors column. If the transaction type you want to record isn't available, click the Create plus sign (+) icon at the top of QBO and select the type of transaction you want to record.

Looking at Expense and Bill payment Methods

- Use **Bill**, then **Pay bills** to pay bills later.

- Use **Check or Expense** depending on how you made the payment for expenses that need to be paid right away or that have already been paid.

Bill payments

- Use **Pay bills** to close a bill if you initially logged it in QuickBooks. You can use your credit card to make a payment or print a check.

CUSTOMERS	VENDORS	EMPLOYEES	OTHER
Invoice	Expense	Payroll ↑	Bank deposit
Receive payments	Check	Single time activity	Transfer
Estimate	Bill	Weekly timesheet	Journal entry
Credit Memo	Pay bills		Statement
Sales receipt	Purcha...er		Inventory Quantity Adjustment
Refund receipt	Vendor Credit		
Delayed credit	Credit card credit		
Delayed charge	Print checks		

Show less

NOV '18   DEC '18   JAN   FEB   MAR   APR   MAY   JUN   J

- When a bill payment is entered through Pay Bills, the Vendor amount is reduced properly.
- Using a check or an expense could result in the bill still reflecting as unpaid on your reports.
- Enter **EFT** in the **Check n**o. area if you paid a bill electronically.

Checks or expenses

- A transaction is reported by both **Check and Expense** as both an expense and payment at the same time.
- Checks and expenses are for services or items that are paid immediately, whereas bills are for payables (received services or items that will be paid later).
- Record an expense as a **Check** rather than an **Expense** if you need to print a check.
- Use **Expense** if you made a credit card payment.
- Use a **Check or Expense** even if you paid something via **EFT. EFT** can be entered in the space for **Check No**.

For instance, if you purchased goods from Office Depot and paid for them right away, you should record the transaction as a Check or Expense. Since Office Depot isn't owing any money, you can forgo entering and paying payments.

146

Understanding the Transaction Types

A transaction type in QuickBooks describes the sort of transaction that took place, such as a customer transaction, a bill payment, or a bank transfer. You enter a transaction code to indicate a transaction when you submit it. Not all transaction types, though, have a corresponding code. You can filter your transactions in your reports by setting a transaction type.

Customer Transactions

The core of your business is customer transactions, so you should record every kind of transaction. An "RCPT" code is a generic code for sales receipts; an "ITEM RCPT" specifies an item receipt, which shows that you have received items from a vendor without an invoice; and a "TAXPMT" code represents a sales tax payment. An "STMTCHG" code identifies a statement charge you have billed to a customer, while a "CREDMEM" shows a credit memo you have issued.

Bills and Invoices

To keep track of the money you owe or are owed, some of the kinds are used to represent transactions between you and your vendors. The "BILL" type denotes an unpaid bill from a vendor; the "BILLPMT" type denotes a paid bill from a vendor; the "BILLCRED" type denotes a credit extended to you by a vendor, and the "INV" type denotes an invoice you have issued to a client or vendor.

Checks and Credits

You should also keep track of your payroll and any other business-related expenses if you have staff. A "CC" type denotes a credit card charge, whereas a "CC CRED" type denotes a credit card credit, possibly if you've had to return purchases. The "PAY CHK" type identifies each paycheck you provide to your employees. Payroll tax and other liabilities transactions are displayed in a "LIAB CHK."

Generic Types

The other transaction categories don't include dealings with other people directly. The "CHK" type denotes checks, while "DEP" stands for a deposit to your bank, and "TRANSFER" is for a transfer between two balance sheet registers. "DISC" stands for a discount you've offered consumers or vendors in exchange for early payment.

Based on your customer or vendor settings, QuickBooks automatically calculates the discount amount. Last but not least, "GENJRNL" denotes a general journal entry, which you use in situations where none of the other transaction kinds apply.

Purchase orders, estimates, pending assembly builds, and waiting bills are additional transaction types in QuickBooks. Because you never need to use these types when publishing to an account, they do not have corresponding transaction codes. Instead, you use these for subsequent reference or to manage your finances and resources.

Entering an Expense

QuickBooks Online makes it simple to record business expenses in addition to sales tracking. A more detailed view of your business and profit is provided by entering your income and expenses.

Enter a cost as a business expense if you have already paid for it. On the other hand, enter the expense as a bill if you want to pay for it later. These particular transaction types instruct QuickBooks on how to record each transaction. These are the steps for entering expenses in QuickBooks.

Record an expense

If you have already paid for a business expense and need to register it in QuickBooks, follow these steps:

- Choose **+ New**. Next, choose **Expense**.

- Pick the **vendor in the Payee field**. Leave this box blank if the transaction includes many petty cash expenditures.
- Choose **the account** you used to cover the expense in the Payment account area.
- Enter the **date of the expense** in the **Payment date section**.

- Choose your method of payment in the **Payment method area.**
- Enter a **ref number or permit number** if you want detailed tracking. This is not required.
- Enter your preferred label for classifying your money in the **Tags area**.
- Enter the **expense information** in the **Category details area**. Choose the **cost account** you use to keep track of spending transactions from the

Category selection. Add a description after that. To categorize the expense, you can also insert specific goods and services in the Item details box.

- Add the **tax and the amount**.
- Select the **Billable checkbox** and type the customer's name in the **Customer field** if you intend to bill them for the expense.
- Click on **Save and close** when you are through.

Writing a Check

In QuickBooks, writing checks, and tracking them as expenses keeps your checking account tidy. You must enter a check-in QuickBooks if you wish to print a new check or make a purchase with a handwritten check. This makes sure that all of your business transactions are recorded and that your accounts are up to date.

Follow the steps below to create a check;

- Choose + **New**.

- Choose **Check.**

- Select the **Payee** using the drop-down menu.
- Choose the account that the check will draw funds from the **Bank account option**.

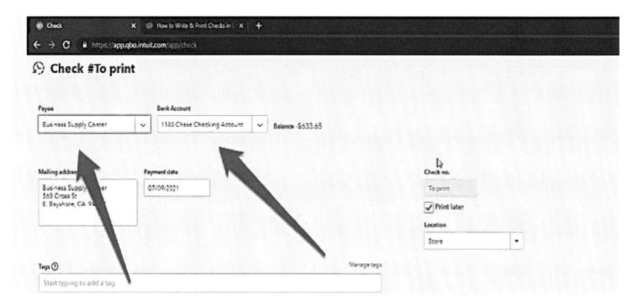

- Fill out the necessary checkboxes.
- If you want to immediately open the check queue for printing, use the **Print check option**. Alternatively, if you want to print the check later, tick the **Print later box**.
- The check window can be closed by selecting **Save and close**.

Entering a Bill

QuickBooks Online makes it simple to record business expenses in addition to sales tracking. A more detailed view of your business and profit is provided by entering your income and expenses.

Enter the expense as a bill if you intend to pay for it later. You have the option of recording one bill at a time or several bills for various merchants all at once. If you have already paid for a business expense, on the other hand, you should record it as an expense. These particular transaction types instruct QuickBooks on how to record each transaction.

Paying Bills

Here's how to record a bill you receive from a vendor:

- Choose **+ New**.
- Choose **Bill**.

Craig's Design and Landscaping Services

CUSTOMERS	VENDORS	EMPLOYEES	OTHER
Invoice	Expense	Payroll ↑	Bank deposit
Receive payments	Check	Single time activity	Transfer
Estimate	Bill	Weekly timesheet	Journal entry
Credit Memo	Pay bills		Statement
Sales receipt	Purchase order		Inventory Quantity Adjustment
Refund receipt	Vendor Credit		
Delayed credit	Credit card credit		
Delayed charge	Print checks		

Show less

- Choose a **vendor from the Vendor selection**.
- Choose the terms of the bill from the **Terms menu**. When is the anticipated payment date for your vendor?
- Enter the **Date, due date, and bill number** exactly as they appear on the bill.
- In the Category details area, enter the bill's details. Choose the cost account you use to keep track of spending transactions from the Category selection. Add a description after that. To itemize the bill, you can also specify individual goods and services in the Item details area.
- Add the **tax and the amount**.
- Select the **Billable checkbox** and type the customer's name in the Customer field if you intend to bill them for the expense. find out more about chargeable costs.
- When finished, choose **Save and close**.

Uploading bills from computer

- Go to **Bills** after selecting **Get paid & pay**.
- Pick **Upload** from the computer from the **Add bill dropdown menu**.
- Files can be uploaded by dragging them into the **Upload window** or by choosing the **Upload option** to pick files from your computer.

152

Paying two or more bills at once

- Go to **Bills** after selecting **Get paid & pay**.
- Choose the **Unpaid tab**.
- Choose **Schedule payment** next to the bill you want to pay, then follow the on-screen instructions.

Writing a check to pay a bill

- Choose + **New**.
- Choose **Check**.
- Choose **the vendor** you paid from the **Payee dropdown menu**. This brings up a popup displaying all of their unpaid debts.
- To add an open bill to the check, **select Add**. Select the tiny arrow next to the amount if you can't see this. You can also add credit from the Credits section if you have credit with the vendor.
- Choose **the account** from which you made the check payment from the **Bank/Credit** account selection.
- Enter the **check's amount** in the **Amount area.**
- Pick the **invoices** that the check payment was made in the **Outstanding Transactions** section. Select the checkboxes next to the bills they cover if it applies to numerous bills. Splitting the payment allows you to specify a different amount in the Payment column for each bill.
- When finished, choose **Save**.

Recording Vendor Credits and Refunds

How you record your purchases will determine how you enter the credit. Select the relevant section from the list below.

Entering a vendor credit

If you enter bills to keep track of your costs, follow these instructions. By doing this, you ensure that the credit is applied to the expense account you use for this vendor.

- Choose + **New.**
- Choose **Receive** vendor credit or **Vendor credit.**

- Choose your seller from the **Vendor dropdown menu**.
- Enter either the **Category data or the Item details**, depending on how you track your purchases from this merchant. This is typically the category, item, or service for which you are receiving credit.
- Select **Publish and close**.

Applying vendor credits against bills

A vendor credit may be used to pay any current or upcoming invoice. Here's how to use the credit once you're ready.

- Choose + **New**.

- Alternatively, choose to **Pay a bill**.

- From the list, pick a bill for your vendor. The Credit Applied section is where you can see the credit that is offered by this business.

- Fill out the remaining fields in the usual manner.

Recording vendor refund checks and payments

Vendor send you a refund check for a bill that has been paid already

- Record a **Deposit of the vendor check**

- Select **Make Deposit**s from the **Banking menu** after going there.
- Select **OK** if the **Payments to Deposit** window opens.
- Choose **the merchant** that sent you the refund from the **Received drop-down menu in the Make Deposits window**.
- Choose the **appropriate Accounts Payable account** from the **From Account** drop-down menu.
- Enter the **precise amount** of the vendor check in the **Amount column**.
- Insert a **memo, check number, payment method,** and class if need be.
- Click on **Save & Close**.

- Record a **Bill Credit** for the refunded amount;

  - Choose **Enter Bills** under the **Vendors menu**.
  - To record the return of items, select the **Credit radio button**.
  - Insert the name of the vendor.
  - Enter **the Accounts f**rom the original bill under the **Expenses tab.**
  - Put the right sum for each **Account in the Amount column** (the amounts may have to be prorated).
  - Click on the **Save and Close option**.

- Link the deposit to the Bill Credit

  - Select **Pay Bills** from the **Vendors menu** to begin.
  - Verify that the deposit amount is the same as the **vendor check.**
  - Apply th**e Bill Credit y**ou previously made by selecting **Set Credits**, then **click Done**.
  - Then click **Done** after selecting **Pay Selected Bills.**

The vendor sends a refund check for inventory items that were returned

- Record a **Deposit of the Vendor check;**

  - Select **Make Deposits** from the **Banking menu** after going there.
  - Select **OK** if the **Payments to Deposit window opens.**
  - Choose the merchant that sent you the refund from the **Received** drop-down menu in the **Make Deposits window.**

- Choose **the appropriate Accounts Payable account** from the **From Account** drop-down menu.
- Enter the precise amount of the vendor check in the **Amount column**.
- Fill out the **Deposit** with the remaining details.
- Click on the **Save & Close option.**

- Record a **Bill Credit** for the items that were returned;

  - Select **Enter Bills** from the **Vendors menu**.
  - To record the return of items, select **the Credit radio button.**
  - Insert the **name of the vendor**.
  - Choose the **Items Tab**
  - The same amounts as the reimbursement check should be entered for the returned products.
  - Click on the **Save & Close option**.

- Link the deposit to the Bill Credit

  - Choose **Pay Bills** from the **Vendors menu**.
  - Verify that the deposit amount is the same as the vendor check.
  - Apply the **Bill Credit** you previously made by selecting **Set Credits**, then click **Done**.
  - Then click **Done** after selecting **Pay Selected Bills.**

Vendor sends the refund as a credit card credit

- Select **Enter Credit Card Charges** from the **Banking menu.**
- Choose the **credit card account** from the **Credit Card drop-down menu.**
- Choose **Refund/Credit from the radio buttons.**
- Enter the **Date, Ref No., and Amount** after selecting the proper **Vendor name**.
- Write a suitable memo to explain the transaction.
- Select the Item tab and input the Items and **Refund Amounts** if you return any items.
- Select the **Expenses tab**, choose the **appropriate Accounts**, then input the Amount if the refund doesn't include any Items.

- Click on the **Save & Close option**.

Managing Recurring Transactions

Have you set up recurring transactions to automatically log regular purchases and outlays, such as monthly rent? Open a Recurring Template List report to view all of your recurring transactions in one location. You may find out from this which accounts on your chart of accounts they are connected to.

- Select **Reports** from the **Business overview menu**, or go directly to Reports.
- The **Recurring Template List** can be found and opened.
- Select **Customize** to make the report your own.
- Select the **Filter section** to make it larger.
- The **Distribution Account checkbox** should be selected. Additionally, you can choose particular accounts from the dropdown.
- Click on **Run report**.

The templates for your recurring transactions are now included along with their associated accounts, amounts, and quantities.

To operate, a firm also needs money. To make money, you must spend money. You must have learned about the different approaches to managing money and spending sensibly when operating a business in this chapter. You should be able to enter expenses, create checks, insert and pay bills, record vendor credits, and refunds, and deal with transactions that appear to be recurring. You should also be more familiar with the different sorts of transactions.

Activity

1. Configure expense and bill payment methods.
2. Describe the various transaction types.
3. Insert an expense in your QuickBooks Online.
4. Write a check in your QBO.
5. Highlights the steps involved in paying a bill in QBO.
6. Create a bill on your computer with the excel sheet and upload it to QBO.

7. Describe the steps to inserting a vendor credit.
8. How can a vendor check and payment be recorded?

CHAPTER 8

PAYING EMPLOYEES AND CONTRACTORS

It's a huge choice to decide whether to recruit someone as an employee or an independent contractor. It affects taxes, payroll requirements, and more. There are numerous laws governing this, but here is a brief summary and a list of resources that might be useful.

A person hired by an employer is known as an employee. An employee is typically under more employer control. An independent contractor is a self-employed individual who, typically under their terms, renders services to enterprises.

If your employee is a worker, you must:

- Payroll taxes, such as income, Social Security, and Medicare taxes, should be withheld.
- Pay the same Social Security and Medicare taxes as the employee.
- On employee earnings, pay federal and state unemployment taxes.
- Publish a Form W-2 after the year has ended.

If your employee is a self-employed person:

- Payroll taxes shouldn't be withheld at all.
- Federal and state unemployment taxes shouldn't be paid by you.
- A 1099-MISC form needs to be sent out each year.

Getting Started with QuickBooks Payroll

You have more control and flexibility with QuickBooks Online Payroll's automation and dependability. You'll have more time to devote to giving your clients advice and expanding your business while also letting your clients know that their payroll is handled correctly.

From QuickBooks Online Payroll, you can manage payroll, access health benefits, and provide HR support for your clients.

For smooth business administration, use QuickBooks Time to access accounting, payroll, and time tracking.

Payroll will begin to operate automatically after initial setup. Utilize clear notifications and alerts to stay in control of your finances.

By combining accounting and payroll in one location, you can handle your client's finances with ease.

When you need them, use the integrated suite of QuickBooks products.

Access a full range of employee services, including workers' compensation and health benefits, all administered directly from your payroll account.

You may approve payroll at any moment because of the seamless integration of automated timekeeping provided by QuickBooks Time with QuickBooks Online Payroll.

Eliminate tax penalties, decide how to pay your employees, and set up your own payroll system to position yourself for success.

Payroll taxes are automatically calculated, filed, and paid on a federal and state level.

- Payroll will operate automatically following the initial setup. With simple alerts and messages, Auto Payroll makes it simple to maintain control.

- Pay W2s and 1099 contractors in a single transaction. Online pay stubs are also accessible to employees.

Turning on QuickBooks Payroll

A popup to accept the New Pricing and Billing Terms and Conditions will appear once you log in to your new QuickBooks Online Payroll account. Accept the terms so that your payroll can be processed without interruption. Once the terms and conditions have been accepted, your new billing date will begin.

Below are some icons on the toolbar navigation to help you out;

- **Search**: in this section, you can search for a particular employee or payroll transaction rather than having to make use of the navigation menu.
- Notifications: in this part, you will be able to see all the important reminders or alerts about dates of tax, product news, and more.

- **Settings**: in this part, you can configure your payroll preferences, manage users on your account and also change companies.
- Log in as the **Primary Admin** when **QuickBooks Online** opens.
- Then **click Account and settings under Settings.**
- Choose **Billing & Subscription**.
- The second box contains the name of your payroll plan.

We are aware that entering your payroll data into QuickBooks takes time. As a result, the configuration is made to let you enter information whenever it's convenient for you and save it as you go.

Almost any order can be used to complete the tasks. If you have already paid your employees this year, there are a few extra tasks.

To do these tasks:

- Select **Overview** after going to **Payroll**.
- On the assignment you wish to work on, click **Start**.

Setting payroll preferences

To suit your accounting requirements, you can alter how you track your payroll wages, taxes, deductions, and corporate contributions in your chart of accounts.

To manage your payroll accounting settings if you're using Core, Premium, or Elite payroll without accounting turned on, check out **Export your payroll data into QuickBooks.**

Step 1: Determine what account type you would like to use for your payroll transactions

Your payroll liabilities and costs are recorded in default accounts that QuickBooks Online Payroll automatically generates. However, you can create a new one to your QuickBooks Online Chart of Accounts if you'd rather record it in a separate register or account.

Be aware that QuickBooks won't let you use a different account type, like the cost of goods sold, for liabilities, or payroll expenses.

Step 2: Add or edit your payroll account register

If you only want to modify the type or name of the account, edit the current one. If you'd rather utilize a different account for a certain payroll item, you can also add a new account.

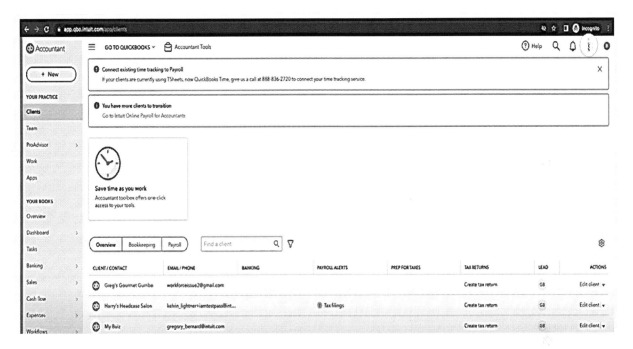

For instructions on how to add or change a payroll account, read on. You can skip to step 3 if the account you want to use is one you already have.

- Go to the **Chart of accounts under Settings**.

- To add a new one, select **New**. Alternatively, perform a search for the account you wish to modify, then choose **Edit** from the **View register dropdown**. You are creating a sub-account if you see the New category window rather than the Account window. Change to accountant view if a new parent account needs to be created.

- Select **Expenses or Other Current Liabilities** from the **Account Type dropdown menu**.

- Select a **Detail** type based on the account type you chose.

- In the Name area, you can add or change the account name.

Step 3: Update your payroll accounting preferences

- Enter **Payroll settings** from the **Settings menu**.

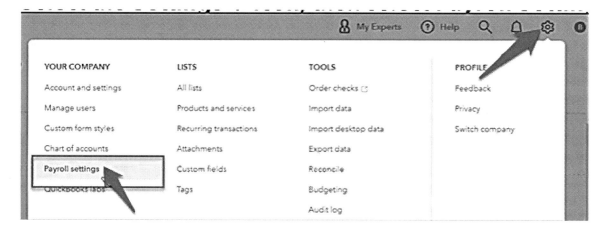

- Select **Edit** when **Accounting is selected**.

- To update a specific section, choose **Edit**.

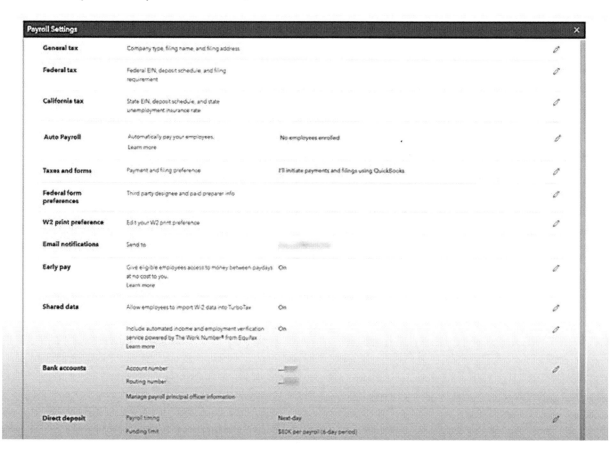

- Select the **account** to which the transaction for that particular payroll item should go. **Next,** click **Continue**.

If you would like to make changes to past transactions;

- If you would like to make changes to the already existing transactions click on **Edit**.

- Specify a **Start Date**. With the exception of the Bank Account section, we'll modify every account.

Setting up payroll taxes

The state payroll taxes that you and your employees must pay depend on where your employees live and work. Local taxes, state disability insurance, state unemployment insurance, and paid family leave may all be included in your state taxes.

Following are the steps to add a new state to your payroll product if you have an employee in one.

Step 1: Find out the state taxes that apply and obtain the information

It can be challenging to calculate the correct state and municipal taxes. Every circumstance and condition is unique.

The state withholding and unemployment insurance offices as well as any relevant municipal tax offices should be contacted where your employees reside and are employed. Which taxes are relevant to your case can be determined by the agencies. Additionally, they will assist you in obtaining the account numbers you will need to file the papers and pay the taxes.

To set up the new state in your payroll product, you'll need the following information, depending on the state taxes that apply:

- Account number(s)
- How often you might be required to make tax payments.
- Tax rates.

Roaming employees

During a given time period, roaming personnel are employed in multiple states. In each state where they work, your employee may be required to pay State Unemployment Insurance (SUI) or local taxes. Only one SUI tax or local tax jurisdiction per employee can be handled by our payroll tools. We advise against applying any workarounds since they can interfere with your state tax forms.

Step 2: Set up or make changes to your employees

You can add a new employee or make modifications to an existing one once you've decided which state or local taxes you need to file and pay.

Step 3: Set up your new state taxes

If you want us to file your forms and pay your taxes electronically, you must finish the state tax setup.

You don't need your account numbers to set up state taxes. Until you enter the account numbers, you will have to manually file the paperwork and pay the taxes.

Step 4: Sign new state authorization forms

You might be required to sign consent forms before we can file your paperwork and pay your state taxes, depending on your payroll service.

Preparing Payroll

Step 1: Navigate to Payroll

You should head to the "Payroll" tab after signing in to your QuickBooks account to get going.

There is a "Get Started" button if your QuickBooks Online subscription was just purchased. To move on to the following screen, click on it. The system will ask you a few questions when you first sign up for QuickBooks Payroll, such as if you need HR support and whether you need to keep track of employees' working hours.

You can manually choose one of the plan's three payroll alternatives, but these questions will assist match you with the appropriate one. You can sign up for a 30-day free trial of QuickBooks, and it will suggest the best payroll plan for you.

Step 2: Enter General Information About Paying Your Employees

The system will ask you whether you have already paid staff for the current calendar year in the following stage. You must select "Yes" if you're transferring from a manual system or another payroll program to QuickBooks Payroll.

Keep in mind that later on in the setup process, the system will want you to provide year-to-date (YTD) payroll information as well as tax payments made for each employee. To guarantee that your W-2 forms are accurate at year's end, you must provide information about earlier paychecks that were sent to employees before the start of your QuickBooks Payroll subscription.

You can get detailed pay records from your former payroll provider in addition to getting YTD data from the most recent payroll you submitted for each employee.

The system will ask you to specify the date that you intend to conduct your first payroll in QuickBooks, in addition to payments to employees in the current calendar year. The physical address of the workplace where the majority of your employees are located will also need to be entered.

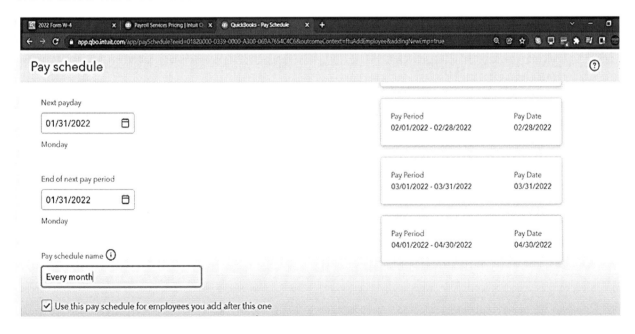

Step 3: Add Employees

When you enter your workplace, a new window that allows you to enter basic personnel data and payroll information into the system will open. To begin entering the necessary information for each person on your payroll, even those who are no longer employed by your business but were paid during the current fiscal year,

- click the **Add an employee button**.

Step 4: Complete Employee Information

You have the option to enter your employees' email addresses as you enter basic staff information into QuickBooks. This enables the system to send them a link so they may access QuickBooks Workforce, the provider's self-service web portal, to check their pay stubs and W-2s. Even better, the solution has the ability to allow workers to use QuickBooks Time to monitor and record their working hours.

You must complete the employee information fields shown below in order to set up QuickBooks Online Payroll.

Pay schedule:

- By selecting the **create pay schedule button** under **How often do you pay** (employee), you can specify a payment schedule for your staff. Choose the appropriate timetable from the dropdown menu, which includes options like weekly, twice a month, and monthly. Additionally, you will have the choice of having the plan you just made serve as the standard schedule for subsequent employees who are added to the system.

Employee pay: In the

- **How much do you pay** (employee) area, enter the employee's salary. Additionally, you need to provide the staff's default workdays and hours per day.

Employee deductions/contributions:

- Select the **relevant contributions and deductions** in the **Does (employee) have any deductions box**.

Employee withholding information: Use the data from Form W-4s in the section titled "What are (employee's) withholdings." Choose whether you need the tax form for the current year or one from a previous year when you click "Enter W-4 form." The form changed in December 2020 as of the time of this writing, and QuickBooks keeps both the new and old forms. This makes it possible for you to print one straight from the system to distribute to employees and record the appropriate data.

YTD payroll information: Use the facts from the most recent payroll check to enter the YTD payroll information into the system if you paid the employee this year. The sums paid during the current quarter but before you started using QuickBooks Payroll will also be requested by QuickBooks, so take note of this.

Payment method: There is a dropdown menu in the "How do you wish to pay (employee)" section where you may choose between direct deposit and (manual) check to pay the employee. Use the data from the direct deposit authorization form and the voided check that you requested from the employee if you decide to use direct deposit.

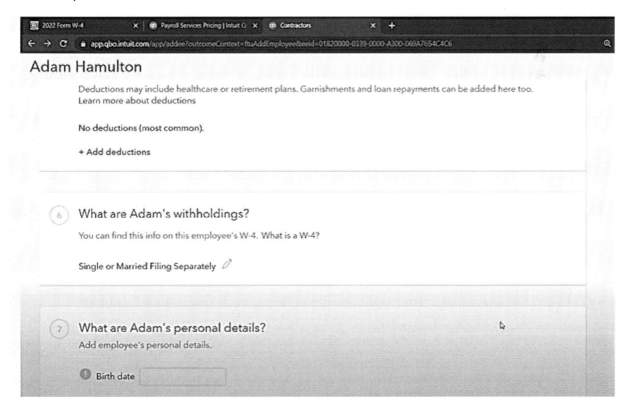

Step 5: Click on "Run Payroll"

- Click the **Run payroll button** in the top right corner of the screen while you are on your "Payroll" dashboard.

Step 6: Insert Current Hours

It should be noted that for salaried employees, the system will automatically fill in the total hours depending on the employee's initial setup's preset amount of work hours. You must manually enter the actual working hours for hourly employees in the "Regular Pay Hrs" column or transfer the time data from your time tracking software to the system.

Your staff's work hours will immediately display in QuickBooks Payroll when you subscribe to the Premium or Elite plans of the software and utilize QuickBooks Time (included in both tiers) to record and track employee attendance. Please feel free to update the system if the staff's working hours change.

Step 7: Review and Submit Payroll

Your final opportunity to evaluate and make changes to the payroll data is at this stage. Check the payment method to make sure that employees who should be paid by direct deposits and paychecks show up correctly, in addition to the number of hours worked and other payment information. Review the employee and employer tax contributions as well.

- Click the **Preview payroll option** at the bottom right of the screen once you have done checking the time data and payment information for your employees.

If everything appears to be in order,

- press the **Submit Payroll button** in the bottom right corner of the screen.

After that, you can print the employees' payroll cheques and/or direct deposit remittance advice. If you use QuickBooks Online as your accounting program, a bill will be generated immediately for each payroll handled, making it simple to reconcile your payroll account.

Recording payroll information

Journal entries are a useful workaround for keeping track of the accounting data for your payroll.

An illustration of how to enter a payroll transaction into a journal may be found below.

Example: Five people work for Fred's Residential Remodeling Company. You would use the employees' gross compensation for the journal entry. In this case, the total sum is $4055.00.

- Click on **+ New**.

- Choose **Journal Entry**.

- Beneath **Date**, choose **the payroll payment(s) date**.

- Insert **Entry #** for a journal entry.

- Debit and Credit accounts:

    o Use a debit expense account to keep track of gross pay. ($4,055.00)

    o Account used to track Employer Contribution is a debit expense (e.g. CPF, EPF, etc.). ($251.41)

    o Payroll deductions are made from a credit bank account. ($4306.41)

    o Note: The next two stages explain how to save the transaction to make entering simpler the next time. Please skip these steps if you just want to complete the transaction once or if you have QuickBooks Online Simple Start.

- Click on **Make Recurring**.

- Insert a **memorable Template Name then configure Template Type to Unscheduled; click on Save Template**.

- Choose **Save**.

Using the same example, the lines on the journal entry would read as follows if the employer was in charge of covering the liability:

- Use a debit expense account to keep track of gross pay. ($4,055.00)

- Account used to track Employer Contribution is a debit expense (eg. CPF, EPF, etc.). ($251.41)

- Medicare spending account used for tracking. ($58.80)

- Payroll liabilities are tracked using the credit liability account. ($1228.67)

- By the net amount of the payroll payments, credit the bank account used for processing payroll. ($3136.54)

Currently, $1,228.67 is waiting to be paid in a liabilities account. You would direct the liability account used in the journal entry when writing the checks to settle the responsibility. The responsibility will be eliminated as a result or reduced to the present balance owed.

Enabling employee time tracking

Use this feature to keep track of and charge clients for the time spent on a project or activity. How? Read on.

- Select **Account and settings under Settings**.

- Choose the **Time tab**.

- Select **Edit** in the **General or Timesheet section.**

- Decide how you want to log your time;

  - **First day of the work week**: this part affects how employees and contractors see weekly time sheets.

  - **Show service field**: when this is turned on, employees and contractors who complete the timesheets can indicate services that were performed.

- ○ **Make time billable**: when this is turned on, employees and contractors who complete the timesheets can indicate if activities should be billed to a customer.

- ○ Show billing rate to users entering time: this section is optional.

- Click on **Save then Done**.

Once the above settings have been completed, you can now add a time-tracking user;

- Choose to **Manage users under Settings**.

- Choose to **Add user**.

- Select **Only Time tracking**.

- Choose **Next**.

- Locate the worker or vendor you wish to add, click **Next**, and then fill out their contact information.

- Choose **Save**.

Note that A Time Tracking Only user's user type cannot be changed. If different corporate access is required for a time tracker, remove the user and re-add them using the new user type.

Reviewing and generating payroll checks

You must continue to track those paychecks in QuickBooks even if you use another service for payroll in addition to QuickBooks for accounting. Third-party paychecks are what we refer to as payments made using providers other than QuickBooks, such as ADP or Paychex.

You may import paycheck data directly into QuickBooks using several payroll systems. We'll teach you how to manually monitor these payments as journal entries if your provider doesn't offer this option. Your payroll and account information is kept in one location as a result.

Step 1: Create manual tracking accounts

Follow the instructions to add additional accounts to your Chart of Accounts if you haven't done so you can keep track of your payroll liabilities and costs.

Make the following expense accounts. Decide on the account type of expense:

- Payroll Expenses: Wages

- Payroll Expenses: Taxes

Step 2: Insert the payroll paychecks into QuickBooks Online

Make a journal note after paying your staff outside of QuickBooks.

- Obtain payroll reports or pay stubs for your employees from your payroll service.
- Choose **+ New**.
- Select **Journal Entry.**
- Put the date of your paycheck under the Journal date.
- Enter the **paycheck number** in the Journal no. area if you want to monitor it.

Make the journal entry using the data from your paycheck report. You can combine all of the paycheck totals for any employees you paid during the pay period into a single journal entry. If you need to break out the specifics, you may also write separate diary entries for each employee.

Establishing or correcting payroll exemptions

Did you know that QuickBooks Online Payroll Core, Premium, and Elite all allow you to adjust previous payrolls? Depending on how the employee was paid and whether any system blocks are in place, you may be able to invalidate, edit, or remove a paycheck.

You can choose to;

- Void, Edit, and Delete all paper paychecks.
- Void processed direct deposit paychecks.

- Edit or Delete unprocessed direct deposit paychecks.

If you would like to gain access to payroll corrections;

- Locate the **Paycheck list page**.
- Navigate to the **specific paycheck** you would like to correct.
- Click on the **down arrow** on the far right of that row.

The system will automatically recalculate your taxes due after a correction is made and make any required adjustments with the following payroll run.

Printing payroll reports

To print payroll reports;

- The payroll report you want to print is accessible.
- Select **Share**.
- Select **the printing options** for your report;

  - **Export to Excel**: Choose this if you wish to print your report as an Excel document. Downloading an excel file, opening it, and printing the report.

  - **Printer Friendly**: Select this option, then choose **Print** to print your report exactly as it appears in your payroll account.

Managing Payroll Taxes

When it's time to pay your payroll taxes, QuickBooks Payroll (QP) informs you of the amount due and assists you in creating the payroll tax papers you need to submit to the appropriate revenue agency.

Paying payroll taxes

- Payroll tax can be found under Taxes so **click on it**.
- Click on **Pay Taxes**.
- All unpaid taxes will be shown in this.
- To record a payment for a tax item, click **Record Payment** to the right of the tax item.

- After reviewing the data on the following screen, choose **Record and print**.

Viewing payroll tax forms

- Payroll tax can be found under Taxes.
- Select Monthly, Annual, or Employer Forms from the Forms area.
- You can produce quarterly or monthly tax forms and worksheets for monthly forms (i.e. PD7A).
- You can produce T4s and the T4 Summary report for Annual Forms.
- You can construct Records of Employment for Employer Forms (ROE).

Paying Contractors

An independent contractor is a self-employed individual who, typically on their own terms, renders services to enterprises.

Setting up 1099-eligible contractors

Add a contractor as a vendor

In QuickBooks, add the contractor as a vendor if you haven't already:

- Select **Contractors** under **Payroll**.
- Click on **Add a contractor**
- Enter the **information** for your contractor or choose the **Email** this contractor button to have them complete it.
- When finished, choose **Add contractor.**

Track contractor payments for 1099s

You must begin keeping track of the contractor's payments now that you have added them as a vendor.

- Click on **Sales or Get paid & pay**, then select **Vendors**.
- Open **the profile** of the seller you want to keep an eye on.
- Choose **Edit.**
- The Track Payments for 1099 checkbox must be chosen and checked.

Reporting on 1099 vendor payments

You can use the reports in QuickBooks to assist you to get ready to produce your 1099s. Here's how to run these reports to determine who needs 1099 filed for them.

See all your 1099 vendors:

- Select **Reports** from the Business Overview menu, or click **Report** and look for the Vendor Contact List option.

Choose Customize.

- Select **Change columns** under **Rows/Columns**.
- Check the box next to Track 1099.
- Click on **Run Report**.

To see 1099 totals, accounts, amounts, and other details;

- Select **Reports** from the **Business Overview menu** or go directly to **Reports**.
- Enter **"1099 Transaction Detail Report,"** **"1099 Contractor Balance Detail,"** or **"1099 Contractor Balance Summary"** into the search bar.

To see all payments to vendors that have a need to go on a 1099

- Select **Expenses** under **Transactions**, under **Bookkeeping**, or directly under **Expenses**.
- Select **Contractors** after choosing **Vendors or Payroll.**
- When you reach the window titled "Check that the payments add up," click **Prepare 1099** and then selec**t Continue.**
- Change the type of contractors to 1099 Contractors below threshold or 1099 Contractors that meet the threshold by selecting the arrow next to the filter icon at the top of the table.
- You can now determine which contractors are eligible for 1099.

Preparing 1099s

You may produce your 1099s using the data you already have in your accounts with the help of a time-saving function in QuickBooks Online. When you pay contractors in cash, you must file tax paperwork with the IRS called 1099s.

Create your 1099s (1099-MISC and 1099-NEC) in QuickBooks Online by following the procedures listed below. We handle mailing a printed 1099 copy to your contractors so they can use it for their tax filing when you file with us.

- Select **Contractors** or **Vendors under Payroll or Get paid & pay**.
- Choose **Let's get started**, then choose **Prepare 1099s**.
- Verify that the information on tax notices or letters from the IRS matches the information for your company's name, address, and tax ID.
- Next, after choosing **the boxes** that correspond to the different types of payments made to all of your contractors this year. Important: Be careful when selecting your boxes because there have been modifications to the 1099 forms. The majority of firms will select "Non-employee compensation (Box 1 1099-NEC)," but if you believe you may have made other sorts of payments, check with your accountant.
- Make sure all of your contractors arrive and that their contact information, including their email addresses, is accurate.
- For each box you chose in step 4, check the payment totals. Both 1099-NEC and 1099-MISC forms will automatically receive their respective portions of the payments. Choose Next.
  - **Note**: You won't be able to see the electronic payments you made to contractors (such as by credit card, etc.). This is so that the credit card company, bank, etc. may report them on your behalf. You can double-check the year and threshold directly above the Name column if you don't see all of the expected payments.
- To have me e-file your 1099s, choose **E-File**. If you prefer to print and mail the forms yourself, choose **I'll file myself**.

Without employees working in various departments or occasionally contractors who work for pay, a firm cannot prosper. You may easily arrange for these people's payments using QBO. You should have learned how to use QuickBook payroll, set up some references for using the payroll, configure payroll taxes, prepare a payroll, use employee time tracking, generate payroll checks, deal with some exemptions that may arise with payroll, pay contractors, and learn everything necessary about 1099 payments in the just-completed chapter.

Activity

1. Switch on your payroll in QBO.
2. Configure the various settings as regards payroll preferences.
3. Configure payroll taxes.
4. Record some vital payroll information.
5. Activate employee time tracking.
6. Generate a payroll check.
7. How can payroll exemptions be corrected?
8. Mention the different payroll forms.
9. Configure 1099 contractors.
10. What are the steps to preparing a 1099?

CHAPTER 9

WORKING IN REGISTERS

Account registers are used by QuickBooks to log transactions according to their source. The whole transaction history and current balance of an account are revealed. An excellent example is your check register, which records any transactions you designate as checks. Your chart of accounts is made up of all of your account registries.

Understanding Registers

Account registers enable you to look over all account-related information. To see a thorough, transaction-level picture of your books, open the register. Additionally, you can update current transactions here.

What you can do in the account register is:

- View each transaction made in an account.
- Edit, revoke, or eliminate transactions
- Filter accounts to locate particular kinds of transactions
- Match up specific transactions
- Look over the reconciliation adjustments.

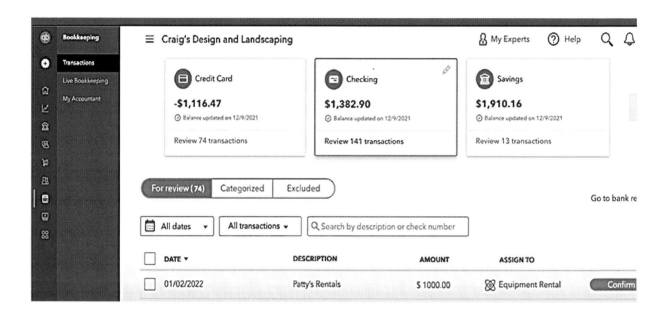

Regularly going over your register can help you find mistakes and make reconciliations much simpler. An account register is commonplace. You might want to check a few of the following account registrations on a semi-regular basis:

- Bank
- Credit Card
- Fixed Assets
- Other Fixed Assets
- Other Current Assets
- Long-term Liabilities
- Other Current Liabilities
- Equity

Several distinct methods exist for entering transactions into QuickBooks. To track the complete sales cycle and the accounting, the primary method is to produce a sales form, similar to an invoice or expenditure. Additionally, you can link your accounts with online banking. After you evaluate the downloaded transactions, QuickBooks inserts them into your account registers.

Some account registers allow you to add transactions directly as well. When evaluating your accounts, account registers are for making rapid changes.

179

Customizing the Register View

You can modify how you view your register in a variety of ways. To find out which of the following options suits you the most, try experimenting with a few of them.

You can make use of the Column headers to;

- Modify the column widths
- Sort by column

You can make use of the Gear icon to

- display and conceal columns
- Show in paper ledger mode the exact place where the most recent transactions are at the bottom.
- Display the transactions in a single line
- Adjust the number of transactions displayed on a single register page.

Adjust column widths

- Click **Transactions > Chart of Accounts (or Accounting > Chart of Accounts, depending on what you see)** in the navigation bar.
- Click the **View registration link** next to the account you wish to look at.
- Hover your cursor over the desired side of the column header. Your pointer transforms from an arrow to a column adjuster with two tiny arrows pointing left and right when you are positioned correctly.
- To adjust the column header's width, click **and drag the edge**.

Entering and Editing Transactions

All previous and ongoing transactions connected to the account are listed in the account history. You can analyze your transactions and make rapid modifications directly from an account history if necessary. Additionally, it provides options for filtering and sorting data to expedite your search.

Entering transactions

- To view your chart of accounts list in QuickBooks Online, click **Chart of Accounts** from the **left menu bar** after choosing **Accounting**.

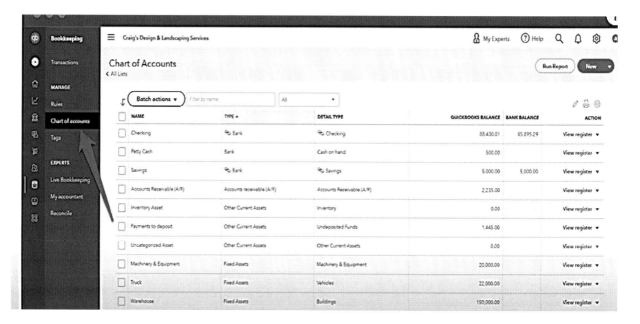

- Select **View Register** in the far right column after locating your bank account in the chart of accounts.

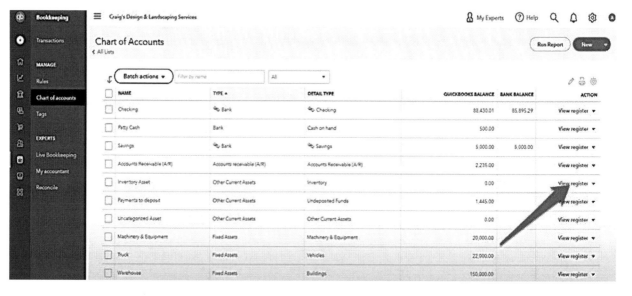

- Regardless of whether you entered the transactions manually into the register, using the relevant input page, or accepted them from your list of imported bank transactions, all transactions that have an impact on your bank balance will be shown in the check register. Date, Amount, Type, and Account are the only fields that must be filled out for each transaction, however, we strongly advise against doing so.

- **Bank register**: Which bank account register you are examining is shown in this area. By clicking the drop-down arrow and choosing a different bank account, you can change bank accounts.

- **Date**: make an indication of the date of the transaction you are inserting.

- **Ref no./type**: As the reference number, enter the transaction number, such as the check number. The transaction type will show up here after being chosen when you create a new transaction.

- **Payee**: For payments, click **the vendor or employee** for this specific field. For deposits, choose **the customer.**

- **Account**: Select **the account** in the chart of accounts to represent the payment or deposit. Choose the rent expense, for instance, if you are submitting a check to pay the monthly rent.

- **Memo**: give a brief description of the transactions. For instance; "July rent check".

- **Location**: Put your user-defined Classes and Locations in charge of the transaction. You must turn on Track Classes and/or Locations if these fields don't show up and you want to track activity by Class or Location.

- **Foreign Currency Exchange Rate**: You can choose to apply your own conversion rates manually for foreign currency transactions or allow QuickBooks Online to do it for you.

- **Payment**: insert the amount of the check or you can also choose to leave it blank.

- **Deposit**: insert **the amount of the deposit** or you can also just choose to leave it blank.

- **Reconciled**: Once you declare during the bank reconciliation that the transaction has cleared your bank, a checkmark will show up in the corresponding column. Never manually add or delete a checkmark.

We advise you to always reconcile your bank account in order to maintain the accuracy of your records.

  - ○ **Balance**: this is the account balance immediately after each transaction

- Select either **a check or a deposit** from the drop-down option that appears directly below the column headers in the check register to add a new transaction. There are numerous additional bank transaction kinds that can be entered through input windows, however, anything entered directly into the check register can only be classified as a check or a deposit.

Editing transactions

Follow the steps below to have transactions edited;

- To widen the view, locate and select **the transaction** in the account register.
- Change **the fields** that are available.
- Select **Edit** to make changes to the sections that are grayed out. By doing so, the entire transaction form is opened, allowing you to make more modifications.
- Select **Save or Save and close** when you are ready.

Direct editing of some transactions is not possible in the register. To make changes, you must choose the transaction and open the entire form.

Reconciled signifies that the transaction has already been marked with the letter R if you want to amend it.

- Click on **the letter-containing field** repeatedly until it turns blank to modify it. then choose **Save**. You can now make changes to this transaction.

Performing Other Register Activities

There are other important activities that can be done in the register. I will discuss some of them in the sections below;

Sorting transactions

The list of transactions can be sorted and rearranged according to date, reference number, payee, or reconcile status. Your most recent transactions are displayed at the top by default.

- Click **and drag any column heading**. You can sort the transactions by the value in that column if a Sort icon (or) appears.

- To sort the account history by any sortable column header in either ascending or descending order, select **the header**.

The Balance column shows n/a if you sort by any column other than the Date or Reconciliation status.

Filtering transactions

You can look for what you're looking for in a few different ways.

- Select **Charts of accounts** under **Bookkeeping**.

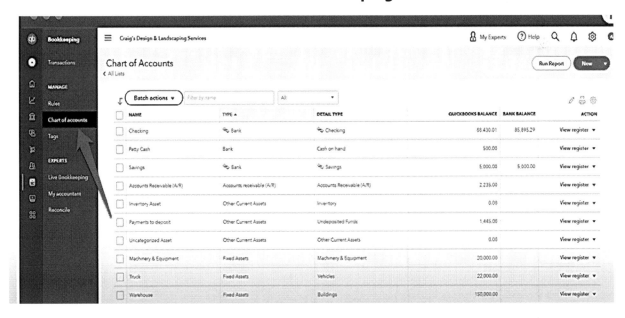

- Locate **the accoun**t that you want to examine. Select **Account history** from the **Action column** after that.
- A filter icon should be chosen. After that, pick the filters you want to use. To conduct a search by value, reference number, or memo, use the **Find field**.

- Select the **X** next to the filter name to remove it.
- Choose **Apply.**

Printing a register

- Beginning on the left side of your screen, click **Reports**. From the list of alternatives, select **Balance Sheet**.
- To print the Register for the bank account we want, click on **the sum** to the right of the account name.
- Then, select **the desired date** range in the pop-up box by clicking **Customize** in the top left corner of the screen. Click **Run Report** to run the **Report**.
- You can then print **the report** after completing the above steps.

Exporting a register

Your check register should be exported to Excel. The report can then be easily converted to the file type you've requested. I'll be happy to show you how.

Evidently, a check register in the format it is available in Quicken is not available in QuickBooks Online (QuickBooks Desktop). However, QBO gives you the freedom to deal with your accounting data; as a result, you can utilize a variety of reports to gather the information you require.

The only problem is that you have to go through this process again each time you need new check register data:

- Access **the report, run it, and then export it**.

On the other hand, you may automate QuickBooks' export of many reports and data without any scripting!

Activity

1. Mention five (5) things that can be done in the account register.
2. Customize your register view to your taste.
3. Insert transactions needed by the business into your QBO.
4. Edit the transactions if need be, and add some more details.
5. Highlight steps to sorting transactions.

185

6. Filter the transactions you have inserted.
7. Export your register to excel and also print it out in order to have a hard copy.

CHAPTER 10

ADMINISTERING BANK AND CREDIT ACCOUNTS

It is easy to add a bank account to pay expenses. By logging into your bank (instantly validated), as well as by inputting your bank account information, we demonstrate how to achieve it (manual entry).

Setting Up a Bank or Credit Card Account

Setting up a bank account

In order to open a new bank account, follow these procedures.

- Log in to your account on **QuickBooks Online**.
- Select **Account and settings under Settings**.
- Choose **Bill Pay**.
- Decide on a **bank accoun**t.
- Choose to **Create a new bank**.

Making a Bank Deposit

I demonstrate how to record client payments and advise using the Undeposited Funds account when entering a Receive Payment transaction. Therefore, your bank account where the money will finally appear hasn't been changed after receiving a client payment and depositing it in the Undeposited Funds account. The updating takes place as you get ready to make a bank deposit.

You must compare the bank's deposits and withdrawals with your own version of deposits and withdrawals when you receive your bank's statement. Your QBO deposits won't match the bank's deposits if you record each customer payment as a deposit in the bank. The bank's representation of your deposits will match your deposits if you deposit client payments into the Undeposited Funds account, though, because you'll shift numerous checks from that account to your bank account to make a single deposit.

Follow the steps below to create a bank deposit;

- Select **Bank Deposit** from the **Create menu** by selecting the **Create button** with the plus (+) sign. The Bank Deposit transaction window is shown by QBO. At the top of the window, in the section labeled **Select the Payments Included in This Deposit**, are existing payment transactions. Add additional payment transactions that aren't connected to an open invoice using the lines in the Add Funds to This Deposit section.

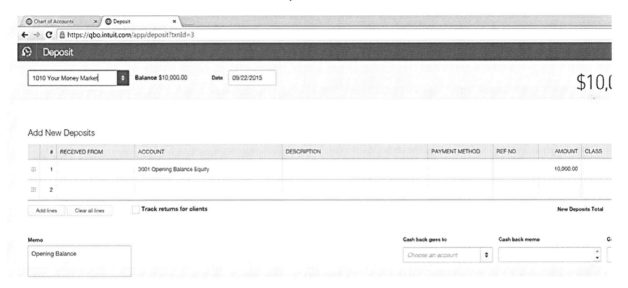

- Choose the account you want to deposit the payments into at the top of the window.
- Click the check box next to each transaction you want to be included on the deposit in the section titled **Select the Payments Included in This Deposit**.
- Choose the **Payment Method** for each transaction you want to deposit.

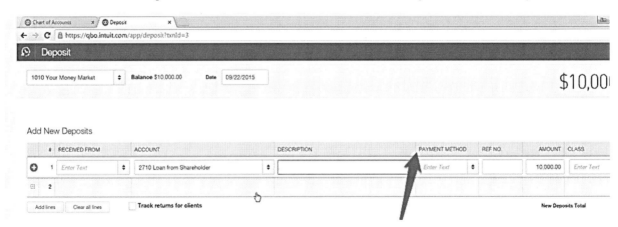

- You can optionally provide a memo and a reference number. Unless you add items to the **Add Funds to This Deposit section**, the sum of the chosen payments and the amount you wish to deposit displays below the **Choose the Payments Included in This Deposit** list.

- In the **Bank Deposit transaction window**, scroll down. Providing a memo for the deposit is optional. Optionally, include a cash return amount that represents the portion of the deposit total that you do not intend to deposit, together with the account where it should be placed and a message outlining its intended use.

- Finally click on **Save and Close**.

Making a Credit Card Payment

In order to process credit cards in QuickBooks Online, you must have a QuickBooks Payments account.

You must enter a credit card payment you made outside of QuickBooks even if you don't use QuickBooks Payments.

Ensure the following before moving on:

- Create an account with **QuickBooks Payments**.

- Where should you keep track of your fees and payments?

There are two methods to use your payments account to process card payments. Whether you use QuickBooks to create invoices will affect how you proceed.

Option 1: Receive a payment towards an invoice

You'll want to get paid if you invoice your clients. You can then apply the payment you make to an open invoice in this manner.

- Choose + **New**.

- Choose either **Receive payment or Receive payment on an invoice**.

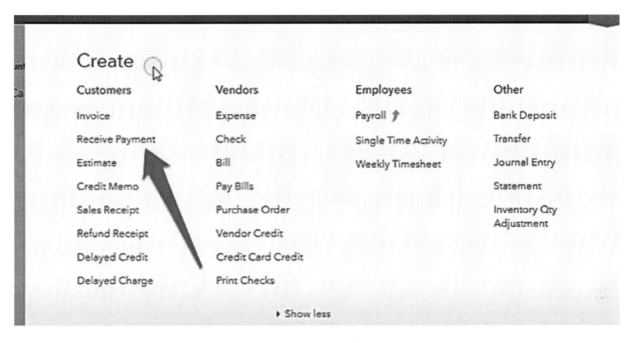

- Insert the **customer's information** and the payment due date.

- Choose **a live invoice** in the **Outstanding Transactions** area to apply for the payment. Enter a different value in the **Amount Received column** to accept a partial payment.

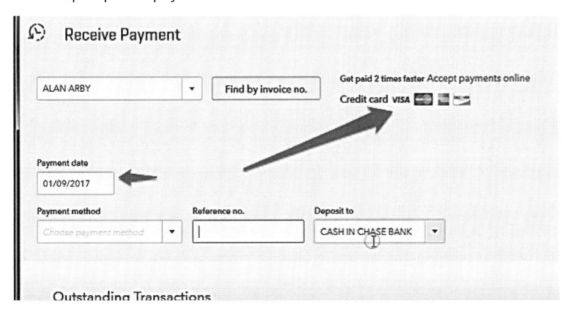

- Choose **a Credit card** from the drop-down option for the payment method.
- Choose **Enter credit card information**.
- Choose **Swipe Card** or enter the **credit card information.**

- Select **Use this credit card** in the future if you want to save this customer's credit card.
- Insert the option to process a credit card.
- Choose **Save**.
- Choose **Save and new or Save and close**.

Option 2: Credit a sales receipt

- Choose **+ New**.
- Fill up the customer information after selecting **Sales receipt or Make a sale**.
- Add a good or service to offer for sale.
- Choose **a Credit card from the drop-down** option for the payment method.
- Choose **Enter credit card information**.
- Choose **Swipe Card** or enter the credit card information.
- Select Use this credit card in the future if you want to save this customer's credit card.
- Enter the option to process a credit card.
- Choose **Save.**

- Choose **Save and new or Save and close**.

Recording a Credit Card Credit

In QuickBooks Online,

- click the **+ New** option in the **Navigation Bar to add a credit card credit**.
- The Credit Card Credit window will then appear once you click the **Credit Card Credit** link in the menu that appears under the **Vendors title**.
- Using the **Payee drop-down**, choose the **merchant** from which you made the purchase.
- From the **Bank/Credit account drop-down menu**, choose the **credit card** you used.
- Then, depending on the account or items you are receiving credit for, enter the appropriate Category details or Item details. To accurately display the credit you the linked account or accounts, make sure to provide the identical account or item information as when you used the credit card to pay the initial transaction or the bill.

- Click the **Save and close button** to save the **credit card information** and then exit the page.
- Alternatively, you can choose the **Store** and new option from the drop-down menu to save the current transaction and open a brand-new, empty **Credit Card Credit** window in its place.

Reconciling a Bank or Credit Card Account

You must check your accounts in QuickBooks to make sure they line up with your bank and credit card bills, just like when you balance your checkbook. Reconciling is the action of doing this.

The transactions on your bank statement will be compared to those recorded in QuickBooks once you have them in your possession. Your accounts are accurate and balanced if everything matches. Every month, you should reconcile your credit card, checking, and savings accounts.

Step 1: Review your opening balance

Review the opening balance if you are reconciling an account for the first time. It must coincide with the balance in your actual bank account on the day you made the decision to begin keeping track of transactions in QuickBooks.

Connecting your bank and credit cards to online banking will save you time by downloading transactions and entering the opening balance automatically.

Step 2: Begin a reconciliation

You can begin reconciling once you have your monthly bank or credit card statement. Reconcile many months' worth of statements one at a time, beginning with the oldest:

- Make sure to categorize and match each downloaded transaction if your accounts are linked to internet banking.
- Reconcile can be found under **Settings** in **QuickBooks Online**. Select **Get started** to proceed if this is your first time reconciling.
- Choose the account you want to reconcile from the **Account menu**. Verify that it matches the one on your statement.

- Examine the **Starting balance**. Verify that your statement's beginning balance matches the one in **QuickBooks**. If they don't match, follow these instructions.

- On your statement, enter the **Ending balance and Ending date**. The final balance is also known as the **new balance** or the **closing balance** by some institutions.
- Review the Last statement ending date if you see it. Your most recent reconciliation's end date is indicated here. The next day is when your current bank statement should begin.
- Select **Start Reconciliation** when you are ready to begin.

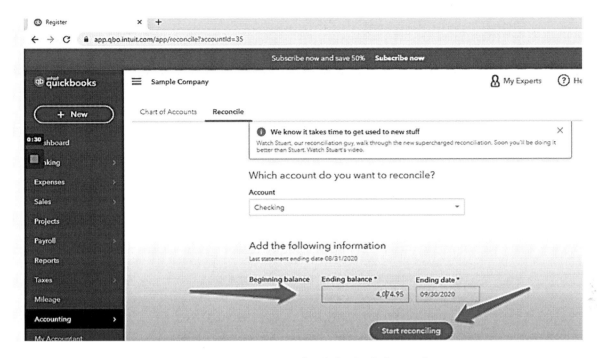

Step 3: **Have your statements compared with QuickBooks**

Simply compare your statement's transactions with those in QuickBooks at this point. Review each one separately. Making sure QuickBooks has the correct dates and transactions so you know everything matches is the tough part.

Reconcile accounts connected to online banking

Since your bank is the only source of information regarding your transactions, reconciling should be simple. Your accounts may already be balanced in some circumstances.

- Start with the **statement's very first transaction**.
- In QuickBooks, locate the identical transaction in the **Reconciliation window**.
- Both transactions should be compared. Put a checkbox next to the amount in QuickBooks if they match. That designates it as reconciled. Transactions that you added or matched from online banking are already chosen for you to speed up the process.
- Don't checkmark a transaction if you can see it in **QuickBooks** but it doesn't display on your statement.

194

- The transactions on your statement should be compared to those in **QuickBooks**. Don't worry if you're positive you've identified a match but a little detail, like the payee, is off. To widen the screen in QuickBooks, choose the transaction. then choose Edit. Make changes such that the specifics support your assertion.
- When you're done, there should be no difference between your statement and **QuickBooks**. If so, click **Finish** right away.

Reconcile accounts that are not connected to online banking

- Start with the statement's very first transaction.
- In QuickBooks, locate the identical transaction in the **Reconciliation window**.
- Both transactions should be compared. Put a checkbox next to the amount in **QuickBooks** if they match. That designates it as reconciled.
- Don't checkmark a transaction if you can see it in **QuickBooks** but it doesn't display on your statement.
- Each transaction on your statement should be compared to what is in **QuickBooks**.
- When you get to the end, the difference between your statement and **QuickBooks** should be $0.00. If you get this, click on Finish now

Since businesses deal with money, they unavoidably require a bank account and a credit account. You must have learned how to set up a bank or credit card account, make a bank deposit, make a credit card payment, and record a credit card charge in this chapter.

Activity

1. Configure a credit card account or bank account.
2. Highlight the steps in making a bank deposit.
3. List the steps in making a credit card payment.
4. Highlight the steps in recording a credit card credit.
5. What does it mean to reconcile a bank or credit card account? Highlight the steps involved.

CHAPTER 11

SYNCHRONIZING WITH FINANCIAL INSTITUTIONS

Online banking, commonly known as "bank feeds," is one of QuickBooks' most effective features. You could spend less time and effort if you used this unique function. Without having to enter any data, easily connect your bank, credit cards, and other financial accounts to your QuickBooks Online account. With the aid of our outsourced accountants, you may enhance QuickBooks and connect it to your bank account online.

Once your financial accounts are linked to your QuickBooks Online account, all transactions conducted through those accounts will be downloaded and categorized automatically by QuickBooks. You will be able to see all of your most recent updated credit or bank card transactions, sales, and expenses included after approving how QuickBooks categorized your accounts.

Connecting QuickBooks Accounts to Financial Institutions

Connecting ...or not connecting

- Access **QuickBooks Online**.
- Choose **Connect** from the banking option on the landing page if you haven't already made an account, or choose **Add Account** if you have.
- Look up your bank (most banks, and even small credit unions, can be connected).

You can try manually uploading your transactions from a CSV file if you can't find your bank on the list but still want to add your transactions to your QuickBooks account.

- After clicking **Continue**, input your online banking login information in the pop-up box and click **Connect**.

It can take a few minutes to link your bank account to QuickBooks online; however, certain banks might need more information for security reasons. In this situation, the screen will display instructions that will tell you what to do next.

- Select **the sort of account** you want to add, such as checking, savings, or credit card. Select **the type** for each card you are connecting if you are linking several credit cards from the same bank.

If the drop-down list does not contain the item you require or if you are unfamiliar with QuickBooks,

- choose **+New** to add a new account to your **Chart of Accounts**.

Follow these steps if you ever need to re-connect QuickBooks Online to your bank account:

- Select **Banking** at the top after finding "Banking."
- After clicking **Add Account**, input the bank's name.
- Choose **the bank with an existing connection** if you plan to use the same login information.
- Choose **the bank using a New connection** with a new login when logging in with different credentials.
- Once you've entered your username and password, click **continue**.
- After selecting **QuickBooks Account** and selecting the checkbox next to the account you want to connect to, a drop-down option will appear. Choose the account from your chart of accounts from the menu.
- Once you are connected, click **I'm done** and then **Connect**. Let's move!

Accessing bank and credit card-related pages in QuickBooks

You can save time by using bank feeds or online banking, which eliminates the need for human data entry. The download and categorization of transactions begin as soon as you link your accounts. All you need to do is provide your approval.

Being Direct: Connecting a Bank or Credit Card Account

- Go to **Banking or Bookkeeping**, then click **Transactions**, then **Bank transactions**.
- Choose a **Connect account**

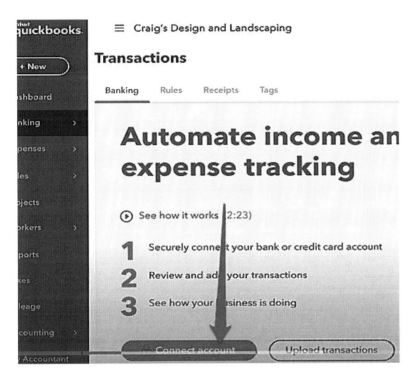

if this is your first time setting up a bank account. Or, if you've already created an account, choose **Link accoun**t.

- Note: For security purposes, if you are switching from **QuickBooks Desktop**, you must connect your bank and credit card accounts once again.

- Enter the **name of your bank, credit card**, or credit union in the search area. Note: You can manually upload your bank transactions if you can't find your bank but still want to add your transactions.

Connect an account

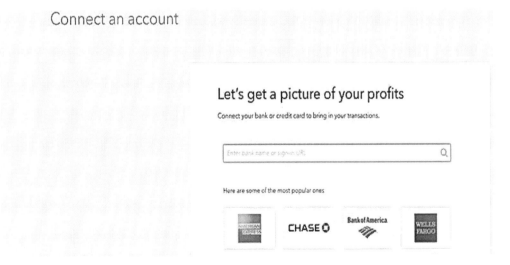

- Choose to **Continue** then use your user ID and password to log in to your bank.
- Take the steps shown on the screen. This could involve the security checks that your bank demands. The connection can take a while.
- Choose **the accounts** you want to link, then pick an account type from the selection. Select **the account type in QuickBooks** that corresponds to your chart of accounts.
- Choose **how many transactions** you wish to download in the past. You can obtain 90 days' worth of transactions from some banks. Others are able to go back up to 24 months.

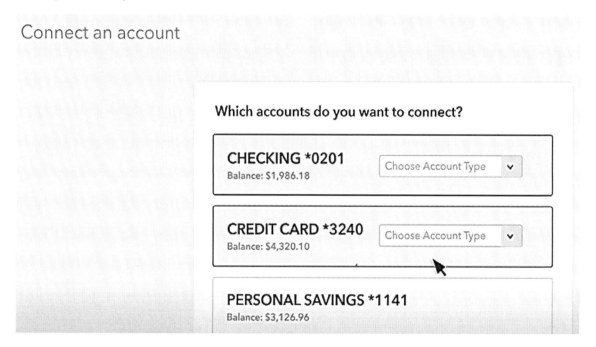

Connect an account

Which accounts do you want to connect?

CHECKING *0201
Balance: $1,986.18
Choose Account Type ⌄

CREDIT CARD *3240
Balance: $4,320.10
Choose Account Type ⌄

PERSONAL SAVINGS *1141
Balance: $3,126.96

- Choose **Connect**.

Managing uploaded or downloaded activity

The most recent transactions are downloaded by QuickBooks immediately after you connect your bank and credit card accounts. It searches for them and makes an effort to match them up with transactions that you've already put into QuickBooks. If it is unsuccessful in doing so, it makes a new transaction record for you. The match or newly formed transaction only has to be approved.

Downloading the latest bank and credit card transactions

Every night at roughly 10 PM PT, QuickBooks downloads the most recent transactions for the majority of banks. Some could require a bit more time. Whenever you want to get the most recent transactions available, you can manually update your accounts:

- Select **Bank transactions** under **Bookkeeping**, then **Transactions**, or go to **Banking**.
- Choose **Update**.

Reviewing transactions

- Go to **Banking or Bookkeeping**, then click **Transactions**, then **Bank transactions**.
- Choose the tile representing the account you want to examine.
- To begin your review, select the **For review option**.

The For review tab is where QuickBooks sends downloaded transactions. Go over each one in detail.

Automating downloaded activity with rules

Utilize bank rules to process transactions from bank feeds more quickly and effectively. Create rules that examine bank transactions for particular information, then give them particular payees and categories. On the page for bank transactions, there are applied rules.

Assume, for instance, that you always pay with a credit card you've linked to a banking institution in QBO while filling up your business-use vehicles at Shell gas stations. In essence, you want to assign your Fuel expense account as the category for all transactions at Shell gas stations.

A rule can be established for QBO to follow, or you can manually assign the category to one of these transactions and wait for it to "learn" your preference. When you create a rule, you specify details like the accounts and the kinds of transactions (money in or money out) that should be covered by the rule. You should be aware that you can make rules that apply to all accounts or rules that only apply to certain accounts.

The next step is to specify the requirements that must be satisfied by each transaction before QBO takes any action. The information that QBO should give to transactions that fulfill the criteria is the last thing you describe. You may, for instance, define a category and a transaction type.

Identical methods are used to set up either type of rule: one that automatically adds transactions based on a rule, and one that suggests changes that you must review.

- Click on **Banking** from the **Navigation pane**.
- Choose **Bank rules** at the top of the list of bank and credit cards.
- Select the **New Rule** button in the upper right corner of the **Bank Rules page**.

- Name the rule and ensure it is a name that has a meaning.

- Choose **the accounts** to which you want the rule to apply after deciding whether it relates to money moving into QBO or out of it.

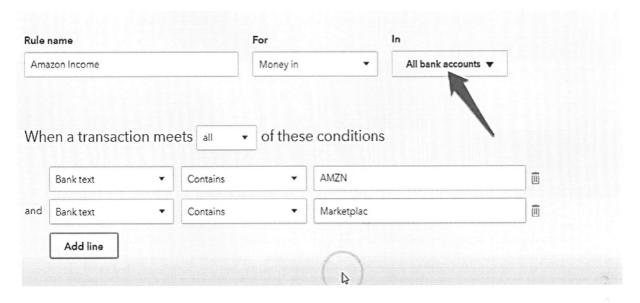

- Set criteria for **QBO** to consider when reviewing downloaded transactions to decide whether to apply the rule to them in the "When a Transaction Meets" part of the Rule page.

- Set the data you want QBO to apply to transactions that satisfy the rule's requirements at the bottom of the Rule dialog box. Choose any of the options below;

  - Choose **the transaction** type that QBO should give it.
  - To apply the rule to transactions that satisfy the requirements, choose the **Payee** and one or more categories.
  - You can optionally add a **Memo** to each transaction that satisfies the requirements of the rule.
  - If you wish QBO to automatically add transactions that satisfy the rule's requirements to your firm, tick the **Automatically Add to My Books check box**.

- Finally click on the **Save button** in the lower right corner of the Rule page.

Once you've created a rule or rules, you can replicate them (so you don't have to write similar rules from the beginning) and delete rules you no longer need using the Actions column of the Rules page. Additionally, to amend a rule, open the Rule dialog box again by

- clicking the **Edit link** in the **Actions column**.

Fixing mistakes in uploaded or downloaded transactions

Since QBO distinguishes between transactions entered manually by rules and transactions added automatically by rules using distinct icons in the Category or Match column, you may quickly identify transactions to which QBO has applied rules on the Bank and Credit Cards page. The Reviewed option on the Bank and Credit Cards page allows you to see how QBO manages each downloaded transaction in your business.

Imagine that you included a transaction in QBO by mistake that you had intended to leave out. Consider another scenario in which QBO miscategorized a transaction. Using the In QuickBooks tab on the Bank and Credit Cards page, you can quickly fix these errors.

You can reverse the process if you include a transaction in QBO that contains errors, such as one that was automatically added to the incorrect category by a rule. Undoing a transaction brings it back to the For Review tab where you can make adjustments and re-accept it. This removes the transaction from the register.

On the Bank and Credit Cards page, select the Reviewed option to cancel an accepted transaction. In the Action column, locate the transaction, then

- click the **Undo button**. When you click **Undo**, QBO notifies you that it was successful.
- Change to the **For Review tab**, locate the transaction, amend it, and accept it once more. If necessary, you may also exclude the transaction from QBO.

Using Indirect Connections to Financial Institutions

Downloading Web Connect and text files

- To download the transaction as a.QBO file, log **in to your bank**.
- Afterward, in your QBDT. Access the **File menu**.
- Click **Web Connect Files** after choosing **Utilities, Import, and then Utilities**.
- Select **Open** once you click the.**QBO file** you saved.
- Choose a **bank account**.
- Then click **Next**.

- The data should have been successfully read into QuickBooks, and you should receive a dialogue window informing you of this. Click **OK**.
- Visit the **Bank Feeds Center** next.

Opening text files in Microsoft Excel or Google Sheets

Using the Open command, you can open a text file that you prepared in another application as an Excel workbook. The title bar of Excel displays the name of the file with the text file name extension, demonstrating that opening a text file in Excel does not affect the file's format (for example, .txt or .csv).

- Navigate to the location where the text file is located by selecting **File > Open**.
- In the Open dialog box's file type drop-down menu, choose **Text Files**.
- Locate the text file you wish to open, then **double-click it**.

    - When a text file (.txt) is selected, Excel launches the Import Text Wizard. After completing each step, click Finish to finish the import process.

    - Excel opens the text file and presents the data in a new worksheet if the file is a a.csv file.

Saving CSV files

- Select **Save As under File**.
- Choose **Browse**.
- Click **Text or CSV** in the Save As dialog box's Save as type box to select the worksheet's text file format.
- Click **Save** after navigating to the spot where you want to save the new text file.
- You're reminded by a popup box that the new file will just contain the present worksheet. Click **OK** if you are satisfied that the worksheet you want to save as a text file is the one you are currently working on. By repeating this process for every worksheet, you can save more worksheets as distinct text files.

If you save the worksheet in a CSV format, you could also get a warning below the ribbon stating that some functionalities might be lost.

Uploading Web Connect and CSV files

- Go to **Banking or Bookkeeping**, then click **Transactions**, then **Bank transactions**.
- Choose the **blue tile** for the **accoun**t that contains the transactions that you want to submit.
- Choose **Upload** from file from the **drop-down menu** next to **Link account**.
- The file you downloaded from your bank should be selected when you choose **Drag & drop or Files**. Next, click **Continue**.
- Choose the account you wish to upload the transactions into from the **QuickBooks account selection**. Next, click **Continue**.
- To match the columns on the file with the appropriate fields in **QuickBooks**, follow the onscreen instructions. Next, click **Continue**.
- Choose which transactions you want to import. Next, click **Continue.**
- Choose **Yes**.
- Select **Done** once you have approved your transactions.

Connecting to Online Providers through App Transactions

You can manage your PayPal transactions the same way you manage other bank transactions with the Connect to PayPal app. Once connected, QuickBooks allows you to effortlessly update, categorize, and match transactions.

- Log in to your account on **QuickBooks Online**.
- Select **Find Apps after going to Apps**.
- Search for **Connect to Paypal**.
- Choose to **Get the app now**.
- Install is chosen once you check the box next to the relevant file.
- Select **Let's do it**.
- Select **Give the authorization** to give Intuit permission to retrieve data from your **PayPal** account.
- Insert the email address associated with your PayPal account then follow and choose the option that best suits you;

- You will be asked to create an account if you don't already have one.

- You must return to QuickBooks Online and start the connection process over if you create a new account.

- Register for a **PayPal account**.
- Select **Agree and Connect** to approve the sync.
- After the connection has been made, choose **Return to Intuit**.
- Click on **Next**, after choosing the **PayPal Bank** where your **PayPal transactions** can be found.
- Select **Next** after choosing the sales tax rate that will be applied to all imported sales transactions.
- In the event that you have historical transactions, choose **the date** you want to import from and then click **Done**. You may import previous transactions going back up to 18 months.

Converting Paper Receipts to Electronic Transactions

Spend less time keeping track of and recording your vendor receipts. They can be uploaded to QuickBooks Online from a computer, a smartphone, or even an email account.

The information on your receipt is extracted by QuickBooks, which then creates a transaction for you to see. Then, in the Receipts tab, you may update the receipt, add it to an account, or match it to an already-completed transaction.

Upload receipts

There are numerous ways receipts can be converted into an electronic transaction.

- Uploading receipts containing private or delicate information, such as credit card numbers and government identification numbers, is not advised.
- Images in JPEG, JPG, GIF, and PNG formats are all supported by QuickBooks. Your photographs may be in the HEIC format if you have a more recent iPhone or iPad. HEIC photos can be converted into a format that is compatible.
- Open **QuickBooks Online** and **log in**.
- To access receipts, go to **Bookkeeping**, then **Transactions**, or to **Banking**, then pick **receipts**.

- Decide whether to upload from your computer or Google Drive. Take note: Only one receipt should be included in each image or file.

You can scan and upload receipts from your mobile device using the QuickBooks Online mobile app.

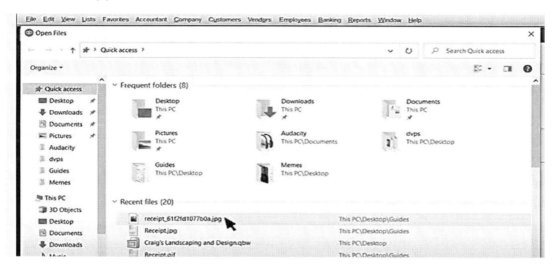

Install the QuickBooks Online app for iOS or Android if you haven't already.

- Launch **the mobile version** of **QuickBooks Online**.
- Select the **Menu icon.**
- Click on **Receipt snap**.
- By choosing **a Receipt camera**, you can take a picture of your receipt.
- Select **Use this image**, then **Finish**.

Activity

1. Connect your QuickBooks Online account to a financial institution.
2. Connect your bank account or credit card account to your QuickBooks Online.
3. With the use of rules, automate downloaded activities.
4. Check if the downloaded or uploaded transactions in your QBO have some mistakes; if they do correct the mistakes.
5. Search for text files in your QBO and open them in Excel or Google sheets.
6. Connect your QBO to online providers via app transactions.
7. Convert your manual receipts to electronic transactions.

CHAPTER 12

WORKING WITH PURCHASE ORDERS, ESTIMATES, PROJECTS, AND TAGS

Working with Purchase Orders

You have the resources in QuickBooks Online to manage every stage of the sales cycle, including purchasing. When you're ready to acquire more goods, you can make purchase orders (PO) and email them to merchants. Purchase orders inform merchants of your intention to buy.

You can input the precise items and quantity you wish to purchase on purchase orders. You may rapidly add a purchase order to an expense or bill transaction in QuickBooks once your vendor accepts it and agrees to the terms. This keeps your accounts in balance and all of the transactions related.

Enabling the purchase order feature

The purchase order feature should be activated if it hasn't already:

- Select **Account and settings under Settings**.
- Choosing the **Expenses tab**.
- Select the **edit icon** under **Purchase orders** in the section.

- Activate the option to use purchase orders.
- Add a default message for vendors and up to three custom fields if you like. These are not required.
- Choose **Save**, followed by **Done**.

Creating purchase orders

- Choose **+ New**.
- Choose **Purchase order**

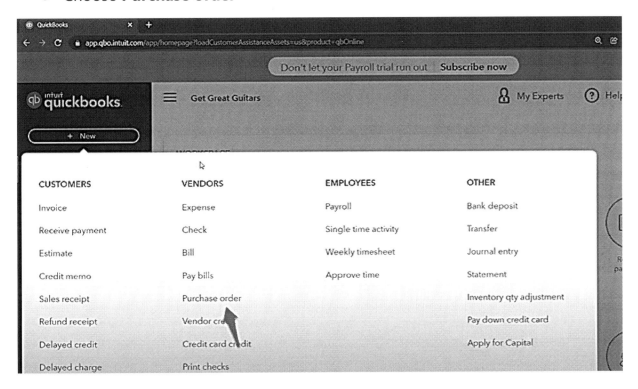

- Choose **the vendor** from the **dropdown list for vendors**.
- Take a look at the mailing address.
- Choose **Ship from the Ship** to drop-down menu if you are sending the products straight to a customer. Make sure the shipping address is accurate by checking it.
- Type the date of the purchase order.
- On the **Purchase Order** form, click **Settings**. Next, click the link to create your own custom fields in the Choose what you use panel.

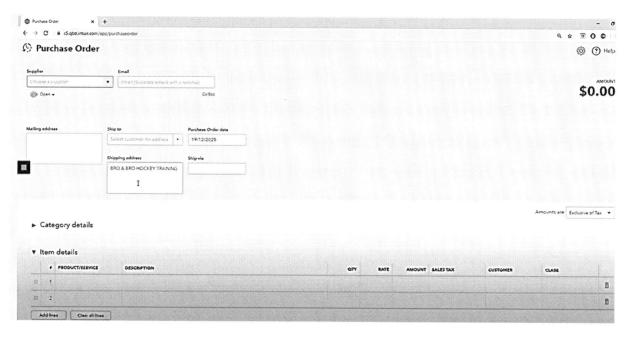

- Enter the items you want to buy in the Item details section. The phrase **I acquired this product/service from a vendor** must be checked in order to add a product or service. Find out more about editing services and products.
- When finished, choose **Save and close**. Or, choose Save and send from the dropdown menu when you're ready to send it.
- Go to **Expenses** if you wish to send the purchase order later. Choose to **Send** in the Action column after finding your purchase order.

Copying an existing purchase order

To copy an existing purchase order, follow the steps below;

- Select **Expenses** from the menu.
- Find the **purchase order** that you made.
- Click **More** at the bottom to select **Copy**.
- Click **Save and close** when finished.

Receiving items against purchase orders

Depending on what stage it's in, a PO has an impact on your inventory. QuickBooks changes your stock levels and product costs in accordance with the items you receive through a PO.

Receive all items from a purchase order

- Go to **Purchase Orders** after **Stock Control**.
- Choose the **Purchase order** from which you want to receive products.
- Choose **Receive All**.
- Insert the date it was received.
- From the **Received option** in the dropdown, pick the **desired location**.
- Choose **Receive**.

Partially receive items from a purchase order

- Go to **Purchase Orders** after **Stock Control**.
- Choose the **Purchase order** from which you want to receive products.
- Select **Not Received Ye**t to clear every box.
- Choose the supplies you want to get.
- Fill out the **To Receive** section with the quantity.
- Choose **Receive Selected**.
- Insert the date it was received.
- From the **Received option** in the dropdown, pick the **desired location**.
- Choose **Receive**.

Closing purchase orders

Purchase orders are non-posting entries. In that case, you can either erase them from your record or immediately close the POs if they won't be accepted.

- Pull up your **purchase orders** first.
- Click to **open the transaction** of your choice.
- Click the **Open drop-down arrow** next to the **Vendor name**.
- Select **Closed** by selecting the drop-down arrow for the purchase order status.
- Close by pressing **Save**.

Tracking open purchase orders

Follow the steps below to track purchase orders that are still open;

- Select **Vendor Center** from the Vendors menu.

- Choose **the name** of the merchant.

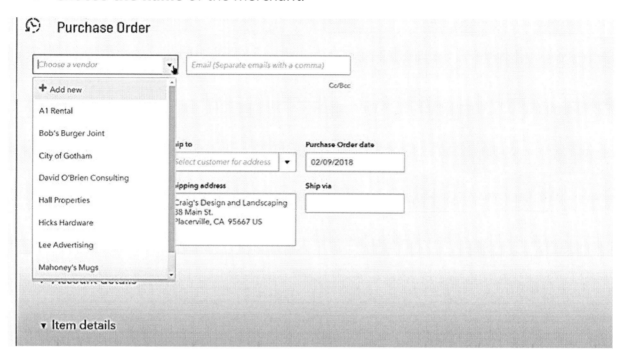

- Locate **the Bill** under the **Transactions tab** in the **Vendor Information section** and **double-click it.**

- Select **Purchase order** by clicking the symbol.

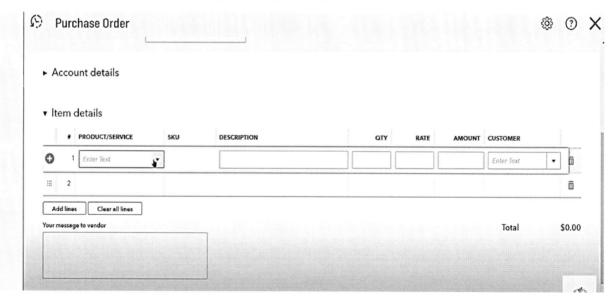

- Verify every purchase order that should be listed on the invoice.

- To save and close, click **OK**.

Working with Estimates

When you want to provide your client with a price, bid, or proposal for work you intend to complete, create an estimate. The form resembles an invoice, but rather than billing your client, you're informing them about your proposal and their expenditures. You may then convert the estimate to an invoice so you don't have to enter it again when the work is finished and you're ready to bill your client.

Preparing an estimate

- Choose + **New**.

- Select **Estimate**.

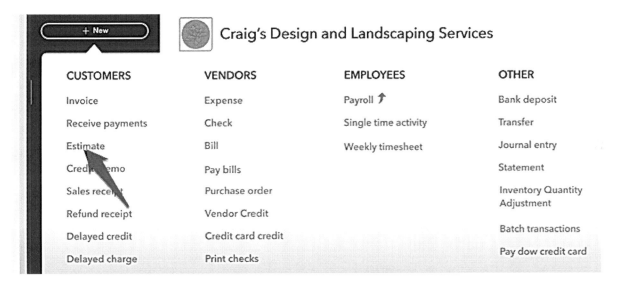

- From the Customer dropdown, choose a **client.**

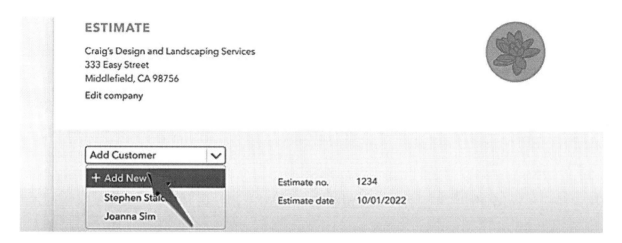

- In the event that the work has already begun, choose a status from the **Pending menu**. This is not required.
- Decide on the **Estimate date** and, if applicable, the **Expiration date**.
- Add the goods and services you intend to market.
- Please enter any further information you require.
- Choose **Save** when you are prepared.

Copying an estimate to a purchase order

Once a customer approves your estimate, you may quickly copy it to a purchase order to streamline your workflow.

Step 1: Turn on the purchase order feature

- Select **Account and settings under Settings**.
- Click on **Expenses**.
- In the area for **Purchase orders**, click the **pencil icon**.
- Use **purchase orders** is switched on.
- Pick **Save**, then click **Done**.

Step 2: Copy estimate to a purchase order

- Choose + **New**.
- Click on **Estimate.**

Craig's Design and Landscaping Services

CUSTOMERS	VENDORS	EMPLOYEES	OTHER
Invoice	Expense	Payroll ↑	Bank deposit
Receive payments	Check	Single time activity	Transfer
Estimate	Bill	Weekly timesheet	Journal entry
Credit memo	Pay bills		Statement
Sales receipt	Purchase order		Inventory Quantity Adjustment
Refund receipt	Vendor Credit		
Delayed credit	Credit card credit		Batch transactions
Delayed charge	Print checks		Pay dow credit card

- Type in the **client and product or service information** then choose **Save**.

- Next to the sum, a dropdown menu with the options Create invoice or Copy to purchase order will display.
- Decide where to copy the order.
- Choose a **Vendor**.
- Select the **same customer** as on the purchase order in the Item details section.
- Select **Publish and close**.

Purchase orders only receive copies of products that have been marked as being purchased from suppliers. Check to see if your goods or services are appropriately tagged.

- On the toolbar, click **Settings,** then click **Products and services**.
- Locate the item or service. then choose **Edit.**
- Select the **I acquire this product/service from a supplier checkbox** in the Purchasing details section.
- Select **Publish** and **close**.

Converting an estimate to an invoice

Change the estimate into an invoice so you may charge the client:

216

- Select **All Sales** by going to **Bookkeeping, Transactions, or Sale**s, respectively.
- Look for **the estimate**.
- Choose to **Create an invoice** from the **Action column**.
- Determining the amount to invoice depends on whether progress invoicing is enabled: If you don't use progress invoicing, skip this step.

    ○ Select **the Remaining sum** of all lines to generate an invoice for the entire estimated amount. Next, choose to **Create an invoice**.

    ○ Alternatively, you may choose to specify a percentage of each line or a specific amount in order to create an invoice for just a portion of the estimate. Next, choose to **Create an invoice**.

- Select **Save and send or Save and close** after making any necessary changes to the invoice.

Adding an estimate to an existing invoice

You can also add estimates to current invoices rather than converting them:

- Choose + **New**.
- Choose **Invoice**.
- From the **Customer dropdown**, choose **the customer**. The Add to Invoice window is then displayed.
- Select **Add** on each estimate you want to include in the invoice in the **Add to Invoice window**.
- Determining the amount to invoice depends on whether progress invoicing is enabled: (If you don't have progress billing, skip this step.

    ○ Select the Remaining sum of all lines to generate an invoice for the entire estimated amount. Selec**t Copy** to invoice after that.

    ○ Alternatively, you may choose to specify a percentage of each line or a specific amount in order to create an invoice for just a portion of the estimate. Select **Copy** to invoice after that.

- Update or modify the invoice as necessary. then choose **Save.**

You can add all of the open estimates you have for a particular customer at once. Your client might, however, prefer distinct invoices for each.

Copying an existing estimate

Instead of entering all the information twice for a customer who receives recurrent invoices, you can duplicate the invoice.

- Select **All Sales** by going to **Bookkeeping, Transactions, or Sales**, respectively.
- Locate **the estimate** or invoice that you wish to copy.
- Select **the dropdown menu** under the **Action column**. then choose **Copy**.
- If necessary, modify the invoice or estimate, then choose **Save**.

You can create recurring transactions in its place if the consumer requests the same invoice on a regular basis. Alternatively, you may generate the same invoice for numerous clients.

Creating a progress invoice for an estimate

You can divide an estimate into as many invoices as you need to with progress billing. You can charge clients for partial payments rather than requesting full payment at the start of a job. Add things from the initial estimate to progress invoices as you finish the work. This keeps project payments connected and structured throughout.

Step 1: Turn on progress invoicing

If you have not already turned on progress invoicing, follow the steps below;

- Select **Account** and settings under **Settings**.
- Choosing the **Sales tab**.
- Select **Edit** in the Progress Invoicing section.
- Activate the switch next to Create numerous partial invoices from a single estimate.
- Select **Update** from the Update invoice template? window.
- Pick **Save**, then click **Done**.

Step 2: Create a progress invoice template

When you enable this option, QuickBooks automatically prepares a progress invoicing template. Every time you make a progress invoice, use the ready-made Airy fresh style template. Follow these steps to build a new template:

- Select **Custom** form styles in Settings.
- To create a new invoice template, first choose **New style**, then choose **Invoice**. Alternatively, find the template and choose **Edit** to make changes to one of your current templates.
- Choose **a catchy name** for the template, such as "Progress invoice template."
- Choose **Change up** the template or Dive in using a template from the Design menu.

  ○ Choose the **Airy new template**. Only this template can be used to create progress invoices.

- Choose **Edit print setting**s or **Print it** out if in doubt.

  ○ Make sure the box labeled "Fit printed form with pay stub in window envelope" is not ticked.

- Choosing the **Content tab**.
- On the form's table section, click **Edit** (the second section with Activity, Rate, and Amount).
  ○ Choose the link for **Show more** activity options.
  ○ If you want to display item details on the progress invoice, tick the box that says "Show progress on line items."

- In the form's footer area, click **Edit** (the third section with Total and Balance Due).

  ○ If you want the invoice to show the estimated amount, the amounts of each progress invoice, and the total amount invoiced thus far, click the Estimate summary checkbox.

- Click on **Done.**

I advise utilizing this as your new default template for all invoices if you send out a lot of progress invoices. To set your newly produced template as your default template:

- Return to **Custom form styles** if you haven't already.
- Select the dropdown menu next to the template in the **Action column**. Select **Make default** next.
- Select **Change template** to confirm your selection.

Note: You can set up a different default template for regular invoices if you intend to use this one only sometimes for progress invoices. Then, you can utilize the progress invoice template when creating a new invoice by choosing Customize straight on the invoice form.

Managing Projects

To monitor the success of your project, use projects in QuickBooks Online. From a single dashboard, you can add project revenue, expenses, and labor costs and run project-specific reports. You can also include previous transactions in fresh or current projects as needed.

Only QuickBooks Online Plus, Advanced, and Accountant offer Projects.

Turning on the project feature

Projects in QuickBooks Online Accountant are a permanent configuration that cannot be changed once they are activated.

- Choose **Settings**. Next, choose **Company Settings**.
- Choosing the **Advanced tab**.
- To extend it, locate the **Projects section** and choose **Edit**.

- The Use project financial tracking toggle should be turned on.

- Choose **Save**, followed by **Done**.

Contrasting projects with sub-customers

You can convert sub-customers into projects and use the job costing tools to manage everything in one place if you're currently using them to track client jobs. Here's how to migrate only certain transactions or sub-customers into projects.

Step 1: Turn on Projects

Step 2: Review your sub-customer settings

- Before converting **a sub-customer**, make the following changes:
- Select **Customers under Get paid & pay** from the menu.
- Find the sub-customer and open it. Make it active if it is currently dormant.
- Choose **Edit**.
- Make sure the Is sub-customer checkbox is checked.
- Review and decide who the key client is. The account that is associated with the project is this one.
- **Bill** with a parent should be chosen in the drop-down option.

Step 3: Check the main customer for the sub-customer

Ensure that the sub-customer has a single primary parent customer. It cannot be a sub-client of a sub-client.

- Select **Customers under Get paid & pay** from the menu.
- The sub-customer you wish to convert should be found.
- Select **Edit** after choosing the sub-profile. customers
- Choose the **primary customer from the Sub-customer dropdown**. The parent customer is another name for this.

Step 4: Convert a sub-customer to a project

A sub-customer can be used to start a new project or be merged into an existing project.

- Creat**e a new project** from a sub-customer

The result is a clean slate. Existing transactions made by your sub-customers won't carry over.

- Select **Customers under Get paid & pay** from the menu.
- Find the message that asks, "Do you structure sub-customers as projects?" and click the **Convert now** button. Alternately, choose **Convert from sub-customer** from the New project dropdown menu under the **Projects menu**.
- The sub-customer you want to convert should be chosen.
- Select **Convert** when you're ready, and then click **Continue** to confirm. Keep in mind that your current transactions won't be carried over.

Merge a sub-customer with an existing project

- Select **Projects** under **Business Overview**.

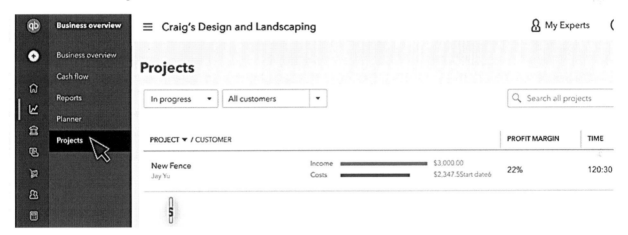

- Locate the project that you want to combine your sub-customer with.

- The project's name should be copied.

- Select **Customers under Get paid & pa**y from the menu.

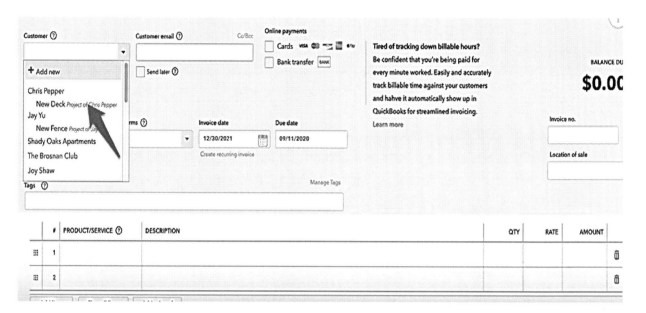

- Find the sub-customer and open it.
- Choose **Edit**.
- Change **the Display name** in the edit box to precisely reflect the project name.
- Select **Save and Yes** to confirm the merge when you are ready.

The project will not receive information about your sub-customers, such as addresses, tax codes, and payment and billing information.

Creating a new project

Projects are enabled by default in QuickBooks Online Plus and Advanced. You must activate projects if you use QuickBooks Online Accountant, though.

- Select **Projects** from **Business Overview**.

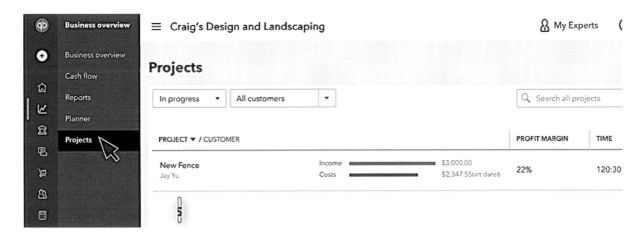

- Choose **New Project**.
- Enter the **project's name** in the **Project Name area**.
- From the **Customer dropdown**, choose the **project's client**.
- Include any project-related notes or information under Notes.
- Choose **Save**.

Adding transactions to a project

You can easily add new transactions to your projects, such as invoices, expenses, or estimations. Projects' classification or impact on your accounts are unaffected by the addition of transactions. Simply designating them as a component of the project allows you to keep track of its revenues and outlays.

New transactions can be added in one of two ways. As usual, you can create the transaction in QuickBooks. In the Customer/Project dropdown, simply type the project name. Alternatively, follow these steps to generate a new transaction from a project:

- Select **Projects under Business Overview.**
- Choose a **project**.
- To add a new transaction, choose to **Add to project**.
- Choose from **Bill**, **Receive Payment, Expense, Estimate, or Invoice.**
- Like you normally would, enter the transaction's details.
- Select **Publish and close**.

Reporting on projects

Project reports can only be conducted by team members with the Manage My Timesheets authority, managers, and account administrators.

This report, which is frequently used to help with task costing, shows the number of hours monitored for each job or customer as well as the team members who worked on each one.

- Select **Project Report under Reports**.
- Select **Run Report** after choosing your **filters**.
- **Note**: After running the report, filters can be added by drilling down on an individual pie chart slice. By choosing **Clear All Filters** at the report's top or the x next to a specific filter, you can remove the filter or filters.

Updating project status

To obtain the data you require in QBO and export it to an Excel file, you must run two distinct reports. Run the Project Profitability Summary report first to display all active projects broken down by clients, projects, and dates. This is how:

- From the left menu, select **Reports**.
- Look for the report on the **Project Profitability Summary**.
- From the **Report period drop-down**, choose the date range.
- Select **Customize** from the menu.
- Select **In progress** from the **Project Status** drop-down menu in the **Filter section**.
- Create a custom start and end date for the project.
- Click **Run Report**.
- Next, choose **Export to Excel** by clicking the **Export icon**.

Deleting projects

- Locate the **Projects menu**.
- Choose the **Delete option** from the **Actions menu** after finding the project you wish to get rid of.
- Selecting **Yes** will confirm.

Tagging Transactions

Tags are labels that you can customize to monitor transactions any way you like. Bills, costs, and invoices can all be tagged. Run reports and group tags to examine the performance of particular divisions of your company. They have no effect on your books. Instead, they allow your staff to monitor the information that is most important to you.

Creating Tag Groups and Tags

Follow the steps below to create tag groups;

- Select **Tags under Settings**.

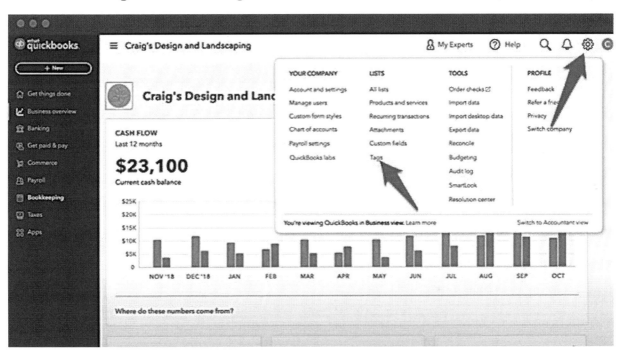

- Pick **Tag group** from the **New dropdown menu** after that.
- Give the group a name.
- Choose **a color** from the drop-down menu.
- When finished, choose **Save**.

Let's say you manage an event organization. You might want to check your earnings and event expenses for this year. Make an event-themed group. After that, make tags for particular events and include them in your events group.

Tagging new transactions

While working on a form, such as an invoice or expenditure report, you can add tags:

- Enter the name of the tag you want to create in the **Tags field**. Next, choose **+ Add**.
- To add the tag to one of your groups, choose **that group**.

This tags the form and creates the tag. Simply put the name in the Tag field and select it to add an existing tag to a form.

Note: You may add as many tags as you like, but each tag group may only include one tag.

Disabling the Tags feature

Go through the steps below to have Tags disabled;

- Choose **Settings**.
- Select **Settings and Account**.
- Choosing the **Sales tab**.
- **Turn off Tags** in the **Sales form content section**. then choose **Save**.
- Choosing the **Expenses tab**.
- Turn off the **Show Tags field** on the expense and purchase from in the **Bills and Expenses** section. then choose **Save**.
- Choose **Done.**

Purchase orders and estimates must be used in all businesses that deal with goods. Businesses typically carry out a variety of initiatives with the goal of improving what they do. You must have learned how to utilize QuickBooks Online to accomplish the aforementioned goals so easily in the just-completed chapter. You must be familiar with using purchase orders, comparing items received to purchase orders, creating estimates, turning estimates into invoices, creating progress invoices for estimates, using the project feature, and many other things. Test your understanding of the just-ended chapter by engaging in the below-mentioned exercise.

Activity

1. Turn on the purchase order feature in your QBO.
2. Create a purchase order.
3. Close the purchase order you have just created.
4. Prepare an estimate deciding on the estimated date and also the expiration date.
5. Copy the estimate you have just prepared for a purchase order.
6. Switch an invoice to an estimate.
7. Create a progress invoice for an estimate.
8. Turn on the project feature.
9. Create a new project.
10. Create a tag
11. Tag the new transactions in your QBO.

PART 3

BUDGETING, REPORTING, AND ANALYSIS

CHAPTER 13

CREATING BUDGETS IN QUICKBOOKS

To compare against their real revenues and expenses, many businesses prepare budgets. You can build budgets using your accounting data in QuickBooks Online Plus. After entering your budgets into QuickBooks, you can analyze and make changes as necessary. Then you may compare your actual sales and expenses to your budget by running financial reports.

Creating a Budget

Register with QuickBooks as a user who has access rights to create, edit, and delete budgets. then adhere to these guidelines;

You can either establish a brand-new budget or replicate one that already exists. If this is your first budget, start here. Once you've added your first budget, we'll show you how to copy one.

You also have the choice to establish a budget by importing a .csv file if you subscribe to QuickBooks Online Advanced. Expand the section below titled "Upload a budget using a.csv file" to find out how.

- Select **Budgeting under Settings**.

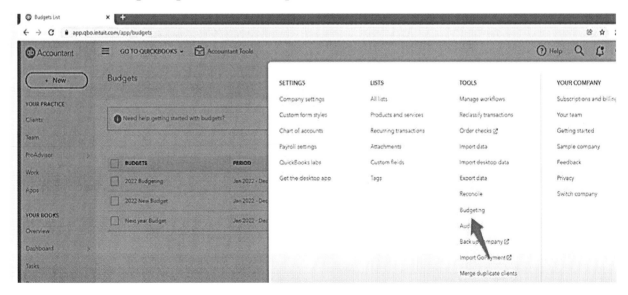

- Choose to **Add budget**

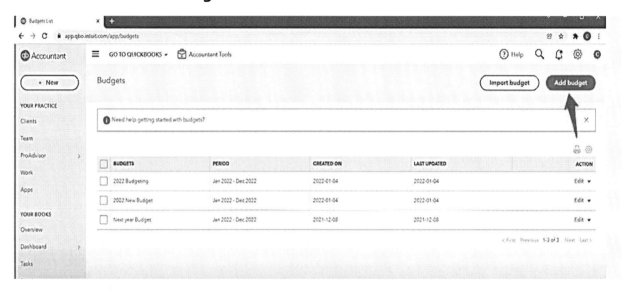

- Give the budget a name in the **Name column**.
- Choose **the fiscal year** for which you are constructing the budget from the dropdown list.
- Choose **whether you want the budget to display monthly, quarterly, or annually** from the Interval dropdown.
- If you would want QuickBooks to prefill your budget with actual data from your chart of accounts, use the actual date year option from the Pre-fill data menu.
- To further divide the budget, use the **Subdivide by dropdown**.
- Choose **Next or Create a Budget** when you are prepared.
- Enter **your monthly budget for each account**. If necessary, go to the report you saved in Step 2.
- If your budget is satisfactory, click **Save or Save and close**.

Budgets are outlined by account in the Budget Overview report. The accounts are summarized along with your actual account totals in the Budgets vs. Actuals report. Additionally, it displays your budgetary surplus or deficit.

Make any necessary edits to a budget in QuickBooks by following the steps below:

- Select **Budgeting under Settings**.

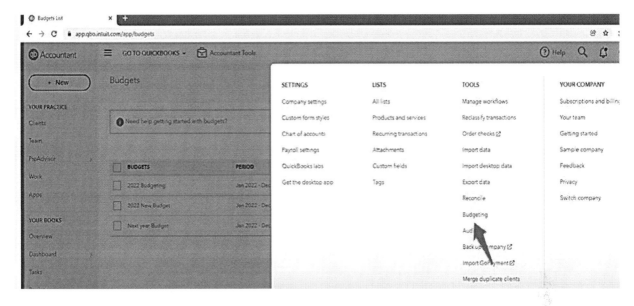

- On the list, locate **your budget**.

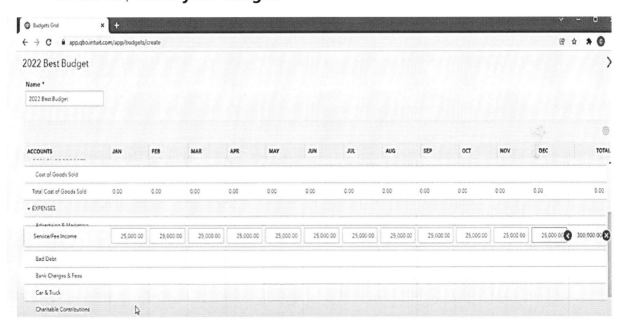

- Select **Edit** in the **Action column**.
- Every month, edit **each account**.
- Choose the **Gear icon** at the top of the budget to switch the time period from monthly to quarterly or yearly. Next, choose **Year or Quarter**.
- Choose to **Save or Save and exit**.

Importing Budgets

You have the ability to upload your budget from a .csv file using QuickBooks Online Advanced. Before you can access the.csv import option if you've never created a budget before, you must first create at least one budget, which can be blank.

Download a budget.csv template before you create your first budget. The template is formatted by QuickBooks using your chart of accounts and fiscal year months. The template can then be used to generate your budget, guaranteeing that your data is compatible and imports well.

- Select **Budgeting under Settings** if you aren't already there.
- Click on **Import budget.**
- To obtain the template, click the link for **Sample.csv**.
- Save the file in a location where you can locate it quickly, such as your computer's downloads folder.

Import your budget back into QuickBooks when you're ready by taking the steps below;

- Select **Budgeting under Settings**.
- Click on **Budget Import**.
- Choose **Browse**, then look for and open the template.
- Choose **Next**.
- Your budget is currently in QuickBooks. Make a brief review.
- Give your budget a name in the Name area.
- Analyze the cells. Verify that each account has the appropriate balances. Select **a field** and make the necessary changes if you need to.
- To save your budget, choose **Save or Save and close** when you are finished.

Basing Spreadsheet Budgets on Actuals

You must access the Budget vs. Actual Report and export it to Excel in order to accomplish this. For the time period you want to view, you must follow the same procedure. For instance, August through January and the entire fiscal year.

You can manually arrange the timeframe using the technique. Then, choose the information you wish to appear in the report.

For the report's creation and export

- Enter **Budget vs. Accruals** in the field box under **Reports** on the left panel.
- Select the appropriate date range by clicking the **Report period drop-down**.
- Select **Export to Excel** by pressing the **Export icon**.
- For the date range you want to use, use the same procedure.

Deleting Budgets

Be cautious if you decide to eliminate a budget. Deleted budgets cannot be recovered.

- Select **Budgeting under Settings**.
- On the list, locate your budget.
- Pick **Delete** from the **Edit menu** in the **Action column**.

In every business and in every person's life, budgets are extremely crucial. Budgets enable us to live a more financially balanced existence by helping us control our expenditures. It's encouraging to know that QuickBook Online shares this opinion and has assisted us in this chapter in learning how to establish budgets and import budgets into QBO if we have already created them elsewhere, such as in excel.

Activity

1. Create a budget in your QBO.
2. Import a budget you have elsewhere in your QBO.
3. Delete the budget you have created and create another.

CHAPTER 14

UTILIZING QUICKBOOKS REPORTS

It should come as no surprise that you utilize reports to assist you to assess the health of your company. Maintaining QBO up to date with your daily operations will assist ensure that accurate information shows on the reports you run because the reports mirror the information in QBO.

Looking at the Reports Page

There are three tabs for reports, and by default, you see the Standard tab (more on that in the following section). You'll find reports categorized in the following groups as you scroll down the Reports page:

- Favorites
- Business Overview
- Who Owes You
- Sales and Customers
- What You Owe
- Expenses and Vendors
- Sales Tax
- Employees
- For My Accountant
- Payroll

Whether you have a payroll subscription will determine the payroll reports that are provided to you. If you don't, you'll only see an Employee Contact List and two reports about time tracking on the list of payroll reports that are readily available.

Finding the Report You Want

In QBO, reports are divided into three groups:

- Standard
- Custom Reports
- Management Reports

Examining standard reports

Based on your QBO subscription level, the QBO features you use, your choices, and any add-ons you have installed, QBO displays all reports that are accessible to you on the Standard tab of the Reports page.

Note the star that is filled in next to the Balance Sheet report. The star appears gray at best in my black-and-white book but is green on your screen (and mine as well). The Balance Sheet report can be found in the Favorites area of the Standard tab; it has a filled-in star to indicate that it has been recognized as a favorite.

When you select Reports in the Navigation bar, the default page opens. Use the Favorites section to move the reports you use the most frequently to the top of this page. Simply click the empty star next to a report to star it; QBO will fill in the star and place the starred report at the top of the Standard tab in the Favorites group.

Finding customized reports

The Custom Reports page lists any customized reports you've printed to a printer or your display and saved, either as individual reports or as a report group. Until you customize and save a report, the Custom Reports tab is empty.

If you previously used QuickBooks Desktop, be aware that saving a report in QBO corresponds to memorizing a report in that product conceptually, and saving a report to a group in QBO corresponds to creating a memorized report group in that product.

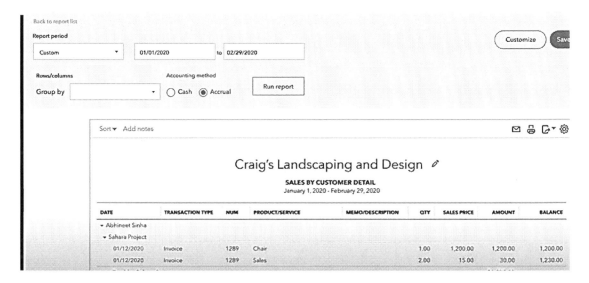

Reviewing management reports

By selecting the View link in the Action column, you can prepare and print any of the three predefined management report packages that are listed on the Management Reports tab.

These report packages are actually rather nice; each one includes multiple reports related to the report package's name, a table of contents, and a cover page that has a professional appearance.

- The Profit and Loss report and the Balance Sheet report are both included in the Company Overview management report.
- The Profit and Loss report, the A/R Aging Detail report and the Sales by Customer Summary report are all included in the Sales Performance management report.
- The Profit and Loss report, the A/P Aging Detail report and the Expenses by Vendor Summary report are all included in the Expenses Performance Management report.

A PDF version of a management report is normally created by QBO when you select View in the Action column next to it. To open the report in the PDF viewer you have installed on your computer, click the PDF link at the bottom of the browser or in the Print Preview window that displays. In the event that you are unable to print the management report straight from QBO, your PDF viewer will undoubtedly provide the ability for you to scroll through and print the report.

237

These reports can also be altered; to see your options, click the downward-pointing arrow next to a report. If you decide to alter a report package, you can change the cover page to incorporate your logo, add extra reports, include an executive summary, and add end notes.

Searching for a report

To find a report, you don't need to use the tabs. Instead, you can use the Find a Report by Name box in the top right corner of the Reports page to click and input the name of the report or a specific section of it. When you do so, QBO presents all reports that satisfy the criteria you specified, listed alphabetically in a drop-down list.

- Click **the desired report** when you see it, and QBO will show it to you on screen. If the report you're looking for isn't there, you can modify or add more criteria in the Find **Report by Name box**, and QBO will once more look for and display report titles that correspond to the keywords you entered.

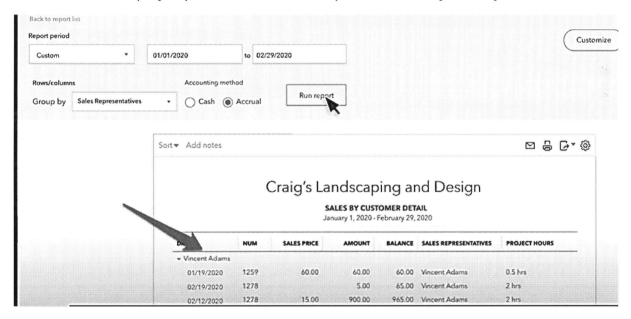

- Additionally, once you choose **Reports** in the Navigation bar, you are not restricted to just searching for reports. Regardless of the page, you are on, you can search for a report using the Search button at the top of the QBO screen (next to the Gear menu).

Printing a Report

- Simply **click any report's title** to generate it.

Using default settings, QBO shows the report automatically.

- Click the **Back to Report List** link located above the report's settings, or select **Reports** from the **Navigation bar,** to reopen the **Reports page**.

You can usually delve down into reports to see the specifics that lie beneath their figures. For instance, you can choose any Income or Expense account amount from the Profit and Loss report, and QBO will show the transactions that contributed to that number.

Duplicate the tab containing the summary version of the report before drilling down to examine details if you want to maintain the original summary version of the report open in addition to viewing the details from drilling down. You can close the tab holding the details after you've finished working with them.

- Right-click a tab and choose **Duplicate** from the context menu in Chrome. Right-click the tab and choose the **Replicate tab** from the context menu in Firefox to duplicate.

  The browser refresh button is located at the left border of the address bar. You may also click it while holding down the **Ctrl key**.

Customizing Reports

Most reports can be altered in a number of different ways. List reports aren't financial reports; thus you won't find an option to select the accounting method on these reports. For the majority of financial-based reports, you can choose to run the report using a Cash or an Accrual basis accounting technique.

For all reports, you can alter the time period that the report covers by either selecting a date range in the Transaction Date list box or entering a specific range of dates in the From and To boxes. Once you've made your choice, click Run Report to update the report and limit the information it displays to the date range (or other criteria) you've chosen.

For any report, you may set up more specific custom parameters; in this section, I talk about the customization choices in regard to the profit and loss report.

At the top of the report, select Customize. The Customize panel for the chosen report is displayed by QBO. It's critical to realize that based on the report you are modifying; different settings will appear in the Customize Report window.

- Click the **right-pointing caret** next to the section name, **Rows/Columns**, to see the settings that are accessible there. You can modify the rows and columns that show on the report from the Rows/Columns section. A variety of comparison columns can also be added.

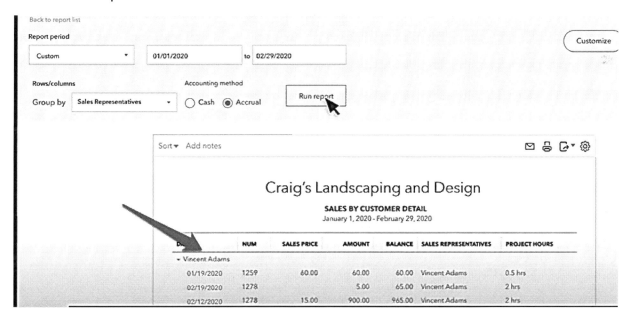

- You can choose which items from the Account, Customer, Vendor, Employee, and Product/Service list QBO includes on the Profit and Loss report by using the Filter section.

When you're done configuring the report,

- click **Run Report** in the lower right corner of the **Customize Report panel**. QBO then uses your personalized settings to display the report on the screen.

Saving a customized report

Once you've customized the report to your liking, you might want to save it so you don't have to repeat the process every time you run the report. To display a panel, click the Save Customization button at the top of the report page.

Give the customized report a name. You can use the QBO name for the report, but it would be preferable to include some details that will make it easier for you to remember the customizations. This is in contrast to the name I used in the figure, which really only tells us that the report isn't the standard Profit and Loss report.

The report can be added to a group you make; groups are helpful if you wish to email multiple reports at once.

- Click the **Establish New Group option** to bring up the **New Group Name box** and add a new group.
- After doing so, click the **Add button** after entering the group's name in the **New Group Name box.** Simply choose the group name from the **Add This Report to a Group list box** in the panel the next time you want to add a report to the group you made.

Additionally, you can choose to share the personalized report with the other users on your account, and accountants can choose to share with clients by selecting All in the Share With list box.

The stored report can be found on the Custom Reports tab of the Reports page when you save your settings in the Save Customizations dialog box. Additionally, the report displays any groups you may have made.

Exporting Reports from QuickBooks

Exporting to Excel

You can easily export your reports and lists from QuickBooks Online. This implies that downloading the information you typed into your file to your local hard disk is simple.

The following reports and lists can all be exported at once into separate Excel files that are compressed into a zip format. To export your list or report:

- From the toolbar, click the **Settings icon**.
- Go to **Tools** and choose **Export Data**.
- Set the date range on the **Reports tab**.
- By moving the slider, you can add or remove items from the Reports and Lists tabs.
- Click **Excel Export**.

Exporting to Google Sheets

- Open your **QuickBooks Online account** and **log in**.
- Select **Reports under Business overview** in the left navigation.
- The report you want to export to Google Sheets should be opened.
- From the Export drop-down box, choose the **Google Sheets export option**.
- Finally, insert the verification sent to you. Your Google account will then be opened.
- If asked, log into **Google**.

Your QuickBooks Online account is connected to Google Sheets, which also permits data export.

Custom Reporting with Spreadsheet Sync

Spreadsheet Sync allows for the creation and customization of reports for QuickBooks Online. The pivot tables are not part of them.

- Additionally, you have the option to download transaction or account data from QuickBooks Online Advanced into a data table.

- These tables and reports are categorized.

Activity

1. What are the three types of reports in QuickBooks Online?
2. Check through the three types of reports and make some recordings.
3. Print any of the above-described reports.
4. Customize a report and save it.
5. Export reports to either Excel or Google sheets.

CHAPTER 15

ANALYZING QUICKBOOKS DATA IN EXCEL

A very flexible accounting tool is QuickBooks. Despite all of its features, there are still occasions when we wish MS Excel could be used to perform a few calculations or generate a unique report.

The good news is that you are not forced to pick between them. The program makes exporting reports from QuickBooks to Excel incredibly simple. You may take advantage of all of QuickBooks' benefits while still being able to complete some tasks in Excel.

Automatically Opening Excel Reports Exported from QuickBooks

From a different QuickBooks Online company

- Log **into the account where your lists are stored**.

- Select **Reports from Business Overview**.

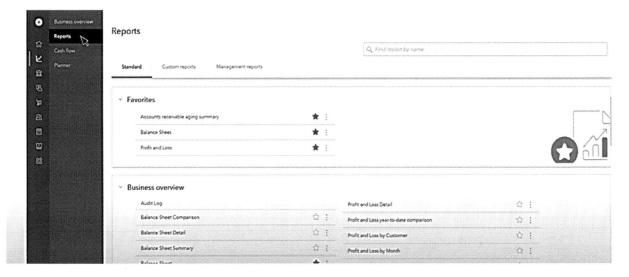

- Find and run **the Account List, Customer Contact List, Supplier Contact List, or Product/Service List reports**, depending on the list you need to export.
- Create **a column layout** for the list report. Choose each report from the list below to see how the columns should be arranged.

- Export your report after saving it.
- Open **Excel and the exported report**.
- To remove your company name and the title of the report from the sheet, delete rows 1-4.
- Your report should now be saved as **Excel or CSV**.

Sifting through Excel Reports

Utilize a specified custom field to view each transaction. You could use a custom field you built for a client loyalty program, for instance, to search through all transactions.

Filtering data

- Select **the magnifying glass-shaped** icon for search.
- Insert the name of the custom field. Select **the Gear icon on any page**, then choose **Custom fields** to get a list of your active custom fields.
- Choose **a transaction** in the list of results.
- Select **Advanced Search** to view the complete list of transactions. From the dropdown menu next to the Contains or Equals field, choose the custom field. Select **Search next**.

Use custom fields while running reports to gain more insight into your company. For instance, you can filter a report to just display the information that interests you.

Guarding against tricky traps

Two of the largest issues facing small business owners are data security and fraud prevention.

Scammers can use stolen security codes, PINs, and credit card data to conduct fraudulent purchases. Social Security number theft, identity theft, tax ID theft, data mining, and even a loss of control over your accounts can all result from a data breach at your small business.

Small firms are just as vulnerable to a data breach as larger organizations, contrary to popular belief. In fact, when compared to larger enterprises, small businesses lose nearly twice as much money annually, according to the Association of Certified Fraud Examiners.

Slicing your data

- Ensure that you are logged in as an administrator to QuickBooks Online.
- You can erase the data for a single QuickBooks Online company using these methods. If you want to completely remove all of your Intuit data, learn more about data management or visit our privacy center.
- Learn more about migrating your lists to a new firm so you can continue using your current lists after starting over.
- Don't use these procedures if you have a QuickBooks Online Accountant. To start afresh, import a brand-new QuickBooks Desktop file.

Creating Custom Reporting with Pivot Tables

- Access QuickBooks Online **by logging in as an administrator.**
- Select **Reports from the Business Overview menu**, or go directly to Reports.

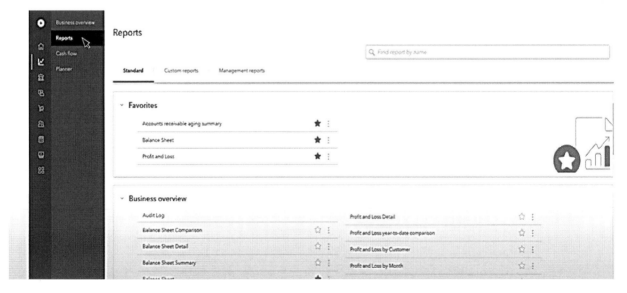

- Select **Make a fresh report**.

- Type the **report's name** here.

- A date range can be chosen from the dropdown.

- Choose **Customize**.

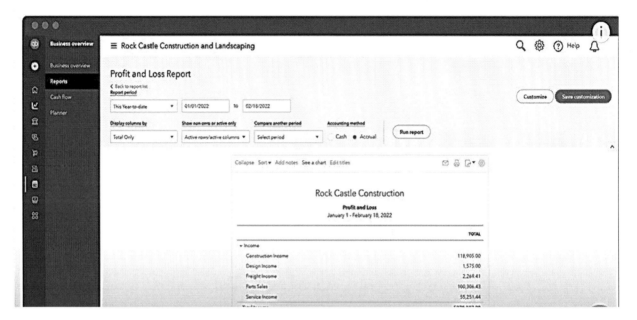

- To expose the available fields, choose **Column**s, search for the subject you wish to report on, and then pick it.

- Any fields you want to see in the report should be **selected**.

  ○ It's possible that some fields won't cooperate in a report. Non-compatible fields won't be available when you choose one.

  ○ Custom fields that you have used show up in this list.

  ○ To eliminate all fields, choose **Clear All**.

- Select **Layout**, then select and drag **the listed field**s into the desired order to change the order in which the selected fields display.

- Utilize a pivot table to add up and total the data in your report.

  ○ Select the **value field** you wish to summarize after choosing the fields to categorize in the rows and columns.

  ○ To add a totals row or column, choose **Show totals**.

- After choosing Rows, Columns, and Values, a pivot table will appear in place of the report view. To restore the report to its default view, toggle off the Show pivot table.

- To group and subgroup line items by any column, use Group.

    - To compute totals, averages, or percentages for numerical groups, select **Edit group computations**.

    - Select **expand** to see the details inside a group when a report is grouped.

- To examine only particular entries, use **Filter**. Select **the action**, decide what you want to filter by, and then pick a value from the list. You can use several filters.

- The Save option will save your report. The report can be changed at any moment.

- To export the data to a spreadsheet, choose **Export.**

Understanding pivot table requirements

- The Pivot Table must-have titles for each of its columns.
- One row should contain only the title.
- Each item in a column needs to be of the same data type (numbers, dates, or strings).
- There shouldn't be any merged cells in the data table.
- Subtotals and grand totals shouldn't be shown in the data table (unless you use a dynamic table).
- There shouldn't be any empty rows or columns in the table (if an empty row or column remains, Excel will treat the table as two different ones).
- Don't alter the field titles after establishing a pivot table because doing so will cause the values to be lost.

Adding fields

To make the data easier to read and scan for details, you could choose to improve the report structure and format after establishing a Pivot Table and adding the fields that you want to study. You can alter the PivotTable form as well as how fields, columns, rows, subtotals, empty cells, and lines are shown to alter the layout of a PivotTable. You can use a predetermined style, banded rows, and conditional formatting to alter the Pivot Table's appearance.

- In the field section, tick the box **next to each field's name**. The field is positioned by default in the layout section, however, you can move the fields around if you'd like.

  Online Analytical Processing (OLAP) date and time hierarchies are added to the Column Labels area by default, while text fields are added to the Row Labels area and numeric fields to the Values section.

- After performing a right-click on the field name, choose the necessary command. To position the field in a particular location in the layout section, choose to **Add to Report Filter, Add to Column Label, Add to Row Label, or Add to Values**.

- When dragging a field between the field section and an area in the layout section, click and hold **the field name** while doing so.

Removing fields

- Click on the **Pivot table**. This causes the ribbon's PivotTable Tools tab to appear.
- If necessary, click **Field List** in the **Show group of the Analyze or Options tab** to show the **PivotTable Field List**. The PivotTable's Show Field List option can also be chosen by performing a right-click.
- One of the following actions can be taken in the PivotTable Field List to remove a field:
  - Uncheck the box next to the field name in the **PivotTable Field List**.
  - Click the field name in a layout area, then select **Remove Field**.
  - In the layout section, select a field name and hold it while dragging it away from the pivot table field list.

Spreadsheet Sync

- Go to **Data > Pivot table on your Google Sheet** after opening it.

- Choose the **data range** from which you will build the pivot table. I have chosen the suggested range in this case, which contains all of the sheet's data. Select **"OK."**
- To set up the pivot table in the current sheet, select **Existing sheet**, or to build it on a different sheet, select **New sheet**. I decided to make the pivot table in the current sheet because this dataset had space for it. Click Create after that.
- Choose where your pivot table will be placed on the current sheet. Click **OK** and then **Create** when you're done.
- Your pivot table and the **Pivot Table Editor** should now be visible on the sheet's far right side.
- You can choose the data to view in the pivot table and how to view it by clicking the **Add button** that is located next to each table feature. Select the data you want to use in your pivot table by clicking **Add next to Row.**
- You can choose how you want to calculate the data in "Values." You can compute and create new values that aren't already contained in your data using the Calculated Field.

Activity

1. Open excel reports you have imported to QuickBooks automatically.
2. Look through the Excel reports and also filter the data, and slice the data in the report.
3. What are pivot tables?
4. Create a custom report with the use of pivot tables.
5. List five (5) requirements for a pivot table.

PART 4

FEATURES FOR ACCOUNTANTS

CHAPTER 16

INTRODUCING QB ACCOUNTANT

The needs of an accountant are different from those of a customer; for instance, accountants must operate in numerous QBO companies, whereas clients typically only work in one.

Additionally, accountants must perform tasks for clients' businesses that the clients are not required to perform, such as creating journal entries to accurately classify income or costs and write off bad debts. They utilize QuickBooks Online for Accountants to meet the requirements of accountants (QBOA). You, the accountant, can open client QBO firms using the front-end interface that QBOA offers. The features for the client's subscription level Simple Start, Essentials, Self-Employed, Plus, or Advanced are available to you when you open a certain client's firm.

Getting Started with QuickBooks Online Accountant

It costs nothing to create a QBOA subscription account, and the subscription is cost-free as long as you use it. For more information, speak with Intuit. You can enroll in the Intuit Wholesale Pricing program to earn lower QBO pricing for each client subscription you oversee.

A free QBO company that you can use for your own QuickBooks company is one of the benefits of signing up for a QBOA subscription account.

Open your browser and go to http://quickbooks.intuit.com/accountants/online to set up a QBOA account. Click the Sign Up for Free link on the left side of the website that loads.

A free QBO company that you can use for your own QuickBooks company is one of the benefits of signing up for a QBOA subscription account.

Open your browser and go to http://quickbooks.intuit.com/accountants/online to set up a QBOA account. Click the Sign Up for Free link on the left side of the website that loads, then click

Setting up your Team

Ensure that everyone in your company has access to QuickBooks. Here's how to update and add team information.

- Activate QuickBooks Online Accountant by **logging in as the administrator or as a user** with full access rights. For your accounting staff, find out more about access levels.
- Select the **Team menu**.
- Choose to **Add user**.
- Enter **the information for your teammate**, then click **Next**.
- Choose **an access level** from the **Access menu**. Next, choose **Next.**
- Choose **the clients** for which you want your team member to have administrator rights.
- When finished, choose **Save**.

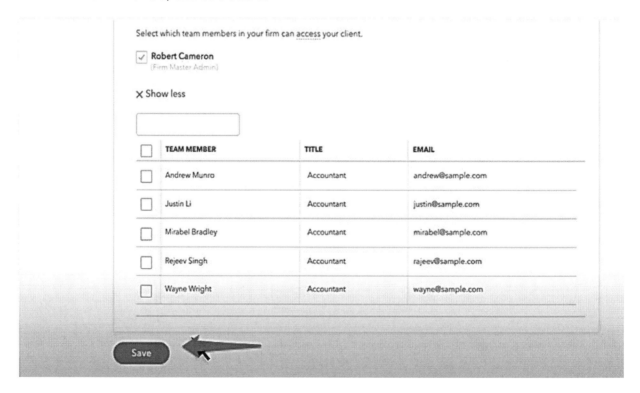

Assigning lead accountants

You can designate lead accountants for particular clients in QuickBooks Online Accountant. Lead accountants manage their clients' QuickBooks bookkeeping while serving as their main point of contact. To appoint a lead accountant to a customer, follow these steps.

Step 1: Assign a lead accountant to a client

You can instantly become a lead accountant in one of two ways:

- If a client personally asks you to serve as their accountant.
- Adding a customer and making a corporate file for them.

The lead accountant has access to the client's books in both situations. Tip: If your company's other accountants have access to the customer's books and can evaluate them, they can also perform bookkeeping for the client.

The primary admin function and the role of the head accountant are entirely distinct. Sometimes, but not usually, the same person fills both positions.

Step 2: Change a client's lead accountant

- Become a principal admin **by logging into QuickBooks Online Accountant**. Lead accountants can only be assigned by firm administrators.

- Select **Clients** from the menu.

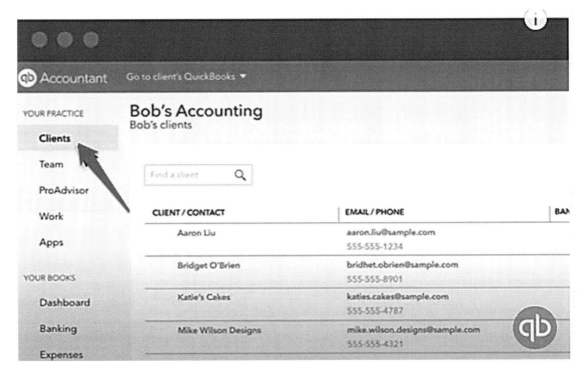

- Choose **the filtering icon**.
- Choosing **Edit leads**.
- Locate the customer for whom you wish to change the lead.
- In the Lead column, choose a **new lead accountant.**
- Choose **Save**.

You can also choose to assign more than one client to the same lead accountant;

- For each client, check the **appropriate box**.
- Choose the **lead accountant** from the **Assign to menu**.
- Choose **Save**.

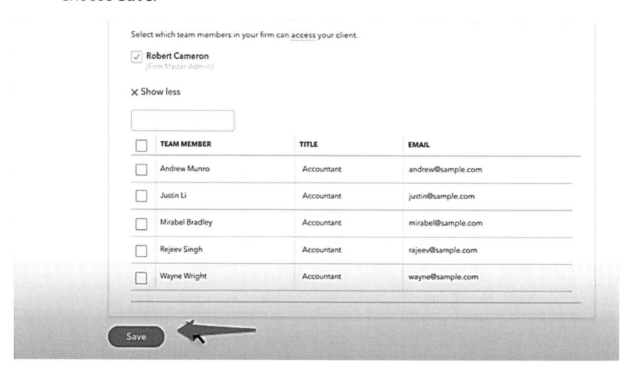

Examining the QB Accountant Interface

The QBOA interface is designed to provide accountants with the resources they require to manage numerous clients. Regardless of where you are working in the QBOA interface, two things consistently appear:

- The navigation bar is located on the page's left side.
- On the left and right sides of the green QBOA toolbar, which runs across the top of the page, are tools. The toolbar at the top of the website is black when you work for a client QBO company.

The different pages of QBOA are displayed using the Navigation bar. The Your Practice and Your Books views are two options in the Navigation bar that show several views and modify the toolbar options in QBOA. The Navigation bar and the QBOA toolbar are discussed in detail in the following two sections for each of these views.

Using Your Practice commands

When you first log in to QBOA, the Clients page of the Your Practice view is displayed on the QBOA Home page by default. Your clients are listed on the Clients page. You would utilize the Navigation bar and click Clients under Your Practice to get to this page if you wanted to return to the list of your clients after seeing another section of QBOA.

You can look up a client, examine a summary of each client, and open a client's QBO company on the Clients page. The Clients page's appearance can also be modified.

Toolbar commands

A toolbar with the following buttons may be seen at the top of the interface, from left to right:

- **The accountant button**: You can view the Client List in another fashion with this button, which features the QuickBooks logo.

- **The Menu button**: This button, which is made up of three horizontal lines, toggles the visibility of the Navigation bar.

- **The Go to Client's QuickBooks drop-down button**: This list box allows you to show a list of your clients; clicking a name in the list brings up the client's business.

- **The Search box**: A list of recent transactions or reports is displayed when you click in this box; you can either click an item in the list or type in the box to search for a specific transaction or report.

- **The plus sign (+) icon**: With the help of the Create menu, which is accessible from the QBOA Home page, you can create a client or a user. You can generate transactions and more using the Create menu while working in your own QBO company or one of your clients' QBO companies.

- **The Gear button**: To view the Gear menu, click this icon. The options you can choose for your own business, your client's business, and your QBOA account are displayed in the Gear menu. You may also access the QBO sample firm from the Gear menu; read more about doing so in the section that follows this chapter for more information.

- **The ProAdvisor Profile button**: You can set up information that Intuit includes in the ProAdvisor directory by clicking this button, which appears to the right of the Gear button. This is the spot to brag about yourself since prospective clients can find you through the ProAdvisor directory.

- **The Help button**: To access the Help menu and do a search for assistance on any subject, click this button. In QBOA, all screens include access to help that is based on the current context. The options that are given when you select Help from a transaction screen depend on the kind of transaction you were viewing at the time.

Adding Companies to the Client List

The individual who creates the QBOA account, known as the master administrator in QBOA jargon, can set up as many other users as you need if your accounting company has more than one person who needs access to client QBO firms. The other users can access the customers that the master administrator designates with their own login information, and for those clients, the QBOA user can access the accountant tools.

Inviting you to be the accountant user

When adding additional users to a QBOA account, the master administrator or any firm member who has full access rights does so. QBOA then sends an email to the additional firm members, who I will refer to as invitees for the purposes of this article. As soon as an invitee accepts, QBOA prompts him to create his own QBOA login information. To create a new user in a QBOA account, adhere to the following steps:

- Sign **in to QBOA**

- Select **Team in the Navigation bar.**

- Select the **Add User button**.

- Enter the name, email address, and title of the team member you wish to add on the **Add User wizard's first page.**

- Choose **Next.** The Add User wizard's second page opens. You provide the privileges connected to your company that you want to grant the team member on this page. You can choose to put up a team member with customized access; this team member has access to particular clients' books but not to the firm's books or to firm administration tasks.

- Choose **the type of access** you want to give to the team member. You can provide Basic, Full, or Custom access; the right side of the page features descriptions of each category of access. Give those team members who need access to your own company's books Full Access. To grant a team member access to only QBO customer companies, assign Basic access.

- Click **Next** in the lower right corner of the page.

- Deselect **clients** as needed.

- Tap **Save**. The new user is added to your team by QBOA, who also gives them the status of Invited. Additionally, the Status column on the Team screen shows that QBOA issued the user an email invitation to join your team. The user's status on the Team page in QBOA changes to Active after responding to the QBOA invitation.

When the recipient clicks the Accept Invite button on the email invitation they received from QBOA, a screen displaying their user ID or email address appears, asking them to create a password and, if they have been given full access, a security question and answer. The login information is set up by QBOA and displayed along with a Success message once the invitee fills out the form and clicks Create Account. The invitee then hits Continue. The team member is then logged in by QBOA with the customers he has been given access to as well as his allotted rights.

Adding a client to your practice

A new client is wonderful. Using QuickBooks to connect with clients makes keeping track of their books much simpler. To get their information, add them to your company. If a client asks you to be their accountant, you can also make direct changes to their accounts.

Add clients who already have QuickBooks

Ask your client to accept you as their accountant if they already use QuickBooks Online or Self-Employed:

- The invite should be sent to the email address you use for your **QuickBooks Online Accountant business**, so ask your client to do that.

- Click the **Accept Invitation link** in the invitation email after opening it.

- Use your **login name and password to log in**.

- Choose the **QuickBooks Online Accounting company** you want to connect your client with if you have multiple.

QuickBooks links their accounts to your business and adds them to your customer list when you accept the invitation. Now that their books are out for evaluation and revision.

Adding clients who don't use QuickBooks

Add your client to your company even if they don't use QuickBooks so that all of their information is in one place:

To access the Clients menu in QuickBooks Online Accountant, click.

- Select **Client Add**.

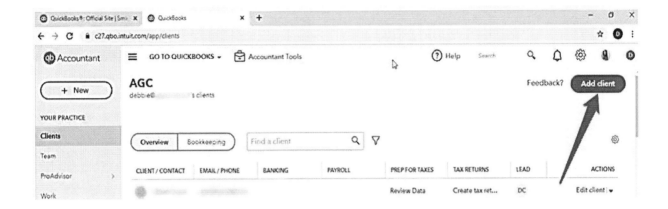

- Choose between **Business and Individual**.

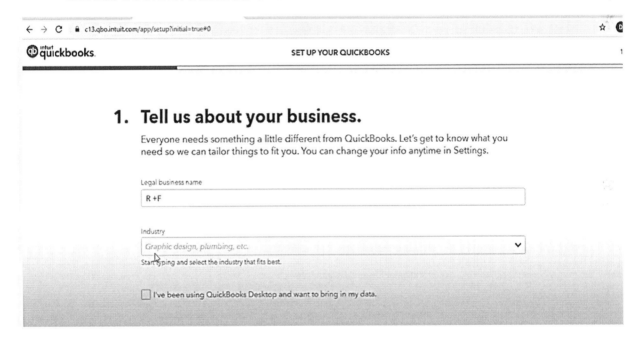

- Enter **the client's information**.
- Choose **No subscription** from the Products section.
- When finished, choose **Save**.

Accepting primary admin rights from your client

The main user with access to every area of the QuickBooks account is the primary admin. The most privileged user type is this one. They can perform all administrative duties and manage all users. The account's initial creator is automatically designated as the principal admin.

Here's how to switch this role to another QuickBooks user if you need to replace the primary admin.

You can give an existing QuickBooks user the principal admin position. Alternatively, if the person isn't already a user of QuickBooks, you can add them as a new user. Once they have been added, give them the primary admin role.

To transfer the primary admin position, you must be able to login in as that user. You can ask to be the principal admin if the one who is currently in that role has left the organization. To assign the role to an existing user, follow these steps.

Log in to QuickBooks Online as the primary administrator on hand. You can retrieve your user ID or password if you're having trouble logging in.

- Choose **Settings**.
- Choose to **Manage users**.
- Locate the user you want to serve as the main administrator.
- Verify that they are labeled as an administrator in the User Type field. If not, choose **Edit** to modify their role to the administrator.
- In the Action area, click the tiny arrow. Select **Make primary admin** after that.

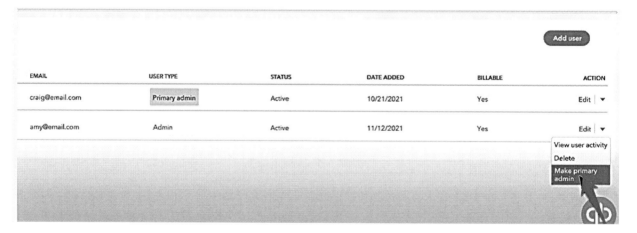

- Selec**t Reset primary** admin to validate the modification.

- Exit **QuickBooks now**.

Transferring primary admin rights to your client

You can also take on the role of their main administrator when a client asks you to serve as their accountant or when you set up a company file for them. This enables you to undertake administrative duties for them, such as managing rights and data.

- You can transfer the role if your client wants to take over as the main administrator for their company file. Here's how to give them their original admin access back.

- Join QuickBooks Online Accountant as the main administrator for the client's business.

- Go to **QuickBooks** by clicking **the link**.

- Choose and open **the QuickBooks Online company** for your client. Tip: You can also find your client in the Clients menu, then pick the QuickBooks icon to the right of their name.

When you're in the QuickBooks Online company of your client:

- Choose **Manage** users under **Settings**.
- On the list, locate **your client**.
- Make primary admin by selecting the selection in the **Action column**.
- To approve the transfer, adhere to the on-screen instructions.

Working with the Client List

Your clientele is constantly expanding. It's simple to keep your client list current in QuickBooks Online Accountant. Keep in mind that the system has a cap of about 2000 clients per QBOA firm. We advise consolidating the client list for larger firms with 2000 or more clients and setting up a new QBOA firm to handle the additional clients.

- Click **Clients Menu** in QuickBooks Online Accountant.

- The customer list includes information about your clients, including the name of their head accountant. You can also check the progress of tasks like tax returns and tax preparation.

- Select **a client's name** to view additional information. You can see what QuickBooks products they have, documents you've emailed them, and tax return information by clicking on the tabs on their profile.

Customizing the Client List

Why should your customer list in QuickBooks Online Accountant (QBOA) appear that way when you wouldn't prefer to see your clients as a single, lengthy alphabetical list? Using the new client groups functionality in QBOA, you can control and customize how your clients are displayed.

You can classify and display your clients using this functionality in a way that is appropriate for your practice. You will be able to establish grouping names and then just drag and drop clients into the proper category, whether you choose to organize your business by client type or frequency of activity.

Make a big list much easier to manage

You may quickly create and add your clients to groups using the client list capability. You may add, update, and reorder groups by simply

- clicking on **manage groups**.

Drop and drag with ease

By choosing your customer records and dropping them into your new group, you can add multiple clients to it. Additionally, you can easily move big groups by using the "move to group" button at the top of the client list display.

The client's name, email address, and phone number have been updated on the client list page as well, putting company contact information in your fingers. You only need to click the "edit client" option to make changes.

Practice right in your pocket

Never before has it been so simple to contact clients on the go. You can use your mobile device to access QuickBooks Online Accountant, keeping you updated at all times. Simply open your client list on your mobile device and tap the call, text, or email button to get in touch with a client. Easy!

Removing Clients from Your Client List

You can permanently delete clients if you're the main administrator for your QuickBooks Online Accountant company. You are no longer able to use their services or complete any work in areas like tax preparation. The subscription to QuickBooks Online is not terminated when a client is deleted.

Follow the steps below to have a client deleted;

Make sure your client names a new primary admin if you are now the company's primary administrator.

- Remove the client from your ProAdvisor discount program if they are a part of it. After updating their billing information, your client has complete access to their accounts.

- Log in as an administrator to **QuickBooks Online Accountant**.
- Choose **Clients**.
- Locate and choose **the name of the client** you wish to remove.
- Choose to **Delete permanently** from the Edit client dropdown menu.
- To confirm, click **Yes**.

Only the client's QuickBooks profile is deleted when you delete a client who is also connected through ProConnect Tax Online. Their ProConnect profile is unaffected.

ProAdvisor Preferred Pricing versus ProAdvisor Revenue Share

Signing Up for ProAdvisor Preferred Pricing

The new ProAdvisor Preferred Pricing program, which is solely offered to accountants, offers the only permanent discount option for QuickBooks Online and all associated QuickBooks goods and services.

For subscriptions you add, upgrade, or downgrade using QuickBooks Online Accountant, ProAdvisor Preferred Pricing is applicable.

For QuickBooks Online, QuickBooks Online Payroll, and QuickBooks Time, your business and clients will receive the best long-term price. Select the strategy that works best for you and your clients by billing the subscription alongside the services provided by your organization or by offering your clients special discounts directly. When you add clients, you may make sure they are initially set up with the appropriate QuickBooks goods and services.

Adding existing clients to your consolidated billing

You can add clients to your ProAdvisor Preferred Pricing if they currently subscribe to QuickBooks Online on their own or are still covered by the wholesale or ProAdvisor discount plan from their prior accounting company.

When you add a client who already has a QuickBooks Online subscription to the ProAdvisor Preferred Pricing program, we'll charge them at the standard price rate without any special offers. The costs and billing for them are now handled by your company.

- Request that the main administrator of your client log into QuickBooks Online.
- Select **Account and settings under Settings**.
- The **Billing & Subscription tab** should be chosen.
- Choose the link that says **Allow billing transfer to your accountant.**
- The accounting company you want to transfer billing to should be chosen.
- Choose **Allow transfer**.

You can complete the transfer if your client gives you the go-ahead:

- Select Subscriptions and billing under Settings in **QuickBooks Online Accountant.**
- The Your subscriptions tab should be chosen.
- Choose to **Add current clients**.
- For the clients you want to add, tick the appropriate box.
- Choose **Add Clients**.

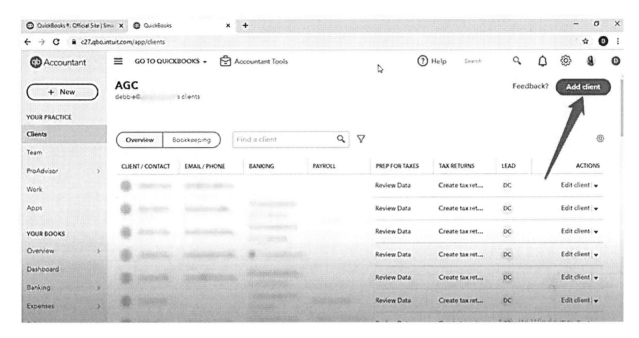

Removing clients from your consolidated billing

Your client may withdraw their request if they change their mind and you haven't agreed to the transfer:

- Request that the main administrator of your client log into **QuickBooks Online**.
- Select **Account and settings under Settings.**
- The **Billing & Subscription tab** should be chosen.
- Choose the link that says **Allow billing transfer to your accountant**.
- Select **Cancel permission** next to the name of your company.

Stopping consolidated billing

Subscriptions can always be taken out of your client discounts. By navigating to Account & Settings in QuickBooks Online and choosing "Discontinue," the QuickBooks customer may at any moment cancel their membership. The prorated refund will not be sent to the QuickBooks customer. The client discount for the subscription cannot be removed without also terminating the user rights of the QBOA customer.

Signing up for ProAdvisor Revenue Share

Subscriptions can always be taken out of your client discounts. By navigating to Account & Settings in QuickBooks Online and choosing "Discontinue," the QuickBooks customer may at any moment cancel their membership. The prorated refund will not be sent to the QuickBooks customer. The client discount for the subscription cannot be removed without also terminating the user rights of the QBOA customer.

With this subscription, you can give your customer a 50% discount for three months combined with a free month, as well as 30% off base costs and 15% off employee fees for a full year. Since the client pays the subscription directly, you can spend less time maintaining subscriptions.

- Open **QuickBooks Online Accountant and log in**. choosing the gear icon
- Select **Billing and Subscriptions**.
- Click the **Get started** button after selecting the Revenue share distributions option.
- Complete the **application and submit it.**

Using Your Free QuickBooks Online Advanced Subscription

The most robust QuickBooks Online package, QuickBooks Online Advanced, was created to give complicated and expanding organizations more insights, increased productivity, and peace of mind so they can concentrate on making important decisions. The 60-Day Money Back Guarantee from Intuit is bundled with these potent features.

The features available in this subscription include;

- Includes 25 users plus up to 3 accountant seats
- QuickBooks Priority Circle & 24/7 support
- On-demand online training
- Integrates with premium apps
- Advanced business analytics & insights
- Automatic data backup and restore
- Track income and expenses
- Batch invoices & expenses

- Customize access by role
- Track project profitability
- Automate workflows
- Invoice & accept payments
- Track inventory
- Chart of accounts entries (unlimited)
- Tracked classes & locations (unlimited)
- Capture & organize receipts
- Batch invoices & expenses
- Manage 1099 contractors
- Track time and miles
- Track sales & sales tax

Activity

1. What is the difference between QuickBooks Online (QBO) and QuickBooks Online Accountant (QBOA)
2. Activate QBOA and set up a team for your company.
3. Pick a lead accountant.
4. What are practice commands?
5. Add companies to the client list.
6. Add any client of your choice to your practice.
7. Transfer your admin rights to the client you have added.
8. Customize your client list.
9. Add a client and then remove the client again from the client list.
10. What is the difference between ProAdvisor preferred pricing and ProAdisor revenue share?
11. Sign up for either ProAdvisor preferred pricing or ProAdisor revenue share.

CHAPTER 17

MANAGING YOUR CLIENTS' BOOKS

When seen with QBOA, a client's QBO company has a somewhat different appearance. This chapter examines the user interface that appears when a client QBO firm is opened from QBOA. In order to ensure that everything goes smoothly for both of you, it also covers several aspects of a client QBO company that you might wish to review for your client.

Opening a Client's Company

From the Clients tab, open a client's company by clicking the QuickBooks logo on the client's line in the list (the circle with the letters q and b in it). As an alternative, you can use the Go to Client's QuickBooks list on the QBOA toolbar, which is always available and makes switching between client QBO companies simple. Open the list, then choose the name of the business you wish to open.

Utilizing the Client Overview page

You can use this website to gain a sense of the situation at your client's QBO company. Use the Go to Client's QuickBooks list box on the QBOA toolbar to access the client's QBO company and display the Client Overview. Next, select Overview from the Navigation bar's tabs. Information on the client's subscriptions and associated apps is displayed at the top of the Client Overview page.

The client's financial activity is detailed in the list of accounts in the middle of the client overview page; these accounts can either be set up as bank accounts or credit card accounts. The client QBO company's status in relation to difficulties you frequently encounter in client QBO companies is displayed at the bottom of the client overview page, providing you with leads on data you might need to investigate in the client QBO company.

Be mindful that the Client Overview page does not have any links other than the View Chart of Accounts link at the bottom. Although you will undoubtedly want to check the client's Chart of Accounts, I advise you to first review the company setup information.

Examining company setup information

To ensure that the customer QBO company employs the proper accounting technique, employer EIN, and legal business organization, you evaluate company setup information. You can also choose whether to include account numbers in the Chart of Accounts (you can choose to do so, but I've never met an accountant who wished to do so). Reviewing company settings involves the following steps:

- Check out the client QBO firm by opening it. On the QBOA Clients page, you can either use the list of clients in the toolbar or the QuickBooks logo.

- To access the Settings menu, click **the Gear button** on the right side of the QBOA toolbar.

- Click **Account and Settings** in the Your Company group on the **Gear menu's left side**. The Account and Settings dialog box's left side displays the Company tab. (When you create a company for a client, QBO shows the Company Profile dialog box and asks you to provide the company's email, address, city, state, and zip. Although the dialog box must be displayed, you can close it by clicking the X in the top right corner of the form.)

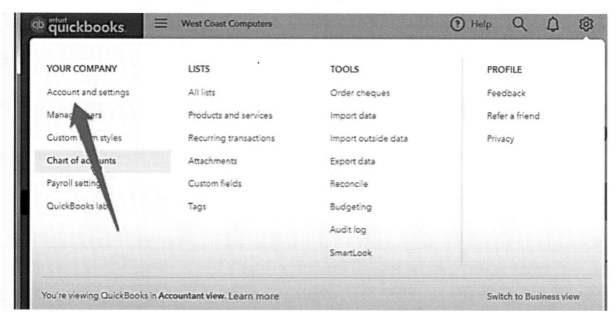

- Go over the settings again. Set or correct the Company Name, Legal Name, and Employer ID in specific (EIN). Click **any setting** or the pencil that appears in the area of the settings' upper right corner to make changes. The setting options are made available by QBO; make your selections and then click Save.

- Click on **Usage** located on the left side of the **Account and settings dialog box**.

- Select **Advanced** located on the left side of the **Account and Settings dialog box**.

- Review the settings. Configure or make corrections to the following

  - The options in the Accounting section, specify the QBO company's accounting technique and financial and tax year details.

  - The tax form setting is found in the Company Type section.

  - You can regulate how numbers are used in the Chart of Accounts by adjusting the parameters in this area.

  - When duplicate check numbers and bill numbers are used, warnings are displayed, according to the settings in the Other Preferences section.

- Examine any further options you believe may want your attention on any of the pages in the Account and Settings dialog box.

- To save your changes, click **Done**.

Taking a look at the chart of accounts

You should probably inspect your client's Chart of Accounts to make sure it displays the way you want it in addition to checking the company settings. To access your client's Chart of Accounts, click the link at the bottom of the Client Overview page. The Navigation bar is another option:

- Click **Accounting Chart of Accounts** in the client QBO company Navigation bar. A page with the Chart of Accounts appears. Be advised that a screen can appear inviting you to peek inside; if this happens,

- click the **See Your Chart of Accounts** button.

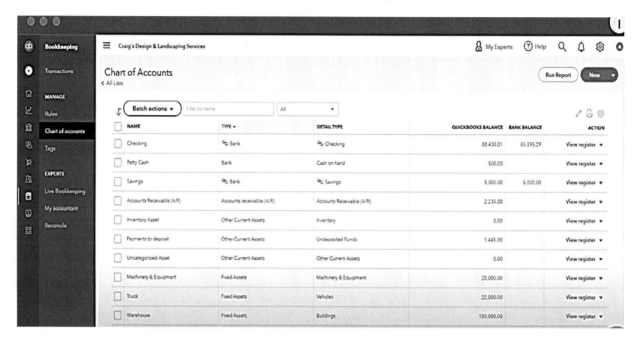

The Chart of Accounts page displays a column for account numbers at the left side of the page if you decide to select the option to use account numbers while examining company settings, and the Batch Edit button is visible in the top right corner and has the appearance of a pencil. The Batch Edit button can be used to add account numbers.

Reviewing list information

You can also look at the list's details. You can obtain a summary of information about clients, partners, and workers by clicking on the links in the Navigation bar.

- Click **Sales** in the Navigation bar (it may also say Invoicing, depending on the selections made when the organization was created), then

- click **Customers** to view customers.

- Clic**k Expenses** in the Navigation bar, followed by Vendors, to access vendor details. Click **Workers in the Navigation bar, followed by Employees**, to access employee data. When you select **Workers > Contractors**, QBO shows the 1099 suppliers that the customer has configured.

The status bar at the top of the page can be used on any of these pages, with the exception of the Contractors page (where payroll must be configured before you can use it), to show activity over the previous year. If you click one of the elements on the status bar, QBO filters the list so that you can view that specific subset of the list. To view just clients with past-due invoices or only customers with unbilled activity, for instance, you can filter the list of customers on the Customers page. Additionally, you can execute batch activities using the Batch Actions button (located directly above the table), such as sending a batch of emails to customers.

If your list is lengthy, you can search for a specific list entry using the text box next to the Batch Actions button. Click the appropriate heading under the Batch Actions button to sort the list by name or open balance. Be aware that a people list can import names.

- Click the **Gear button in the QBOA toolba**r to view **additional listings**. You can choose to examine any of three typical lists in the Lists area of the Gear menu that opens (the Products and Services list, the Recurring Transactions list, or the Attachments list). Alternatively, you can display the Lists page, which you can use to browse any list other than a people-oriented list, by clicking **All Lists** at the top of the Lists section.

Discovering QuickBooks Online Accountant Tools

Discover the specific tools available to accountant users. Only accountants who use QuickBooks Online Accountant have access to these resources.

These tools improve the efficiency of evaluating your QuickBooks Online clients' accounts. They enable you to accomplish more in less time.

Reviewing reports

Although QBOA provides various reports of particular interest to accountants, reports in QBO operate similarly to those in QBO. When you open a customer QBO firm and choose Accountant Reports from the Accountant Tools menu, the Reports page is displayed. When you scroll down, all of the reports are arranged into different groups, with the reports that have been designated as favorites appearing first. You might be especially interested in the Reports in the For My Accountant group because they include reports like the Adjusted Trial Balance report, the

Adjusting Journal Entries report, and others. You need to scroll down the page when reading these reports because I couldn't show them all.

Basic Company Financials and Expanded Company Financials are two tailored management-style reports that QBOA lists when you select Management Reports from the Accountant Tools menu or click the Management Reports button that appears on the Reports page. Each report has a table of contents and an appealing cover page that displays a collection of reports. To view either report onscreen or download it as a PDF file to your computer, click the View option in the Action column.

The P&L, Balance Sheet, Statement of Cash Flows, A/R Aging Detail, and A/P Aging Detail reports are all included in the Expanded Company Financials report. All reports aside from the Aging Detail reports are included in the Basic Company Financials report. You can add or remove reports, change the appearance of the pages in the report, and choose whether or not pages like the table of contents display in the report by selecting Edit after clicking the down arrow in the Actions column. You can email these reports, export the data to PDF or DOCX files, and duplicate them so that you can create your own set of management reports by using the same down arrow in the Action column.

You may access customized and saved reports by selecting My Custom Reports from the Accountant Tools menu or the Custom Reports option on the Reports page. Additionally, you may define default report dates and the accounting basis by selecting Reports Tools from the Accountant Tools menu. Additionally, you may examine and modify the company's closing date information as well as the status of account reconciliation for credit card and cash accounts.

Examining voided and deleted transactions

The Audit Log can be seen by selecting Voided/Deleted Transactions from the Accountant Tools menu. The Audit Log's default view provides details about transactions that have been nullified or removed. However, you may establish a range of additional filters by selecting the Filter option in order to observe other types of transactions and events.

Looking at Books Review

The incomplete transactions, reconciliations, and account balances are the three key bookkeeping areas that the Books review tool concentrates on. It outlines important tasks so you may prioritize work and quickly tie up any loose ends. You can also add your own custom tasks for review. Using QuickBooks, you may even communicate with your client directly about transactions, send and receive messages, and upload documents.

Step 1: Clean up clients' books

If your client's books need cleaning up, start there by selecting the Setup option. In order to produce high-quality books and avoid duplication of effort between monthly bookkeeping and cleanup, use a bookkeeping setup.

- Open a **QuickBooks Online account** for a client.

- Review of **Select Books**.

- Choose the **Setup tab**. Select the **Monthly option,** then choose **Cleanup** if you can't see it.

- To display a different month, select **Edit** next to the date. Reviews of books are typically for the preceding month by default.

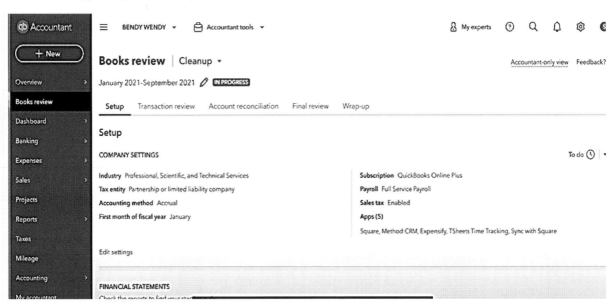

Step 2: Fix incomplete transactions

Transactions with erroneous or missing information are displayed in the Transaction review tab. Uncategorized transactions, transactions without payees, and unapplied payments are all flagged by QuickBooks.

There will be a blank line in the column if there is no data. To open a transaction and make changes, choose it. You can work together with your clients to fill up any gaps in transaction-level data. This is how:

- Choose a **single transaction or more**. Pick **Ask client** in the Actions pop-up that appears.

- The name and description fields on the Create a request form are automatically filled out together with the request for lacking transaction-level details. These parameters can be changed, including the deadline for a client response and the inclusion of new documents.

- Choose to **Create**. Your client receives an email asking them to access QuickBooks Online and reply with any further transactional information (s).

- In order to access the Requests tab, your customer must first log into QuickBooks, then select My accountant. They can open each request here and describe what they purchased and why.

- You can find the response from your client in the Books review once they have answered your request. View all requests after choosing Client requests.

Step 3: Finish reconciling accounts

Go to the Reconciliation of Accounts tab next. The accounts on this list need to be reconciled.

To begin reconciling an account, choose the account you would like to reconcile. To determine how much work has to be done, use the information in each column as a reference. The Unreconciled column lists unreconciled transactions.

Step 4: Check account balance issues

The financial reports you should review each month are listed on the Final review tab. Open a report by

- selecting **Review**. For the month you choose, **QuickBooks filters report automatically.**

Step 5: Wrapping up clients' book review

In order to prepare your customer for another successful Books review, you may construct and send them a report package through the Wrap-up tab. You can empower yourself to assist and direct your clients in making smart business decisions by using the reports you generate using the Wrap-up tab.

You can close the books, generate reports, and transmit the reports package from here. On this screen, you may also alter the report template.

For each of your clients, you can quickly check the status of the most recent book reviews:

- In QuickBooks Online Accountant, click **Clients**.
- Decide which tab is for bookkeeping.
- Review the column's status for book reviews.
- To view the jobs that are completed or unfinished, choose **the icon** in the Books review column.

Reclassifying transactions

The Reclassify Transactions page opens when you select Reclassify Transactions from the Accountant Tools menu. You don't need to be concerned about the company's closing date if you utilize this page to reclassify transactions.

To filter for the date range and kind of accounts (Profit and Loss or Balance Sheet) you wish to take into consideration, utilize the data in the Accounts section on the left side of the page and the Transactions part on the right side of the page. Following your selection of an account on the page's left side, QBOA shows transactions that match your criteria on the right side of the page. Transactions that show a green circle can be reclassified either individually or collectively.

To reclassify transactions, take the following actions:

- Set **the date range** you want to take into account and the accounting basis on the left side of the page.

- Choose **the type of account** you want to take into account from the View list box: profit and loss or balance sheet accounts.

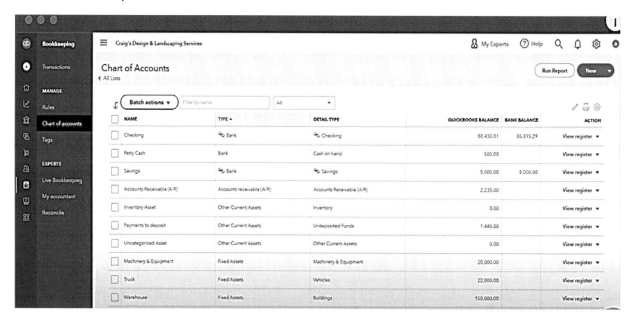

- To view an account's transactions, click **the account name** in the list below the View list box.
- Set filters to display the categories of transactions that you might think about reclassifying above the list of transactions on the right side of the page.
- Select the **transactions** by checking the box next to them to make multiple changes at once.
- Select the **For Select Transactions**, Change check box under the transaction list.
- Taking into account choosing a different account to list.
- Click on the **Reclassify button**.

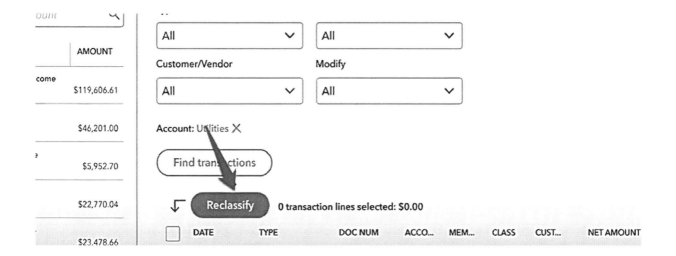

Writing off invoices

The Write Off Invoices page is displayed when you select Write Off Invoices from the Accountant Tools menu. From there, you may view any invoices you might want to write off and write them off to a specific account. You choose filters to display the invoices you want to see at the top of the page. To examine the invoices, choose the age of invoices to view the following;

- Greater than 180 days
- Greater than 120 days
- In the current accounting period
- In a custom date range you set

Date, invoice age, invoice number, client name, original invoice total, and the balance outstanding are all displayed by QBOA on the invoice. Select any bills by checking the box next to them to write them off. Select the account you want to use to write off the bills at the bottom of the page, and then click the Preview and Write Off option.

The Write Off feature makes modifications in the period in which the transaction was originally created rather than the current period, which may have an adverse effect on closed periods.

The Confirm Write-Off dialog box is displayed by QBOA.

- Click **Write Off** if the data in the dialog box is accurate. If not, press **Cancel.**

Closing the books

The Advanced page of the Account and Settings dialog box for the QBO company is displayed when you use the Close Books command from the Accountant Tools menu. The Accounting section's fields, including the field for the books' closure date, can be edited by clicking anywhere inside that section.

Setting a closing date gives you the option to either demand a password to enter changes before the closing date or to enable changes prior to the closing date once QBO offers a warning. To save your changes, click Done.

Understanding the Prep for Taxes page

Before preparing the client's taxes, you evaluate and amend accounts using the Prep for Taxes tool. The Trial Balance page has been replaced with the Prep for Taxes page.

- To preserve the accuracy of the data, the values in the Unadjusted Balance column are locked on the page. You can generate adjusting journal entries for an account by

  - clicking the **Make Adjustment link** in the **Actions column** next to the relevant account by clicking the carats next to the various headings. In the journal entry window that opens when you click the link, QBOA automatically chooses **Is Adjusting Journal Entry check box** so that you can enter the adjusting entry. QBOA displays the Prepare for Taxes page again after you save the entry and notifies you that you changed something.

- Any dollar amount that appears as a link can be clicked to obtain a summary of all the transactions that make up that balance. You can go down to a specific transaction from the report and alter it if necessary.

  - Click the **Back to Prep for Taxes link** at the top of the report page to reopen the Prep for Taxes page after saving the transaction and displaying the report once more. Once more, QBOA alerts you to your adjustment and, once you accept it, changes the Prep for Taxes page to reflect the modification.

- To add notes and attach files to a specific line, use the down arrow in the Actions column. This aids in recalling the rationale behind a specific change.

Make sure that your client's accounts are correctly mapped to lines on tax forms if you use ProConnect Tax Online, Intuit's cloud-based tax preparation software, to prepare their tax return. For corporations using IRS Form 1120 (for corporations) or 1120s, partnerships using IRS Form 1065, nonprofit organizations using IRS Form 990, and sole proprietorships using IRS Form 1040, the Prep for Taxes tool automatically maps the majority of account balances to lines on those tax forms.

Other sorts of business organizations can have accounts manually assigned to tax form lines. Additionally, you can manually allocate tax line assignments on tax forms for accounts that the program does not identify. If you haven't chosen a tax form for the QBO client firm yet, you should be aware that the View Tax Return button doesn't appear to be available.

- Click the **Allocate Tax Line link** to assign an account to a tax form line or to change the line to which an account is assigned. The right side of the screen is where QBOA displays the **Assign Tax Line panel**, which has a list box where you can choose the proper tax form line before clicking **Save**.

After reviewing the Prep for Taxes page and making any necessary corrections, you can transfer the information to ProConnect Tax Online and create a tax return by

- clicking the **Create New Return or Update Existing Return button** (as appropriate) after selecting the **Choose Tax Option button** in the top right corner of the page. You only pay when you print or electronically file a return using **ProConnect Tax Online**; there is no fee to utilize the Prep for Taxes function.

Take a brief look at other accountant tools

A few other tools that simplify the work of accountants may be found in the Accountant Tools menu, like the Reconcile page, where you can choose to reconcile a selected account or check previous reconciliation reports. You can also open the

Journal Entry window or the Chart of Accounts window by selecting one of these options from the Accountant Tools menu. To open a new window in QBOA rapidly, you can use the New Window command.

The last option is ProConnect Tax Online, which opens a new browser window and takes you to the Tax Hub of ProConnect Tax Online where you may view the status of your customers' tax returns. This option can be found under the Accountant Tools menu. ProConnect Tax Online is a separate product with its own options in the Navigation bar, however, it connects to your QBOA account.

Activity

1. Open a client company in your QBOA.
2. Make use of the Client Overview page.
3. Examine company setup information.
4. Make a review of the reports in QBOA.
5. Examine voided and deleted transactions in QBOA.
6. Make a comprehensive study of the book review.
7. What are those things you need to take note of when writing off an invoice?
8. Mention at least four (4) accountant tools.

CHAPTER 18

PRACTICE MANAGEMENT

Look at the Work page in the Navigation pane, which serves as a practice management tool, before getting started with using the QBOA capabilities accessible while you are working in a client's QBO organization. The availability of the Work page in QBOA to all team members in your company makes it possible for you to centralize practice management by utilizing such a tool.

Introducing the Work Page

You can keep track of what has to be done for both your clients and your own company on the Work page. And while the Work page uses the term "projects," keep in mind that these projects are not the same as the ones your clients can create in QBO.

Creating templates

Use the QuickStart templates in the Work menu for a simple project and task setup. To meet the needs of your business or client, you can also develop or modify templates. Utilize them for your ongoing projects to maintain a regular workflow and finish work on schedule. How? Read on.

You can design your own templates. They are utilized to specify the tasks required for a workflow. A unique template can be used for numerous projects.

- Choose **Work** from the **Your Practice section** of the left menu.
- Choose the **Manage templates option**.
- Choose to **Create a template**, then give the template a name.
- Use the options that appear to define the gap between due dates after selecting Repeat to set up recurring due dates.
- In the Details area, enter any details or comments for your team.
- Selec**t Add a task** under the **Tasks heading.** Give the task a name.
- Pick a date from the **Due date drop-down**.

- Set later in order to indicate that the task due date has been configured when a project is set up.

- Offset in order to tie the task due date to the project due date. Insert the number of days before the project due that the task will be due.

  - Include all of the tasks needed in the template.
  - Choose **Save template**.

Creating client requests

You can send your customer a client request if you need them to do something for you, such as respond to a query, upload a document, or perform work for you at their company. The My Accountant tab of the client's firm has it.

- Go to **Work**.
- To create a client request, select **The client request creation** panel.
- Complete the fields.
- (optional) Select **Add document**, then **Close** to attach a file. The maximum file size is 30 MB each.
- Select the **Notify client checkbox** to inform your client about the request.
- Pick **QuickBooks** for the client to publish to.
- Enter **the email, topic, and message** in the preview window.
- Select **Emails that are published** and **sent**.

Managing projects and tasks

Projects can be used to keep track of the work your team has to finish. The work that your team needs to execute to finish the project is represented by tasks, on the other hand. These won't affect the business of your clientele.

- Then click Create **project** under Work. The panel for creating projects appears.
- Complete t**he fields**.
- (Optional) Switch the **repeat button**, then choose the interval, day, and end time if you want your project to repeat at regular intervals.
- Choose **Save**.

You can add tasks to organize the project's work before giving a team member a specific task to do.

- Pick **Add a task** from the Task area.
- Choose **the deadline date** after entering the task's name.
- Choose **the team member** to whom you will assign the assignment from the Assigned to the dropdown menu. For their name to appear in the menu when you assign a job to a new team member, they must first sign in to the account.
- To add particular details, choose to **Add details**.
- Choose **Save**.

You can edit a project in the Work tab if modifications need to be made.

- Select **a client request** after clicking on Work. A panel to edit client requests emerges.
- Select **Close** after making your changes.

Duplicating a project

To duplicate a project's tasks, duplicate the original project. To swiftly create new work items, you can delete or modify them.

- Then select **a project** by going to Work. The project panel for editing appears.
- Choose **Duplicate**.
- Edit the new project's fields.
- Choose **Save**.

Deleting a project

You can remove a project or request from your workboard if it is no longer required.

- Then select a project by going to Work. The customer request or edit project panel appears.
- Select **Delete** after selecting the trash can icon.

Looking at Work page views

Grid View

When you select Work from the Navigation bar, QBOA shows the page in its standard Grid view. Task cards are displayed in the Grid view in date ranges (Due Today, This Week, Next Week, and in the Next 30 days).

Some of what you see on the Work page's Grid view is under your control. For instance, you can filter the page to see information for your company, a certain client, or a member of your team. The Work function also uses information from client QBO companies to automatically provide due dates and tasks for you to complete, such as payroll due dates and related banking transaction reconciliation. You can select the From QuickBooks slider to hide this automatically generated data from view.

You won't notice any sort of visual relationship between activities because the Grid view groups tasks by the due date; in other words, no lines connecting tasks to one another appear because the Grid view isn't a flow chart.

List View

On the Work page, click the List View button in the top right corner to view your projects and tasks in List view (just below the Create Project button). You can access additional filters from this view. You have the option to filter by status and choose a date range of interest in addition to selecting a customer, a team member, and the type of work (project, task, or client request). Additionally, you may still edit any project or task by clicking anywhere on its line to bring up the Edit Project window.

Calendar view

The tasks that are due on any given date are shown in the Calendar view. You can see how many tasks are due on each date on the calendar. When you select a date, QBOA displays the tasks that are due on that day using the right side of the Calendar view.

Communicating with Team Members about Work

The importance of communication in a team setting cannot be overstated, at the risk of sounding obvious. With QBOA, you may send email notifications for a range of events connected to the tasks and projects that are displayed on the Work page. Click the Notifications link at the top of the Work page to open the Notifications tab of the Company Settings dialog box and specify the notifications you want QBOA to deliver to your team.

To toggle email notifications for different actions that happen on the Work page, click the pencil in the upper right corner of the Email section. When finished, click Save before selecting Done to return to QBOA.

Each team member has the ability to manage his notifications. Each team member automatically receives notices of new assignments and due dates, but you may customize the other notifications by having each member log into his or her individual QBOA account.

You may integrate Slack with QBOA if your company utilizes it. Slack is a collaboration tool that fosters team communication. By selecting Connect Now on the Work page, you may add the app to QBOA. Click the Connect Work to Slack button on the Notifications tab of the Company Settings dialog box if you have previously hidden the Slack advertisement.

Activity

1. Create a template that can be used on the work page.
2. Create client requests in your QBOA.
3. Create a project in QBOA and also duplicate the project you created.
4. Mention two (2) views in the work page view.
5. What is the importance of communicating with team members?

CHAPTER 19

AUTOMATING QUICKBOOKS ANALYSIS WITH POWER QUERY

Introducing Power query

A data preparation and transformation engine is Power Query. Power Query includes a Power Query Editor for implementing transformations as well as a graphical interface for obtaining data from sources. The location where the data will be saved depends on where Power Query was utilized because the engine is integrated into many different products and services. You can process data through extract, transform, and load (ETL) using Power Query.

Connecting to QuickBooks Reports

By selecting Settings -> Connections and adding a new connection in the API Server administrative console after deploying the API Server and the ADO.NET Provider for QuickBooks, you can supply the authentication values and other connection properties required to connect to QuickBooks.

There are no connection properties that must be set when connecting to a local QuickBooks instance.

Through the Remote Connector, requests are made to QuickBooks. The Remote Connector utilizes a small, embedded Web server to accept connections while running on the same system as QuickBooks. Users can establish secure connections from distant machines because the server supports SSL/TLS.

- Set **up the API Server** to utilize a variant of the OData protocol that Power Query can understand. Click **Settings -> Server** in the API Server administrative console and set the **Default Version property's value to 3.0**.

- Click **Power Query -> From Other Data Sources -> From OData Feed** from the Excel ribbon, type **the OData URL, then click OK.**

- Define authentication credentials and privacy levels in the following wizard step. Choose Basic authentication, then input the login information for a user who is permitted to submit requests. Enter the user's auth token in the Password field and their chosen username in the Username field.

  Click **Power Query -> Data Source Settings** to modify Power Query's authentication method. Click **Edit Credential** after choosing the **OData stream** from the list. On the Data Source Settings page, from the menu, choose the **privacy level**.

- Power Query now allows you to access QuickBooks data. Expand the OData feed node in the Navigator, right-click a table, and select **Edit** to launch the **Query Editor.** The table data will be shown after this.

Removing header rows

From the Power Query Editor, you want to ignore or eliminate a few unnecessary top rows. You have a choice here between doing it manually and dynamically based on your requirements.

- Go to the **Home tab,** click on **Remove Rows**, and then select **Remove Top Rows** in Power Query to manually ignore the top rows.

- The next question is how many rows you want to remove from the top. Enter your preferred number of rows, then press the **OK button**. The query editor will then no longer display the specified top rows.

Promoting headers

Power Query examines the contents of the file while constructing a new query from unstructured data sources, such as text files. Power Query will attempt to elevate the first row of data to be the column headings for your table if it finds a different pattern for the first row. This section describes how to manually promote headers from rows because Power Query does not always correctly identify the pattern.

The table's top rows must be removed before you may promote the headers. To accomplish that,

- choose to **Remove top rows** from the table option in the preview window's upper-left corner.

Enter the desired number of rows in the Number of rows box of the Remove top rows dialog.

Removing unwanted columns

You can eliminate columns from your query if you don't need them. You can choose to pick one or more columns before removing the selected columns or the unselected ones, or both, i.e. the other columns.

Think about the distinction between eliminating one column and removing further columns. If you opt to remove additional columns before refreshing your data, any new columns that have been added to the data source since the last refresh operation may go undetected since they would still be regarded as additional columns when the query's Remove Column step is run again. If you specifically remove a column, this circumstance won't happen. Data Preview would still display the new columns that have been introduced since the last refresh.

- Locate a previously loaded query from the Power Query Editor, choose a cell in the data, and then choose **Query > Edit** to launch the query.

- Do one more of the following;

  - Select **the column** you want to remove, then choose **Home > Remove Columns > Remove Columns** to remove it.

  - Select the columns with **Ctrl + Click or Shift + Click** to remove many columns at once. The columns may or may not be continuous.

  - Select one or more columns, then choose **Eliminate Other Columns** to remove all columns except the one you've chosen.

Filtering unnecessary rows

You can click Transform Data to launch the Power Query Editor window and eliminate the rows with blank values.

- By selecting the **Remove Empty transformation** from the drop-down menu on the column header, you can remove the entire row if the value of that row in the selected column is empty. This implies that values in other columns which may or may not be blank are not taken into account at all.

Remove Blank Rows is a preferable choice if you want to eliminate the row only if all values (across all columns) are null. It is listed under Remove Rows.

Returning the data to Excel

Data must be transformed in some way to satisfy your data analysis needs. You could, for instance, delete a column, alter the data type, or filter the rows. These actions are all examples of data transformations. Data shaping is another name for the process of applying transformations (and combining) to one or more sets of data.

Consider it this way. A vase begins as a lump of clay that is shaped into a useful and attractive object. Data is identical. It needs to be shaped into a table that meets your demands and makes it possible to create visually appealing reports and dashboards.

Data transformations are facilitated and displayed by Power Query using a special window called the Power Query Editor. In addition to opening when you connect to a data source, create a new query, or load a query, the Power Query Editor also opens when you pick Launch Query Editor from the Get Data command in the Get & Transform Data group.

You can change a lot of things using the user interface. Every transformation is tracked in the background as a step. Using the Advanced Editor's Power Query M Language, you can even edit and create your own steps.

A query is a new representation of the original (and unchanging) data source and is made up of all the transformations you perform to your data connections. Each action is automatically performed when you reload a query. In Excel, queries take the place of the need to manually connect and shape data.

Creating Self-Updating Reports

Setting Power Query to refresh automatically

- Select **Data > Queries** & Connections from the ribbon.
- Select **Properties** from the menu by performing a right-click on the query.
- Select the **Refresh Every n Minutes checkbox** and then type a time frame.
- To close the Query Properties dialog box, click **OK**.

Adding a total row

By checking the Total Row checkbox on the Design tab, you can add totals to a table. The total row drop-down menu also allows you to add a function.

- In a table, pick **a cell.**
- Select **Total Row under Design**.
- The table's bottom is expanded to include the Total row.
- You can choose a function from the total row drop-down menu, including Average, Count, Count Numbers, Max, Min, Sum, StdDev, Var, and others.

Transforming QuickBooks data

- In Excel, select **Data** from the menu.
- Pick **From Additional Sources**.
- Click **From Microsoft Query**.
- To locate the file data source, choose **Browse**. The corporate file and this document are both in the same folder.
- You will be asked to authenticate after choosing the file.

Unpivoting columns

Unpivoting data, also known as flattening data, allows you to arrange similar values in a single column in a matrix format. To make a chart or report, for instance, this is required.

The attribute-value pairs that describe the location at which the new columns cross are unpacked when you unpivot, and you then reorient them into flattened columns:

Follow the steps below to unpivot columns;

- Locate a previously loaded query from the **Power Query Editor**, choose a cell in the data, and then choose **Query > Edit** to launch the query.
- Choose one or more columns you would like to unpivot
- Click on **Transform > Unpivot columns**.

Refreshing reports

You can refresh imported external data to see the most recent additions and deletions in order to keep it current. When you open the workbook or at predetermined intervals are just two of the many options Excel offers for refreshing data.

- Press **Esc** to cancel a refresh. Press the keys **Ctrl + F5** to reload a worksheet. A worksheet can be refreshed by pressing **Ctrl + Alt + F5**.

Activity

1. What is Power Query?
2. Connect Power query to QuickBooks reports.
3. What are header rows and how can they be removed in Power query?
4. Return data imported back to Excel.
5. What are unpivoting data and what are the steps to unpivot columns?

PART 5

SHORTCUTS, TIPS & TRICKS

CHAPTER 20

CHROME & EXCEL SHORTCUTS WORTH KNOWING

officially Chrome The free web browser Google Chrome was developed by Google, Inc., an American multinational company that specializes in Internet-related goods and services like Gmail for email, Google Maps, and Google Docs, to mention a few. Online advertising technologies are where Google makes the majority of its money.

Internet Explorer, Chrome, Firefox, Safari, and QuickBooks Online (QBO) browsers all support using QBO and QBOA. Microsoft Edge is another option, however, it cannot be used to export data to the QuickBooks Desktop version. In my experience, Chrome is the greatest browser for using QBO and QBOA. This chapter is meant to teach you how to use Chrome with QBO and QBOA if you're not familiar with it or haven't used it much. This chapter focuses on guiding you through using and familiarizing yourself with the Chrome interface.

Chrome Keyboard shortcuts

The following are shortcuts used on Chrome keyboard;

Action	Shortcut
Open options in order to print the current page	Ctrl + p
Reload current page	F5 or Ctrl + r
Stop the page from loading	Esc
Browse clickable items moving forward	Tab
Browse clickable items moving backward	Shift + Tab
Browse a file from your computer in Chrome	Ctrl + o + Select a file
Show non-editable HTML source code	Ctrl +u

for the current page	
Return everything on the page to default size	Ctrl +o
Go to the top of the page	Home
Scroll down a webpage, a screen at a time	Space or PgDn
Move your cursor to the beginning of the previous word in a text field	Ctrl + Left arrow
Move your cursor to the next word	Ctrl + Right arrow
Delete the previous word in a text field	Ctrl + Backspace
Open the Homepage in the current tab	Alt + Home
Scroll horizontally on the current page	Shift + Scroll your mouse wheel
Make everything bigger	Ctrl and +
Make everything on the page smaller	Ctrl and -
Turn full-screen mode on or off	F11
Save all open tabs as bookmarks in a new folder	Ctrl + Shift + d

Action	Shortcut
Open the History page in a new tab	Ctrl +h
Open the Chrome Task Manager	Shift + Esc

Set focus on the first item in the Chrome toolbar	Shift + Alt +t
Change focus to unfocused dialog and all toolbars	F6
Open the Find Bar to search the current page	Ctrl + f or F3
Jump to the next match to your Find Bar search	Ctrl + g
Show or Hide the Bookmarks bar	Ctrl + Shift +b
Open the Bookmarks Manager	Ctrl + Shift +o
Set focus on the rightmost item in the Chrome toolbar	F10
Jump to the previous match to your Find Bar search	Ctr + Shift + g
Open the Chrome Help Center in a new tab	F1
Log in a different user or browse as a Guest	Ctrl + Shift +m
Open a feedback form	Alt + Shift +i
Turn on caret browsing	F7
Skip to web contents	Ctrl + F6
Focus on inactive dialogs	Alt + Shift + a
Open a new tab and perform a Google search	Type a search term + Alt + Enter
Move cursor to the address bar	Control + F5
Remove predictions from your address	Down arrow to highlight +Shift + Delete

Opening and activating a new tab

In Chrome, you can have an unlimited number of open tabs. Additionally, you may navigate between and view all of your open tabs. A customized New Tab page based on your browser history appears when you open a new tab.

To move a tab outside of the Google Chrome window, **click and drag it**.

Use the following keyboard shortcut to open a new window:

- **Ctrl + n**

Closing the current tab

At the top right side of the tab,

- Click on the **Close button (X)**. Or make use of the keyboard shortcut; **Ctrl + w**

Navigating to websites faster

Allow Chrome to keep track of your favorite and often visited websites so that you may access them more quickly.

You can access your bookmarks, passwords, and more across all of your devices when you sync to Chrome.

Add a bookmark

- Open **Google Chrome** on your computer.

- Visit the **website** you intend to return to in the future.

- Click **Star Bookmark** this website to the right of the address bar.

Saving open tabs as a bookmark group

To store related pages in one workspace, you can group tabs. Simply right-click any tab and choose Add tab to a new group to create a new tab group.

- Right-click a tab.

- Add **Tab** to **New Group by clicking on it**.

- Select a tab group by clicking its name or by selecting **New Group**.

The tabs in your group will all have the same color when you create them. To find things more quickly, you can give various colors to different groups. To name and select a color for your tab group, simply click the circle next to it.

- To name a tab group, right-click the colored circle next to it.

- Give the tab group a name.

- For the tab group, choose **a color**.

Toggling full-screen mode

By hiding all other programs, Google Chrome's full-screen mode enables users to stop being distracted while using the internet.

Additionally, it conceals the taskbar or dock at the bottom of your screen, making it impossible to launch other programs.

- Open your **Mac or PC and Google Chrome**.

- In the top-right corner of your Chrome window, select the hamburger menu by clicking **the three vertical dots**.

- Next to the Zoom option, select **Full-Screen Mode** by clicking **the button** that resembles an empty square.

- Next to the Zoom option, select **Full-Screen Mode** by clicking **the button** that resembles an empty square.

- In the upper center portion of the screen, an X button will show up. To escape full-screen mode, **click on the box below the screen**.

Opening your home page in the current tab

You may set Google Chrome to launch any page as the startup or home page. Unless you make these two pages identical, they are not the same.

- When you first open Chrome on your device, it displays your startup page.

- When you select Home, you are taken to your homepage.

You might have undesirable software if your homepage, launch page, or search engine has abruptly changed.

Your computer can be infected with malware if you're using it and seeing a startup or homepage that you didn't set. Learn how to prevent Chrome from receiving unauthorized modifications.

Your network administrator can pick your launch page(s) or homepage if you're using a Chromebook at work or school. If that's the case, you can't alter them.

- Open **Google Chrome on your computer.**

- Click **More** in the top right corner, followed by **Settings**.

- Turn on the **Show Home button** in the **"Appearance" section**.

- Choose To utilize the New Tab page or a custom page beneath the **Show Home button.**

Activating a specific tab

- Right-click the tab and choose **Pin** to pin it to the left. The only thing shown on pinned tabs is the site's symbol.

- Right-click a tab and choose **Unpin** from the menu that appears.

- Right-click the tab and select **Move tab** to another window to move it to a separate window. Next, choose the window to which you wish to move it. Ensure that Chrome is open in both windows with the same profile.

Displaying the History page

Chrome allows you to view your browsing history. On a desktop or laptop computer, you can utilize the Journeys view of history to identify similar searches and go on with previously initiated surfing.

The websites you've visited on Chrome in the last 90 days are displayed on your History page. Chrome pages you've visited in Incognito mode, like chrome:/settings or pages you've already erased from your browsing history, are not stored.

Your History page will display websites you've visited over a significantly longer period of time if you're connected to Chrome and synchronizing your history across all of your synced devices. Your Chrome History page won't display webpages from other devices if you've signed out of Chrome.

You can remove some or all of your browsing history from Chrome if you don't want a record of the pages you've viewed there. If you clear your browsing history, it is done across all Chrome-enabled devices where you have signed in and enabled sync. If you'd prefer, you can also turn off the history view for Journeys.

- Open **Google Chrome** on your computer.

- Click **More** in the top right corner.

- Afterward, click **History**.

Your Chrome browser history and searches are categorized and shown in the Journey sections under the "Journeys" tab of your History page. You may quickly locate your prior browsing history here and go on your research with relevant searches. The right side of the page displays a label if you bookmark it or add it to a tab group.

For a look at your journeys

- Open Google Chrome on your computer.
- Enter your search phrases in the address bar.
- When it shows below your address bar, click Resume your research.

The Journeys view is also immediately accessible from the "Chrome History" tab.

- To enable or disable Journeys, select **Turn on Journeys** or **Turn off Journeys** from the **Journeys tab's left menu**.

- To create new tabs for each page of a Journey, Click **More** next to the sought item, and then Open every tab in a new group.

Creating a tab in a new profile

To create a tab in a new profile you have to add a new profile first then follow the steps above to create the tab. Below are steps on how to create a new profile;

- Click **Profile** in the top right corner.
- Select **Add**.
- Select a name and a picture.
- Select **Add**.

Microsoft Excel Keyboard Shortcuts

Many users discover that using an extra keyboard with Excel keyboard shortcuts increases their productivity. Keyboard shortcuts are a necessary substitute for using a mouse for people who have mobility or vision impairments since they can be more convenient than using a touchscreen.

Notes:

- This topic's shortcuts make use of the US keyboard layout. It's possible that the keys on a US keyboard don't exactly match the keys in foreign layouts.

- If a shortcut contains a plus sign (+), pressing multiple keys simultaneously is required.

- When a shortcut contains the comma symbol (,), it signifies that you must press several keys sequentially.

Below are the most used shortcuts in Excel;

To do this	Press
Open a workbook	Ctrl + O
Go to the Home tab	Alt + H
Save a workbook	Ctrl + S
Copy a selection	Ctrl + C

Paste selection	Ctrl + V
Undo recent action	Ctrl + Z
Remove cell contents	Delete
Go to the Page Layout tab	Alt +P
Go to the Data tab	Alt + A
Open the context menu	Windows menu key
Go to the Formula tab	Alt + M

Switching between open documents

It is rather simple to keep organized and move about when working with one Excel file (referred to as a workbook) at a time. Opening a second Excel file could make things a little more challenging. Moving between numerous Excel spreadsheets can be challenging, especially if you need to swiftly look back and forth. Then, rearranging the spreadsheets within several folders will make it more challenging.

As an illustration, consider the process of creating your upcoming budget by using your budget from the previous year or two. It might be rather perplexing if each budget file contains worksheets from various departments. The workbooks can all be opened, but you should only read one at a time. You can also display the workbooks tiled, cascading, side by side, etc.

There are numerous methods for navigating and switching between files. One fantastic feature of many of these techniques is that you can use them to switch between any open files on your computer. The most popular approach is highlighted below.

Switching between worksheets tabs

You can have many worksheets in each of your Excel files (or sheets). Click on the tab of the sheet you want to move to in order to change between them. The tabs are at the left-hand bottom of the screen.

- To access the contents of "Sheet 2," click **the tab** if you are currently on "Sheet 1."

Use the **CTRL + PAGE UP or CTRL + PAGE DOWN** keyboard commands to cycle between the various worksheets if you want to switch between sheets quickly.

Closing an open workbook

All workbooks that you open on a computer that is running a single instance of Excel are opened in a workbook window inside the Excel window. Additionally, you can use the New Window command to create new workbook windows for any worksheet in a workbook (View tab, Window group).

You can either close the workbook as a whole or each of these workbook windows individually (including all of its workbook windows). You can dismiss the Excel window or quit Excel to close all open workbooks.

- The workbook you want to close must be activated.

- Click **Close under the File tab**.

Moving to cell A1 of a worksheet

If the worksheet is large and you want to access a single cell, such as cell A1, you typically have to scroll the page until cell A1 appears, which can take a lot of unnecessary time. In this article, I outline some Excel shortcuts for fast navigating to a particular cell.

From anywhere on the sheet, you can rapidly jump to cell A1 by holding down the Ctrl key and pressing the Home button. The cursor will then instantly move to cell A1 after this.

Saving your work

All of your saving is done on the File tab, whether you want to save your workbook locally or online, for instance.

While you can save an existing workbook using Save or by pressing Ctrl+S in its current place, you must use Save As to create a copy of your workbook in the same or a different location or to save your workbook for the first time in a different area.

- Select **File > Save As**.

- Choose **the location** where you want to save your workbook under **Save As**. Click Computer, for instance, to save to your desktop or a specific folder on your computer.

- To find the desired location in your Documents folder, click Browse. Click Desktop, then select the precise spot on your computer where you wish to save your workbook, to choose a different location.

- Enter a name for a new workbook in the File name box. If you're making a copy of an existing workbook, enter a different name.

- Choose the desired file format from **the Save as type option** (located beneath the File name box) to save your workbook in a different file format, such as.xls or.txt.

- Tap **Save**.

It should be noted that if you attempt to save a workbook with macros enabled (.xlsm) as a standard workbook (.xlsx), macros won't be stored in the new file, which could cause functionality to be lost. VBA macros are an effective approach to automating a sizable amount of work. Until you are certain that the new file provides the capabilities you anticipate, you might want to save the macros or keep the macro-enabled file.

Undoing your work

In Microsoft Word, PowerPoint, and Excel, many activities can be reversed, undone, or repeated. As long as you stay within the undo restrictions, you can still make changes after saving and then save again (By default Office saves the last 100 undoable actions).

- To reverse a decision, press **Ctrl+Z**.

On the Quick Access Toolbar, select Undo if you'd rather use your mouse. If you want to undo several actions, keep pressing the **CTRL+Z keyboard shortcut or Undo**.

Some actions, including selecting options from the File tab or saving a file, cannot be undone. The Undo command becomes Can't Undo if you are unable to undo a decision.

When you wish to undo many activities at once, click the arrow adjacent to the Undo Undo button, choose the desired actions from the list, and then click the list.

Toggling absolute or mixed references

A cell reference is by default a relative reference, which denotes that the reference is relative to where the cell is located. When you refer to cell A2 from cell C2, for instance, you are actually referring to a cell that is two columns to the left (C minus A) in the same row (2). A relative cell reference found in a formula will be altered when you replicate the formula.

Less frequently, you could want to combine absolute and relative cell references by fixing the column or row by adding a dollar sign before either the column value or the row value.

To alter the cell reference's type:

- Choose **the cell** that the formula is located in.

- Choose **the reference** you want to modify from the formula bar Button picture.

- To change between the reference kinds, press **F4.**

In the event that a formula containing a reference is copied two cells down and two cells to the right, the reference type updates as shown in the table below.

Toggling Enter versus Edit mode

In an Excel worksheet, there are four different cell editing modes. There are four different cell modes: "Ready," "Edit," "Enter," and "Point." Excel cells are in the

"Ready" mode by default. When Excel is in Ready mode, it is prepared to accept the data in any worksheet Cell. The default "Ready" mode of an Active Cell can be switched to "Edit" mode by pressing the function key "F2" once. If you hit the function key "F2" once more when in "Edit" mode, the Cell mode will switch to "Enter." The fourth cell mode is called "Point." While creating or editing formulas, the "Point" cell mode enables you to explore a large Excel worksheet and choose the relevant cells.

Edit Mode

In any Excel cell, pressing the function key "F2" will switch the cell's mode to "Edit." Excel cells that have previously been filled with data and are not blank will switch to "Edit" mode when you double-click on them with the mouse pointer.

Pressing the arrow navigation keys will not move the Active Cell to the following cell when you are in "Edit" Cell mode. The text cursor in "Edit" mode moves left or right within the contents of the Cell in the direction of the Arrow key that was pressed. In "Edit" mode, the up and down arrows are ineffective.

Edit mode

The Cell Mode changes to "Enter" mode when a user enters data into a cell. When you double-click with the mouse pointer on a blank (empty) Excel cell, Cell Mode automatically switches to "Enter" mode. When in "Enter" mode, one mouse click will switch the cell mode to "Edit" mode.

- By pressing the function key **F2** while in **Enter mode**, you can transition to "Edit" mode. By using the function key "F2," you can switch between the "Enter" and "Edit" modes.

When in "Enter" mode, typing any arrow key will cause the currently selected cell to become inactive. In the direction of the typed Arrow key, the subsequent cell becomes the active cell.

Calculating a portion of a formula

Considering there are numerous intermediate computations and logical tests, it can occasionally be challenging to grasp how a nested formula produces the final answer. However, you may examine how a nested formula's many components are

309

evaluated in the sequence in which the formula is calculated by utilizing the Evaluate Formula dialog box.

- Choose the cell you want to assess. One cell at a time can only be assessed.

- Click **Evaluate Formula** under the **Formula Auditing** group on the **Formulas tab**.

- To find out the worth of the reference that is highlighted, click **Evaluate**. Italicized text indicates the evaluation's outcome.

- Click Step In to show the other formula in the Evaluation box if the highlighted portion of the formula refers to another formula. To return to the previous cell and formula, click Step Out.

- Continue evaluating the formula until each component has been examined.

- Click **Restart** to view the evaluation once more.

- Click **Close** to end the evaluation.

Summing a range of cells

Allow Excel to handle the math for you whenever you need to add a column or row of numbers.

- To total the numbers, choose **a cell next to them**, choose **AutoSum** from the Home menu, and then press **Enter**.

Excel automatically enters a formula (using the SUM function) to sum the numbers when you click AutoSum.

Notes:

- Select **the cell** directly below the last number in the column to get the total for the column of numbers. Choose **the cell** that is immediate to the right of a row of numbers to add them.

- There are two locations for AutoSum: **Home > Formulas and AutoSummaries > AutoSummary**.

- Instead of repeatedly inputting a formula, you can duplicate it to additional cells once you've created it. The formula in cell C7, for instance, automatically adapts to the new location and computes the values in cells C3–C6 if you copy the formula from cell B7 to cell C7.

- Additionally, you can apply AutoSum to multiple cells at once. For instance, you may choose **cell B7 and cell C7,** choose AutoSum, and total both columns simultaneously.

- In addition, you can sum numbers using a straightforward formula.

Conclusion

You can manage your business from anywhere at any time with QuickBooks Online, a small business accounting program, and app. Over 4.5 million clients use QuickBooks, which offers intuitive tools for running your company. You can manage your finances, send invoices, track inventory, arrange your books, and even process payroll. With the addition of payment services, QuickBooks Online helps you stay organized, save time, and even get paid quickly. The best part is that you may test it risk-free for 30 days.

QuickBooks is a user-friendly program that's simple to use and understand for daily tasks. It has projects that can help you manage the contracts and projects you've taken on, as well as calculate your profits and earnings. It also allows you to calculate your losses on certain projects, which can help you understand why you lost money on them. With the aid of QB, you can arrange your business instruments like delivery notes and purchase orders. You can also create sales orders and acknowledge new orders you have received from customers.

Since it is accounting software, it will assist you in organizing practically everything a large company needs to record, including creating a chart of accounts, product entries for pricing, organizing product inventory, and recording the cost of sales and cost of purchase. It will assist you in calculating the man-hour cost of each employee reporting to finish their Jobs in specific contracts or jobs undertaken that require a specific project completion for contracts services.

If you haven't signed up for this amazing software yet ensure you do that today!

Thank you so much for your order and for taking your time to read this book. We are constantly striving to improve our customer satisfaction, hence, we are curious to find out how helpful this book is to you, if you can spare us a minute to leave us a review, we'd be super grateful.

INDEX

Made in United States
Troutdale, OR
07/12/2023

11176229R00182